A Practical Course in SPOKEN ENGLISH

(with Audio CD)

SECOND EDITION

J.K. Gangal

ELT Expert

and

Director, Centre for Creativity and
Human Resource Development (CCHRD) Delhi

PHI Learning Private Limited

Delhi-110092

2014

₹ 250.00

A PRACTICAL COURSE IN SPOKEN ENGLISH (with Audio CD) Second Edition
J.K. Gangal

ISBN-978-81-203-4654-3

The export rights of this book are vested solely with the publisher.

Fifth Printing (Second Edition) ... ... August, 2014

Published by Asoke K. Ghosh, PHI Learning Private Limited, Rimjhim House, 111, Patparganj Industrial Estate, Delhi-110092 and Printed by Baba Barkha Nath Printers, Bahadurgarh, Haryana-124507.

To
My Friend, Guide and Philosopher
Sadguru Sai Baba

Note to the Reader

A complete list of words often mispronounced and conversations (represented by the symbol in the text) have been recorded on the audio CD.

CONTENTS

PREFACE

Encouraged by the book's wide popularity all over the country and abroad, I decided to come out with the second edition, with some additions such as body language and tips for an effective communication to make it further learner-friendly. I am confident, the new edition of the book will be further useful to its users and all those who are using it on their journey of excellence in the area of effective communication.

Any suggestions or feedback for further improvement of the book may please be directly sent at

jgangal@yahoo.com or jkgangal_consultant53@rediffmail.com.

J.K. Gangal

PREFACE TO THE FIRST EDITION

Need for Effective Communicative Skills

With the globalization of knowledge and culture the need for acquiring good communicative English by one and all has assumed great significance in this twenty-first century. In fact, the demand for learning effective communicative English has never been so great as it stands today. It is interesting to note that during the last two decades the use of English for communicative purposes has not been confined only to the elite group of the society. People from the middle and lower-middle classes are equally keen on learning and using it effectively.

Why this Change

It is because they consider spoken English as a passport for a guaranteed success in life. The craze for learning spoken English has led to mushroom growth of various coaching institutes all over the country. In their advertisement, they very often claim to help an individual learn spoken English within 30–40 days. Well, I need not say that it is just a business gimmick used by these English teaching shops. It is practically impossible to teach or learn good communicative English in just 30–40 days as claimed by some of these commercial coaching institutes.

Learning spoken English does not mean parrot-like repeating some crammed sentences with the help of a limited vocabulary. It means acquiring a skill to generate and use functional English in ever-changing life situations, while speaking. For this, besides acquiring the required sentence patterns and expressions in a given situation a person needs an appropriate vocabulary as well. Naturally, all this cannot be learnt or taught in just 30–40 days time. How much time is actually needed by an individual to be able to communicate confidently and naturally in different situations of life, is difficult to say. It differs with person-to-person and from situation-to-situation. However, one thing is certain that a person needs a minimum of 2–3 hours of rigorous session everyday for 5–6 months before he or she feels confident to communicate in English for various purposes in life. Of course, a strong desire coupled with one-track working is a pre-condition for the successful completion of this project on communicative English.

Although there are a few books available in the market on spoken English, they do not really help an individual acquire the communicative skills. They primarily deal with technical knowledge and the accompanying jargons.

The section on 'Grammar and Usage' in each chapter in this book provides necesssary help to a learner for the understanding of certain grammatical points appearing in spoken English.

Besides dealing with the situations from day-to-day life, the book also attempts to provide its users with the essentials of spoken English, required to speak English with confidence. The following are the areas covered for the purpose:

(a) English sounds
(b) Word stress
(c) Sentence stress
(d) Intonation
(e) Words often mispronounced
(f) Key-symbols used to represent pronunciation of words.

The accompanying CD replaces the need for the physical presence of the teacher for the learner by providing him or her the required help to acquire the listening and speaking competencies. It is a learner-friendly package.

The accompanying CD contains some of the conversations and a suggested list of words often mispronounced. Within the book, the conversations recorded on the audio CD are represented by the symbol . Each time this symbol appears, it means that the conversations and the words often mispronounced are recorded on the accompanying audio CD.

How to use this Book

Each chapter has been divided into different parts to enable the learner to acquire effective communicative English.

Conversation presents a model conversation in a given situation. The learner is expected to read it aloud alone, or with the help of his or her friend to know how he/she sounds while communicating in English. Ideally, it should be read aloud by 2 or more persons depending on the number of characters involved in the conversation. But when it is not feasible, for any reason, an individual may read aloud the dialogues of all the characters as well. Believe me the result will be equally profitable. In order to get the best results it is advised that the learner should first listen to the corresponding chapter on the CD and then read it aloud to facilitate the learner from the book.

Word Meaning provides the meaning of unfamiliar words and expressions appearing in the given conversation.

Comprehension deals with the comprehension of the model conversation. This aims at testing and developing the reading comprehension abilities of the learner with the help of multiple sets of answers to a question. Even those who have poor reading ability can answer these questions easily.

Sentence Patterns/Expressions/For Practice have been provided with a view to giving the learners extra practice in the required sentence patterns and expressions so that they are able to communicate in similar situations in life. As such the more they practise these given patterns, the better it is. They are expected to practise these sentence patterns first as they are, and then with suitable modifications to be able to generate new sentences in parallel situations in life. A pair activity would be quite useful for it. In brief, these sentence patterns will go a long way to serve the learners as a key to enter into the realm of spoken English.

Extended Vocabulary gives a number of useful contextualized words that a learner is expected to know to be able to communicate effectively and naturally in a real-life situation. Many of these words are synonyms of a particular word. The learner is expected to know their exact meanings from a good dictionary-cum-thesaurus and use them appropriately in their conversation in similar situations in life. It may be noted that acquiring vocabulary in the context is much more useful than acquiring it out of context for the purpose of communication—both oral and written.

It would be a good idea if the learner also tries to know the pronunciation of each word while referring to the dictionary for its meaning. For the convenience of the learners the correct pronunciation of most of these words has been given at the end of the book under 'Words often Mispronounced'.

Grammar and Usage discusses the grammatical points arising out of the given model conversation. The learner is expected to go through them carefully to acquire correctness of speech, with fluency in his or her communication. As a thumb rule, it is good to remember that where there is a conflict between a grammatical rule and a usage, preference should be given to the usage. The preference for usage will help the learners use English as a living language.

Activity aims at developing the learner's performance level in spoken English through suggested activities.

When this book is used by a group of people it is suggested that a role play/ group discussion/panel discussion may be frequently used for the benefit of the learners. It will provide them with the opportunity of using English in action. It is earnestly believed that the book being user-friendly will go a long way to help the learners realize their dream of using communicative English effectively and naturally, for which this book has been primarily designed.

The author would welcome any constructive suggestion from the readers of this book at jkgangal_consultant53@rediffmail.com or 011-22241623/ 9899114049 (mobile).

J.K. Gangal

ACKNOWLEDGMENTS

Acknowledging formally somebody's contribution to my growth and progress in life has always been a difficult task for me. Yet, I would be failing in my duty if I do not express my sense of gratitude to those who have helped me in bringing out this book.

To begin with, I would like to extend my heartiest gratitude to Shri Asoke K. Ghosh, Chairman and Managing Director, PHI Learning, New Delhi for having given me this wonderful opportunity of reaching out to all those who aspire to be good communicators but find no way to turn their dream into reality for want of some real good books.

I would also like to express my heartfelt thanks to Shri Sudarshan Das, Editor who went through my proposal of the book and gave his considered opinion in its favour. But for his support, the book would not have seen the light so soon.

My sincere thanks are also due to Mrs Shivani Garg, Editor and her associate Mrs Koyel Chakraborty, who took great pains in editing the manuscript and making this book student-friendly. I think I will be failing in my duty if I do not thank Shri Bijendra Pandey, Copy Editor for introducing me to this prestigious publishing concern.

I am equally grateful to my students and fellow teachers who initially inspired me to write this book for them and for all those who dream of conquering this world with their communication skills. The present book is a sincere effort in that direction.

I would also like to thank, from the core of my heart, my wife, Mrs Shashi Gangal who has always stood by me in all my educational ventures, including the writing of this book. Whenever I was under the clouds of doubt and indecisiveness, she came forward to dispel the same in no time. She always provided me with the necessary strength, peace of mind, besides motivating me to finish this book well in time.

Finally, my heart goes in gratitude to thank my friend, guide and philosopher, Sadguru Sai Baba for all His blessings and minute-to-minute invisible guidance that I have received during my journey to the completion of this book. My heart-felt gratitude for all His blessings and benedictions!

J.K. Gangal

KEY TO PHONETIC SYMBOLS

VOWEL SOUNDS

	Symbol	Examples
1.	/iː/	see, sleep, read, seat, me
2.	/ɪ/	sit, big, hit, will, happy
3.	/e/	red, ten, set, head, said
4.	/æ/	cat, rat, bat, hat, black
5.	/ɜː/	bird, work, turn, first, search
6.	/ə/	arrive, father, mother, announce, colour
7.	/ɑː/	harm, heart, laugh, arm, part
8.	/ʊ/	look, put, foot, could, cook
9.	/uː/	shoe, too, do, shoot, through
10.	/ɒ/	hot, cot, dog, watch, sock
11.	/ɔː/	thought, bought, caught, four, sort
12.	/^/	cup, son, wonder, butter, rough

DIPHTHONGS (DOUBLE VOWELS)

	Symbol	Examples
13.	/eɪ/	name, same, aim, late, tray
14.	/aɪ/	my, try, sky, time, idea
15.	/ɔɪ/	boy, noise, choice, toy, ointment
16.	/aʊ/	now, cow, out, loud, sound
17.	/ɪə/	hear, near, beer, cheer, dear
18.	/eə/	there, chair, pair, bear, where
19.	/ʊə/	tour, pure, fewer, cure, sure
20.	/əʊ/	home, show, low, blow, bone

CONSONANT SOUNDS

	Symbol	Examples
1.	/p/	put, post, hip, lip, pink
2.	/b/	big, book, boy, bangle, band
3.	/t/	two, test, tale, tooth, bet
4.	/d/	dog, dull, do, God, day
5.	/k/	cup, king, cost, come, kind
6.	/g/	good, guest, game, guarantee, go

	Symbol	Examples
7.	/tʃ/	church, catch, chest, chin, change
8.	/dʒ/	age, join, jug, judge, lounge
9.	/f/	face, finger, rough, cough, photo
10.	/v/	love, vest, veg, vehicle, vanity
11.	/s/	sit, signature, same, set, soil
12.	/z/	zebra, zoo, houses, zip, zink
13.	/ʒ/	pleasure, measure, vision, usual, television
14.	/θ/	think, three, through, thank, path
15.	/ð/	this, that, these, those, mother
16.	/ʃ/	ship, sugar, shop, shame, machine
17.	/h/	hot, hear, house, hen, hut
18.	/m/	man, male, money, lamb, lame
19.	/n/	now, name, net, knee
20.	/ŋ/	sing, bring, ring, going, playing
21.	/l/	long, look, while, soil, list
22.	/r/	red, road, write, wrong, rod
23.	/j/	yes, young, yet, year, you
24.	/w/	watch, want, wear, west, wind

- /ˈ/represents primary stress as in the word 'arrange' /əˈreɪndʒ/
  It is put immediately before the stressed syllable.
- /ˌ/ represents secondary stress as in the word, 'academic' /ˌækəˈdemik/
- The symbol two dots (:) shown with a certain vowel symbol indicates that the sound is to be lengthened while producing it.
- The letter 'r' appearing at the end of a word is usually not pronounced except when a vowel follows it. For example, in the word 'car' /kɑ:/ 'r' remains silent. But when we say 'car owner' it is pronounced and indicated by giving the transcription /kɑ:r/

PART I

PHONETICS

[fəˈnetiks]

Learning to drive is important, but knowing about the working of the car you drive is equally important.

1

SOUNDS OF ENGLISH LANGUAGE

[ˈSaundzəvˈɪŋglɪʃˈlæŋgwɪdʒ]

WELL-DEFINED SYSTEM

Like any other language in the world, English has its own well-defined sound system. Since spoken English is nothing but the meaningful use of its sounds, a person speaking English language is expected to master this sound system. In other words, he has to learn what these sounds are and how they are produced. The study of these sounds also helps him to learn the correct pronunciation of the words, besides helping him to stress words and sentences correctly.

The sounds of English, like every other language, can be divided into two major parts—vowels and consonants. The vowels have a further division, i.e., vowels and diphthongs. The diphthongs are also called **double vowels**. A diphthong is a combination of two vowel sounds.

In English, there are 44 sounds, of which 12 are single vowels, 8 diphthongs (double vowels) and 24 consonants. However, to represent these sounds, there are only 26 letters which, at times, causes a problem of pronunciation to the learners of English language. For instance, lays vs. says; bread vs. break.

Thus, in order to overcome this problem, the International Phonetic Association (IPA) has developed 44 phonetic symbols (also called phonemic or phoneme symbols)—one symbol for one sound (phoneme). All standard dictionaries of English use these phonetic symbols only to show how a particular word is pronounced all over the world. As such, the learning of these phonetic symbols would be of great help to those who want to acquire a standard pronunciation, which is called **Received Pronunciation** (RP). It is sometimes said that the learning of these symbols is rather difficult requiring time and some sort of special skill on the part of a learner. But the fact is that the learning of these phonetic symbols is very easy. Anyone can learn them in no time. However, the important thing to remember in this regard is that these symbols must be frequently used after they have been learnt till such time they get fixed in the learner's mind.

VOWEL SOUNDS

There are 12 single vowel sounds. They have been shown by the underlined part in the following words:

1. sit	/ɪ/	2. seat	/i:/
3. set	/e/	4. sat	/æ/
5. book	/ʊ/	6. boot	/u:/
7. cup	/^/	8. heart	/ɑ:/
9. hot	/ɒ/	10. bought	/ɔ:/
11. announce	/ə/	12. curd	/ɜ:/

The two dots (:) used in words like *seat, boot, heart* and *bought* indicate that these sounds are to be little lengthened while speaking as opposed to the sounds shown against words like *sit, set, cup* and *hot*, which are comparatively short sounds. Based on this distinction they are also called short or long vowel sounds.

Diphthongs

Diphthongs are also vowel sounds. But the difference between the two is that a diphthong is a combination of two vowel sounds while a single vowel is just one sound which may be long or short as explained above. In the case of a diphthong, the sound glides from one vowel sound to another vowel sound. The underlined parts in the following words are diphthongs:

1. height	/aɪ/	2. now	/aʊ/
3. boil	/ɔi/	4. page	/ei/
5. near	/ɪə/	6. hair	/eə/
7. home	/əʊ/	8. tour	/ʊə/

Triphthongs

Triphthongs are the most complex of English vowel sounds to produce. In diphthongs, the vowel sound glides from one vowel to another, whereas in triphthongs it glides from one vowel to another, and then to a third without any interruption. For example, while pronouncing the word 'hour', we begin with the vowel sound/ / going to / U / and then end with / schwa, /. Thus, we use the symbols **au**— to pronounce the word **'hour'**.

The triphthongs are composed of the following diphthongs, with the schwa added at the end:

1. eɪ + ə = eɪə	2. əʊ + ə = əʊə
3. aɪ + ə = eɪə	4. aʊ + ə = aʊə
5. ɔɪ + ə = ɔɪə	

As the middle of the three vowel sounds used in a thriphthong (i.e., **i** or **u** part) is hardly heard (unless observed very carefully), the triphthong produced is difficult to be distinguished from some of the diphthongs. However, the following words may be kept in mind as examples of triphthongs while pronouncing them:

1. tower	/aʊə/	2. player	/pleɪə/	3. power	/paʊə/
4. liar	/laɪə/	5. tyre	/taɪə/	6. fire	/faɪə/
7. slower	/sləʊə/	8. lower	/ləʊə/		

CONSONANT SOUNDS

The production of a consonant sound requires some kind of exercise in the speaker's mouth. Unlike a vowel sound, it does not come out freely.

The consonant sounds have been shown by the underlined part in the following words. The phonetic symbols used to represent these sounds have also been shown against them:

1. bat /b/	2. dog /d/	3. finger /f/	4. guest /g/	5. handle /h/
6. kettle /k/	7. lock /l/	8. man /m/	9. nest /n/	10. pink /p/
11. rich /r/	12. sun /s/	13. toy /t/	14. vein /v/	15. *watch /w/
16. zebra /z/	17. three /θ/	18. this /ð/	19. chest /tʃ/	20. jug /dʒ/
21. *year /j/	22. shoe /ʃ/	23. sing /ŋ/	24. measure /ʒ/	

Of the 24 consonant sounds, there are 5 sounds, which the non-native speakers find difficult to produce correctly. It may be due to the fact that some of them are not available in their mother tongue. Thus, to be able to produce these sounds correctly, it is suggested that these sounds be acquired by comparing them with the sounds closest to them. A close study will help the speakers understand the fine distinction between these two minimal sounds, besides helping them to acquire and produce these sounds correctly. These sounds are:

1. /θ/	(three)	vs	/t/	(tree)
2. /ð/	(this)	vs	/d/	(din)
3. /ʒ/	(pleasure)	vs	/z/	(enthusiasm)
4. /dʒ/	(jug)	vs	/z/	(reason)
5. /w/	(wind)	vs	/v/	(vest)

SYLLABLES

The small sound units into which longer words are required to be broken while speaking are called **syllables**. For example, the words like 'wo.man' and 'nut.shell' will require to be broken as shown into two sound units while saying these words—they have two syllables each (as opposed to the words like 'come' and 'hen' which can be said in just one breath). Similarly, the words like 'pho.to.graph' and 'en.gi.neer' will require to be broken, as shown into three sound units—they have three syllables each.

---

* They are also called **semi-vowels**.

In the words of two or more syllables, one of the syllables is said with extra force compared to the other. The syllable which sounds louder because of extra force is called **stressed syllable**.

The stressed syllable is indicated by putting a mark (/'/), called **primary stress mark**, immediately before it, e.g. ce'ment/s'ɪment.

When speaking, normally nouns, full verbs, adjectives and most adverbs are stressed, while helping verbs, determiners, prepositions, pronouns and conjunctions are usually not stressed. Such unstressed syllables are called unstressed syllables.

2

STRESS AND INTONATION

[S'tres n ˌintəʊ'neɪʃən]

STRESS—WHAT AND HOW

When we speak we give more emphasis to certain words of a sentence by making them louder than the rest of the words used in the sentence. Words receiving this extra force of speech are said to be **stressed words** and the words spoken with normal force are called **unstressed words**.

Stress patterns show us which word or parts of a word we should emphasize when we speak. We show stress marks in front of the parts of the word that should be emphasized, e.g., in the sentence, She is the **o**wner, we should emphasize the first part of the word, '**o**wner, and in the word 'de'**ny**' we should emphasize the second part.

Usually in a sentence the following words will be stressed:

(a) All nouns (and some pronouns, especially interrogative pronouns)
(b) Demonstratives (this, that, these, those)
(c) Main verbs
(d) Adjectives
(e) Most adverbs

Examples:

(a) He **plays cricket daily**.
(b) **These apples** are the **juiciest**.

The other words of a sentence such as determiners, helping verbs, prepositions and conjunctions, used to carrying meaning, are normally not stressed. However, when we want to contradict something or stress a particular point they can be stressed like any other stressed words.

Even in case of isolated words, certain syllables constituting that word receive greater stress than other syllables. Syllables receiving this extra emphasis by way of extra force of speech are called **strong syllables** and the syllables spoken with a normal pressure are called **weak syllables**. Further, on comparing weak syllables with strong syllables, we find that the vowel in a weak syllable tends to be shorter and of lower intensity. For example, in the word 'mother', the second syllable is shorter than the first and is less louder. The vowel "schwa" /ə/, the most frequently occurring vowel in English, is always associated with weak syllables.

There are two kinds of stress marks: **primary stress mark** and **secondary stress mark**. The primary stress mark, as already mentioned, is placed in front of the part of the word we need to emphasize, i.e., ˈconduct (n), whereas the secondary stress mark, which shows us the part of the word that has the second most important emphasis, is put below the syllable. It may be noted that we do emphasize the secondary stress, but not quite as much as in the case of the primary stress, e.g., as in the word, 'back-yard' / ˌback-ˈyard/the primary stress is on ˈyard and the secondary stress is on ˌback.

Spoken English shows a noted contrast between its strong (stressed) and weak (unstressed) syllables, which accounts for the rhythmic patterns of the language.

Exercise for Practice

Underline the words in the following sentences that need to be stressed while speaking.

1. How do the lights work?
2. She wants to come and see our new house.
3. It's true he was late, but his car could have broken down.
4. She stood first on the merit list.
5. We celebrate Independence Day in our colony every year.

INTONATION—WHAT AND HOW

Intonation is primarily a matter of variation in the pitch level of our voice. In other words, the rise and fall of the pitch level of the voice while speaking is called **intonation**. It is also called the **modulation of the speech**. The stress and rhythm are also involved in it.

We describe pitch in terms of **high** and **low**. It may be remembered that "high" and "low" are only arbitrary choices in connection with the pitch scale.

Intonation enables us to express our emotions and attitudes while speaking. This is called the **attitudinal function of intonation**. It also serves a grammatical function, distinguishing one type of phrase or sentence from another. For example, "He's dead" is a statement when spoken with a drop in pitch at the end, but a question when spoken with a rise in pitch at the end.

Intonation, coupled with stressed and unstressed syllables, provides musicality to the English language. This is why intonation is also called the **melody** of speech.

The behaviour of the pitch may be described in terms of tones—level tone.

Broadly, we can classify all the English intonation patterns under two types—**falling intonation (tune I)** and **rising intonation (tune II)**. Both normally begin with the first stressed syllable at a fairly high pitch, and then fall step-wise from stress-to-stress until the last meaningful stress is reached.

Tune I (with final fall) is used for statements, remarks, orders and questions beginning with question words. **The falling tune carries a sense of completion and finality.**

Examples: 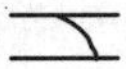

1. She didn't see him leave the house. (statement)
2. Where did you put my pen? (question beginning with the question word)
3. That's the end of the news. (remark)
4. Stop talking. (order)
5. I'm absolutely certain. (statement)

Tune II (with final rise) is used while asking questions beginning with helping verbs.

Examples: 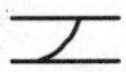

1. Did you meet her before?
2. Can you recite the poem?
3. Do you like him?
4. Is she your teacher?

Fall–rise tune: It is used to express uncertainty and doubt and also to make a request.

Examples: 

1. She <u>may</u> be right. (uncertainty)
2. It's possible. (doubt)
3. Can I borrow it? (request)

Rise–fall tune: It is used to express your surprise and appreciation for something.

Examples: 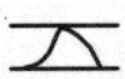

1. She was <u>first to reach</u>. (appreciation)
2. <u>None</u> of them qualified. (surprise)

Exercise for Practice

Put the appropriate symbols indicating the rising/falling/fall–rise/rise–fall tunes in the sentences using the following words:

yes (Fall) yes (Rise) yes (Fall–rise) yes (Rise–fall)
no (Fall) no (Rise) no (Fall–rise) no (Rise–fall)
please (fall) please (Rise)

PART II

ENGLISH CONVERSATIONS

[ɪŋglɪʃ ˌkonvəˈseɪʃən]

Even the 1000 mile journey begins with the first step, and practice makes life perfect.

1

INTRODUCING YOURSELF

READ aloud the following to know how to introduce yourself:

I am Pradeep—Pradeep Aggarwal. I **come from** Aligarh in Uttar Pradesh. I am a **postgraduate** in English with 68% of marks from Lucknow University.

I am a **voracious** reader and can read very fast—about 500 words per minute. Besides reading, I am interested in music, painting and dramatics. I often visit art galleries and various exhibitions to look for new paintings and products. You may also find me in music stores collecting the latest melodies. I regularly **contribute** articles to various magazines and **periodicals**. Recently, I have been awarded for my poem, 'Blood has only one colour' by the Young Writers Club of Uttar Pradesh. By profession I am a science teacher. I am a creative person and quite **enthusiastic** about the works that are beyond the common imagination.

I **look upon** my work as my hobby. For me work is worship. So I always enjoy doing it. I am good at planning and publicity. I am a **dedicated** learner and keep myself always updated with the latest developments in the field of science and technology. Impatience is, however, my weak point.

WORD MEANING

1. **Come from:** belong to
2. **Postgraduate:** M.A/M.Sc./M.Com. (a person with a postgraduate qualification)
3. **Voracious:** one who is always hungry; gluttonous; starving
4. **Contribute:** write
5. **Periodicals:** magazines which are out at a particular time like weekly, monthly, yearly
6. **Look upon:** consider, regard

7. **Enthusiastic:** energetic
8. **Dedicated:** devoted to some task or purpose

COMPREHENSION

ANSWER the following questions:

1. Who is introducing himself?
2. Where does he come from?
3. What is his academic qualification?
4. What percentage did he get in his M.A. examination?
5. What is his profession?
6. What are his areas of interest?
7. What is his per minute reading speed?
8. What has he been awarded for?
9. Which organization has awarded him?
10. Why does he always enjoy doing his work?
11. What is his weak point?

Read aloud the above introduction 3 times before telling about yourself.

EXPRESSIONS AND PHRASES FOR LEARNING

1. I am a self-made man.
2. I hail from the Pink City/Land of Five Rivers.
3. I reside nearby.
4. I am proficient in acting/dancing.
5. I am the only bread-earner in my family.
6. I can compose a poem in no time.
7. I enjoy reading books and magazines and listening to music.
8. Getting disturbed at my criticism is my limitation.
9. My brother is an engineer/doctor.
10. My father is an executive in a multinational company.

EXTENDED VOCABULARY

LOOK up the following words in a good dictionary/thesaurus* to know their different meanings and pronunciations. Also use them while introducing yourself to somebody or a group of people.

Bachelor | Bachelor's degree

*A thesaurus is a dictionary of synonyms and antonyms. Choose a good thesaurus to look for meanings of certain words that you find rather difficult. It is good to have a personal copy of a thesaurus for frequent references.

Belong to
Column
Contribute article
Good at
Graduate from
Hail from
Job
Journals
Magazines
Master's degree
Native
Periodicals
Postgraduate in
Reading is my hobby
Settled in
Social worker
Strength
Voracious reader

GRAMMAR AND USAGE

1. While introducing yourself do not say: "Myself P.K. Sharma". Always say: I am Prabhat Kumar Sharma. Use of 'myself' is grammatically incorrect.
2. We use 'self' for an emphatic purpose, e.g., "I *myself* give the demonstration, I don't invite any expert for it."

SOME USEFUL TIPS TO SPEAK

- Use only small sentences ensuring that the sentence conveys complete meaning in the context.
- The sentence used should not have more than 8–10 words. If you have to give more information on the situation concerned, split your sentence into small sentences.
- Verbs like can, could, will, would, shall, should, do, does, did, has, have, had, need, when combined with NOT are used in contracted forms in spoken English like **can't, won't, wouldn't, don't, doesn't, haven't, hasn't, hadn't, shouldn't, needn't** etc.
- Learn the contextual meanings of new words with the help of a thesaurus.
- Learn both synonyms (words with similar meanings) and antonyms (words with opposite meanings).

EXPRESSIONS AND PHRASES FOR PRACTICE

1. I am ....
2. I come from ....
3. I stay at ....
4. I am a/an ....
6. I am good at ....
7. I can do .... in just half an hour.
8. .... are my hobbies.
9. .... are my strong points.

10. .... in big groups are my limitations.
11. My mother is a ....

Note: ***These expressions may be practised in parallel situations both individually and in pairs in a group.***

ACTIVITY

Imagine you are contesting an election for the position of head boy/head girl of your school. Now introduce yourself to the entire student community of your school in the morning assembly to seek their votes and support. Make sure that you mention all such things about yourself in self-introduction that could influence the students addressed.

2

INTRODUCING ANOTHER PERSON

READ aloud along with your friend the following conversation:

(Rahul takes home his friend, Shalini. He introduces her to his parents)

Rahul: Shalini, let me introduce you to my parents and others.

Shalini: How sweet of you! I'd love to meet them.

Rahul: Shalini, meet my mother. Mom, this is Shalini, my classmate and a very good friend of mine.

Mother: Hello, Shalini! Rahul often talks about you. He says you are a very good dancer and play piano extremely well. Is it true?

Shalini: Well Aunty, there is nothing great about it. **I wonder** if you know that my mother is a well-known Kathak dancer, and my father is a famous **pianist**. Naturally, I have **inherited** these talents from my parents.

Rahul: Shalini, now let me introduce you to my father, Sanjeev Kumar. He works with a multinational company as CEO. Dad, this is Shalini, my friend.

Father: Hi Shalini, nice to meet you! We've heard a lot about you from Rahul. We are glad you decided to come.

Shalini: Thank you Uncle! I always wanted to come and meet you. But somehow, I just couldn't manage to come earlier.

Rahul: Mom, where's Rashmi? Is she back home? I want her to meet Shalini.

Mother: **I'm afraid**, she hasn't returned from the library yet. You can introduce Shalini to her next time. Shalini, I'm sorry, I have to leave you right now. Rahul's dad has to leave for his office and I must give him as usual his packed lunch before he leaves. Hope you won't mind my leaving you so abruptly!

Shalini: Certainly not! Bye Aunty.

Mother: Bye Shalini. Nice meeting you!

WORD MEANING

1. **I wonder:** an expression used to ask a question within one's mind
2. **Pianist:** one who plays a piano
3. **inherit:** which comes from parents with birth automatically
4. **I am afraid:** I'm sorry (to feel sorry for something)

COMPREHENSION

There are three choices for each question. Tick (✓) the choice you consider to be correct.

1. Why does Rahul take home his friend, Shalini?
   (a) Rahul takes home his friend to introduce her to his family members.
   (b) He takes her home to show his house.
   (c) He takes her home to introduce her to his father.
2. While introducing, what does Rahul tell his mother about Shalini?
   (a) He tells her that Shalini is very good at studies.
   (b) He tells her that Shalini is his classmate and a very good friend.
   (c) He tells her that Shalini is a famous Kathak dancer.
3. What had Rahul's mother already known about Shalini before meeting her?
   (a) She comes from a rich family.
   (b) She's a good dancer and plays the piano well.
   (c) She's very good at painting.
4. What's Rahul's father?
   (a) He's a businessman.
   (b) He's working as an executive in a bank.
   (c) He's working as the CEO in a multinational company.
5. Why couldn't Rahul get Shalini introduced to Rashmi?
   (a) Rashmi refused to meet Shalini.
   (b) Rashmi wasn't at home.
   (c) Rashmi was too busy to talk to her.

Read aloud once again the conversation with the help of your friends (Pair activity).

EXPRESSIONS AND PHRASES FOR LEARNING

1. Let me introduce my friend, Anubha. She's my classmate.
2. Meet my friend, Shobha. She's my House Captain.
3. Nice to see you. (We say this to the person at the time of leaving)

4. I'm glad you came/attended the function.
5. Nice to meet you, Shobha.
6. Please meet my colleague, Asha.
7. Raju, this is my new colleague, Anjana. She's a very good singer.
8. Glad to meet you, Anjana.
9. May I have the pleasure of introducing the Chief Guest of today's function, Dr. Awasthy?
10. I am indeed very happy to meet you.
11. I'm privileged to meet you.
12. I would like to go now.
13. I am afraid, I have to leave now.

EXTENDED VOCABULARY

LOOK up the following words in a good dictionary to know their pronunciations. Also use them while introducing people.

Cardiologist:	a doctor who studies and treats heart related problems
Dentist:	a doctor who treats dental problems
Dermatologist:	a doctor who studies and treats skin related problems
ENT specialist:	a doctor who studies and treats problems related to ear, nose and throat
Executive:	a person who manages a business or an organization taking decisions
Gerontologist:	a doctor who studies and treats the medical problems of old people
Gynaecologist:	a doctor who treats women for their sex related illness and problems
Neurologist:	a doctor who studies and treats the diseases relating to nervous system
Obstetrician:	a doctor who is specialised in child's delivery
Ophthalmologist:	a doctor who studies and treats eye related diseases
Orthopaedist:	a doctor who specialises in the diseases and problems related to bones
Paediatrician:	a doctor who treats diseases of children
Pathologist:	a doctor who studies causes and effects of illness by various pathological tests
Physician:	a doctor who treats all kinds of diseases
Physiotherapist:	a person who treats through massage and various exercises
Psychiatrist:	a doctor trained in the treatment of mental illness
Surgeon:	a doctor who operates and does surgery
Urologist:	a doctor who treats people with urinary problems and also men's sexual problems

SOME USEFUL TIPS TO SPEAK

Introduce somebody to something **or** introduce something to somebody.
Examples

1. My friend introduced me to the minister at the party.
2. His first lecture on computers introduced me to the world of computers.

The above expressions may be memorised and practised in appropriate situations.

EXPRESSIONS AND PHRASES FOR PRACTICE (PAIR ACTIVITY)

1. How sweet of ....
2. I would love to ....
3. Meet ....
4. It gives me great pleasure ....
5. I wonder if ....
6. This/That is ....
7. .... can (can't) manage ....
8. .... as usual.
9. Hope you won't mind my/his/her ....
10. Let me have the pleasure of introducing my friend ....
11. I am extremely happy to introduce my friend ....
12. I feel privileged to introduce .... to ....
13. I would like to introduce ....
14. Can I introduce myself/my friend ....

ACTIVITY

1. Note down in your practice notebook all the given expressions and learn them by revising every now and then.
2. Imagine you have to introduce your brother or sister to an old friend of yours who has come to attend the marriage reception of your elder brother. Construct at least six exchange dialogues between the brother/sister introduced and your friend.
3. To facilitate your work write down those exchange dialogues in your practice notebook and read them aloud with correct pronunciation and proper stress and intonation (at least 4–5 times).

3

MEETING A PERSON FIRST TIME

READ aloud along with your friend the following conversation:

Rakesh: Hello, I am Rakesh Mittal. I come from Himachal Pradesh (*shaking hands*)

Amit: How do you do? (*shaking hands*)

Rakesh: How do you do?

Amit: I am Amit—Amit Nehra. I **come from** Chandigarh. What do you do, Rakesh?

Rakesh: Well, I am a student. I am doing MCA from IGNOU. And you?

Amit: I am a student, too. I am doing MBA from Delhi University.

Rakesh: What are your plans after completing your MBA?

Amit: Well, it is very difficult to say anything with certainty these days. However, I intend joining some good multinational company. You know, they are very **good paymasters**.

Rakesh: Wish you all the best, Amit! I think, I must leave now, I am getting late for my extra-class. It was indeed nice talking to you, Amit (*shaking hands*). By the way, can I have your telephone number, please?

Amit: Of course. Here you are! (*giving his visiting card*). Can I also have your visiting card, please?

Rakesh: Why not ? Here's my card, please (*giving his card*). Look! I would like to give you a ring sometime next week. Hope you won't mind it! Then we can **chat at leisure**.

Amit: Certainly not, rather I would love to talk to you. In fact, now that we know each other we should be in regular touch. Don't you think so?

Rakesh: O yes! We must meet regularly. OK, now I **take leave of you**. Bye-bye, Amit!

Amit: Bye-bye, Rakesh!

WORD MEANING

1. **Come from:** belong to
2. **Good paymasters:** pay handsomely
3. **Chat:** talk
4. **At leisure:** comfortably
5. **Take leave of you:** permission to leave

COMPREHENSION

ANSWER the following questions briefly:

1. Who are the two persons meeting for the first time?
2. What does Rakesh do?
3. What does Amit do?
4. What does Amit intend doing after completing his present course?
5. Why do both Rakesh and Amit exchange their visiting cards?
6. What does Amit suggest to Rakesh?

Rehearse the above conversation with your partner 3 times (Pair activity).

EXPRESSIONS AND PHRASES FOR LEARNING

1. How do you do?
2. It was indeed a great pleasure talking to you.
3. Nice seeing you/talking to you.
4. It was nice meeting you.
5. Hi! It's great to meet you, Basu.
6. When can I see you again?
7. When shall we meet again?
8. See you again!
9. Do write to me off and on.
10. Thanks for this wonderful evening!
11. Believe me, it is one of the best evenings I have ever had. We had a wonderful time.
12. Don't be formal, please/there's no need for any formality.

EXTENDED VOCABULARY

LOOK up the following words in a good dictionary for their correct pronunciations

Architect:	one who creates designs and blueprints for making a building
C.E.O:	Chief Executive Officer

Chef: head cook in a hotel
Counsellor: someone whose job is to help and support people who have problems
Defence assistant: a person who argues for the accused in a departmental case
Diplomat: someone who officially represents his/her country in a foreign country
Florist: one who deals in the business of flowers
Male-nurse: a male appointed to look after patients and patients' related problems
Radio/tv jockey: a person who entertains listeners/viewers on Radio/TV
Stenographer: one who takes dictation in shorthand

GRAMMAR AND USAGE

1. The word, "please", can be used both in the beginning and at the end of a sentence, e.g.,

   (a) *Please*, introduce yourself to this board.
   (b) Introduce yourself to this board, *please*.

2. Expressions like:

   (a) Have you got a family? or
   (b) Do you have a family? convey the same meaning.

3. The word, 'Family' does not mean only wife and husband. It also includes children. We also use the word 'family' to refer to children of a couple. So, when you say: "Do you have a family?" or "Have you got a family?" it also means, do you have children?

SOME OTHER USEFUL EXPRESSIONS FOR USE

- What's your name, please?
- May I have the pleasure of knowing your name, please?
  I am Asha — Asha Aggrawal.
- What's your nationality? (*talking to a foreigner*)
- Where do you come from?
- Which is your hometown, please?
- Which is your native place?
  I come from Russia/Jaipur.
  Though we come from .... we've settled in Delhi for the last 20 years.
- What do you do?
- What's the nature of your job?
- What is your profession like?
  I am an/a electronic engineer/architect/doctor/teacher/businessman.
  I am an engineer by qualification but actor by profession.

- What's your mother tongue?
- What language do you speak at home?
  I speak Hindi/Punjabi.
- Are you married?
  Yes, I am.
- Do you have a family?
  Yes, I have two children.
- What's the size of your family?
- How many children do you have?
  I have two children.
- Which school does your son/daughter go to?
  He/She goes to Spring Valley, Lajpat Nagar.
- Where do you stay in Delhi?
- Where are you put up?
  At Patparganj in East Delhi.
- What's your contact number?
- What's your work number?
  22522443
- What's your residence number?
  22241623
- What's the most convenient time for you to speak on phone?
  Between 6 and 8 in the evening.
- Could I have your visiting card?
  Of course, Here you are!
- Is your wife working?
  No, She is a housewife/homemaker Vs. house husband.
- What time do you leave for your work?
  At 8 in the morning.
- What time are you normally back home?
  At 7 in the evening.
- What time do you go to bed at night?
  Around 10 p.m.
- What time are you up in the morning?
- What time do you get up in the morning?
  At 5.

EXPRESSIONS AND PHRASES FOR PRACTICE

The following are some of the useful expressions, sentences and questions to learn to ask at the time of meeting a person for the first time (***Pair activity***):

1. Excuse me, I am ....
2. Could I ....?
3. If you don't mind, may I ....

4. Do you mind if I ask you ....?
5. Convey my regards to ....

ACTIVITY

1. Meet five new students of your class/institution and obtain information about them with the help of the above questions. Also give information about yourself while conversing with them.
2. Note down the given expressions in your practice notebook and keep revising them till they become your friends and you can use them correctly and naturally in appropriate situations.
3. Write six exchange dialogues between two imaginary persons travelling together in a railway compartment of Rajdhani Express from Delhi to Mumbai, using the expressions provided. You are free to use your own vocabulary and expressions.

4

MEETING A STRANGER IN A FAMILIAR SITUATION

READ aloud the following conversation between two strangers meeting for the first time in a familiar situation (Pair activity):

Basu:	Hello, I'm Basu. I'm a teacher and stay at Green Park. How about you?
Radha:	Well, I'm Radha. I'm a student and stay at R.K. Puram, Sector 8.
Basu:	How do you do?
Radha:	How do you do?
Basu:	By the way, how're you related to the **bride**?
Radha:	Well, she is my **cousin**—my uncle's daughter.
Basu:	Incidentally, where's your Dad?
Radha:	He must be at the reception busy welcoming the guests and invitees. When he is rather free I would like him to meet you. He has great regards for teachers.
Basu:	Thanks! Thanks a lot! I would love to meet him!

WORD MEANING

1. **Bride:** the girl getting married (opposite: bridegroom—the boy getting married)
2. **Cousin:** brother/sister (uncle's son/daughter—no cousin brother or sister, only cousin)

COMPREHENSION

ANSWER the following questions briefly:

1. Did Basu and Radha know each other before meeting?

2. Which word does Basu use when he introduces himself to Radha?
3. What is Basu?
4. What is Radha?
5. What expression did they use after introducing themselves?
6. What expression did Basu use to inquire about Radha's relationship with the bride?
7. Which expression does Radha use that shows she will be happy to introduce her father to Basu?

Now read the above conversation once again (3 times) (Pair activity).

EXPRESSIONS AND PHRASES FOR LEARNING

1. Hi ?
   Hello, how are you?
   Hi, how are you?
   How is life?
   Fine, thanks!
   Fine, thank you!
   I am fine, thank you!
   What about you ?
   I'm fine, too.
2. How are you?
   Very well, thank you!
   Fine, thanks! How about you?
3. Haven't seen you for quite some time.
4. It's nice to see you.
5. It's nice to meet you again.

The above expressions may be learnt and practised in appropriate situations.

EXTENDED VOCABULARY

LOOK up the following words in a good dictionary-cum-*thesaurus to know their meanings, synonyms (similar words), antonyms (opposite words) and pronunciations to be able to communicate effectively in similar situations:

Arranged marriage/love marriage/inter-caste marriage
Bachelor/maiden/spinster

* Thesaurus is a dictionary of synonyms and antonyms

Betrothal ceremony/ring ceremony/engagement
Dowry
Groom (bridegroom), father/mother/sister/brother/daughter-in-law/in-laws
Matrimonial
Matrimony
Sacred vows
Wedlock
Widower

GRAMMAR AND USAGE

1. When we meet a person for the first time (a stranger) we greet him or her by saying: How do you do? and the response to 'How do you do' is also: How do you do? However, when we meet that person subsequently, or the person we already know we say: How are you? instead of 'How do you do'? It is a new emerging trend.
2. We use: By the way/incidentally/if you don't mind, please/oh, that reminds me, to change the topic or to refer to something unrelated to what is being discussed or talked about.

EXPRESSIONS AND PHRASES FOR PRACTICE (PAIR ACTIVITY)

1. By the way, ...?
2. Incidentally, ...
3. If you don't mind please ....
4. I would love to ....
5. It's nice ....

ACTIVITY

1. Note down the words provided under 'Extended Vocabulary' with their meanings in your practice notebook and keep revising them for 15 days in your spare time. Also learn with the help of a good dictionary the correct pronunciation of the words appearing in 'Conversation' and 'Extended Vocabulary'.
2. Learn and practise the given words and expressions in similar situation with the help of your friend or learning partner (Pair activity).
3. Construct at least six exchange dialogues between two imaginary persons meeting for the first time at the India Gate, using expressions/phrases given. To facilitate, first write their dialogues in your practice notebook and then read them aloud, with correct pronunciation, proper stress and right intonation as demonstrated in the CD provided along with this book. Read it at least 5 times. (If you have the facility to record, you may also record your dialogue delivery and get the feedback on it from others.)

5

MEETING PEOPLE AFTER A LONG TIME

READ aloud the following conversation between two friends who meet after a gap of two months: Also note how they greet each other.

Heima: Hello Shiva, how're you?
Shiva: Fine, thanks! And you?
Heima: I'm fine, too. Thanks! **Haven't seen you for ages**. **Have** you **been away**?
Shiva: No, I was very much here. I was just busy preparing my project report.
Heima: Is it over, or still working on it?
Shiva: It's **all over**. I have also submitted the report.
Heima: I can **make out** from your face. You **look** so relaxed.
Shiva: Though I was **terribly busy** writing the project report, I **missed** you a lot, Heima.
Heima: **So was here!** Shiva, **shall we** go to the canteen and have our 'brand' coffee?
Shiva: **I'm afraid**, I have to go for my class right now. In fact, I'm already late for the class. **Could we** meet during the lunch, if you don't mind, please?
Heima: **No problem!** It is perfectly **OK**. So now we meet in the canteen during the lunch break. Till then bye Shiva!
Shiva: Bye, Heima!

WORD MEANING

1. **Haven't seen for ages:** haven't seen somebody for a long time
2. **Have been away:** out of station/town
3. **All over:** completely finished
4. **Make out:** can understand
5. **Look:** appear
6. **Terribly busy:** extremely busy

7. **Miss:** feel the absence/ feel sad due to the absence
8. **So was here:** had similar feeling/experience
9. **Shall we:** an expression used to suggest something
10. **I'm afraid:** I'm sorry
11. **Could we:** an expression used to make a request (a polite way of making a request)
12. **No problem/OK:** an expression used to indicate complete agreement

COMPREHENSION

ANSWER the following questions briefly:

1. Who are the two persons involved in the given conversation?
2. How are they related?
3. Why didn't Shiva meet Heima for so many days?
4. How did Heima guess that Shiva had finished his work completely?
5. What was the common feeling that the two friends experienced when they did not see each other for a long time?
6. What expression did Shiva use to express his sad feeling?
7. What expression did Heima use for that?
8. What proposal does Heima make to Shiva on meeting him after a long time?
9. Why does Shiva turn down Heima's proposal?
10. What expression does Shiva use while turning down Heima's proposal for coffee?
11. When do the two friends finally meet to have their 'brand coffee', and where?

Now read the above conversation once again (at least 2 times) (Pair activity).

EXPRESSIONS AND PHRASES FOR LEARNING

1. Hi/Good Morning/Morning/Good Evening/Hello/How are you?
2. How about you?/What about you?
3. Very well, thank you/I'm fine too, thanks!
4. I missed you.
5. So was here!
6. I'm sorry.
7. No problem.
8. OK/all right, is it OK?
9. Never mind!
10. It's perfectly all right.

The above expressions may be learnt and practised in appropriate situations.

EXTENDED VOCABULARY

Assessment
Concerned about
Delayed
Evaluation
In arrears
In time
Presentation of the report
Punctuality
Submission
Teacher-in-charge

GRAMMAR AND USAGE

1. The old distinction between 'shall' and 'will' is no more in use in spoken English these days. Now we use 'shall' for the following purposes only in the question form:
   (a) To seek permission to do something, e.g., It's very cold. Shall I close the window?
   (b) To make a suggestion:
   Now that our last paper is over, shall we go for a picnic?
2. 'Could' is not just the past tense of 'can', it is used to make a request, politely.

EXPRESSIONS AND PHRASES FOR PRACTICE (Pair Activity)

1. I'm afraid ....
2. You look ....
3. Believe me, ...
4. Honestly speaking, ...
5. Shall we .... ? Could we ....?

ACTIVITY

Imagine you unexpectedly meet your school friend at the book fair. Write six exchange dialogues enquiring about his or her well-being and also telling him/her all about yourself after your friend left for UK for higher studies. Use some of the given expressions in your dialogues.

6

ASKING FOR A WAY AND GIVING DIRECTIONS

READ aloud the following conversation:

Tourist: Excuse me, how far is it to the metro station?

Policeman: About 10 kilometres.

Tourist: Thanks! Can you tell me which route number bus goes to the metro station?

Policeman: There are plenty of buses for the metro station. You can take 202, 203 or 405. All go to the metro station.

Tourist: Thank you! How long does it take to get to the metro station by bus?

Policeman: It doesn't take long—just half an hour.

Tourist: How to get to the nearest bus stop?

Policeman: It's nearby. Go along here. Turn left into the ring road. Then take the first turning on your left. Keep going for about 500 metres when you get to the main bus station. From there you get buses for all places, including the metro station.

Tourist: Thank you very much indeed. Supposing, I decide to go by a taxi, how much will it cost me?

Policeman: Around **fifty* bucks**. But you **had better** go by bus. Taxi is not available all the time. Moreover, you have to book it in advance.

Tourist: Thanks for your advice! Bye-bye.

Policeman: It's a part of our duty, Sir. Bye-bye.

WORD MEANING

1. **Fifty* bucks:** (slang) fifty rupees/dollars
2. **Had better:** an expression used to suggest something

COMPREHENSION

There are three choices for each question. Tick (✓) the choice you consider to be correct.

1. Where does the tourist want to go?
   (a) He wants to go to the airport.
   (b) He wants to go to the metro station.
   (c) He wants to go to the bus station.
2. Who does the tourist contact for help?
   (a) He contacts the tourist guide.
   (b) He contacts the Railway Enquiry.
   (c) He contacts the policeman.
3. How far is the metro station?
   (a) It's about 5 kilometres.
   (b) It's about 10 kilometres.
   (c) It's very far.
4. Which route number bus goes to the metro station?
   (a) 202, 203, 405.
   (b) Metro station specials.
   (c) No direct bus goes to the metro station, only taxi goes.
5. What does the policeman advise the tourist to go to the metro station?
   (a) The policeman advises the tourist to go to the metro station by taxi.
   (b) To walk down to the metro station.
   (c) To go to the main bus station to catch the bus for the metro station.

Rehearse the given conversation with your friend 3 times (Pair activity).

EXPRESSIONS AND PHRASES FOR LEARNING

1. (a) Could you please tell me how to get to the airport?
   (b) Please, could you tell me how to go to the railway station?
   (c) Could you tell me which route number bus goes to Connaught Place?
2. Could you guide me how to fix up my appointment with the doctor?
3. Do you mind if I use your phone?
4. Could I leave a message for your husband? or
   I'd be grateful if you could pass on my message to your wife. or
   Please, could you take a message for your husband?
5. Please, could you let me have your answer by Monday?

The given expressions may be learnt and practised in appropriate situations (Pair activity).

EXTENDED VOCABULARY

LOOK up the following words in a good dictionary to know their pronunciations. Also use them in your conversation in appropriate situations.

Botanical garden
Cafe
Cafeteria/restaurant
Cathedral: a church in a city
Chapel: a small church
Church
City centre: main shopping centre
Clinic/nursing home
Coffee-house
Employment exchange
Gas station/petrol pump
Graveyard/cemetery
ISBT (Inter-State Bus Terminus)
Museum
Old age home
Parish: the area that a priest in some Christian churches is responsible for
Picture house/picture theatre
Sports stadium
Stray cattle home: an authorised place for stray animal managed by Municipal Corporation. They are released to their owners only after payment of some fine
Tourist bungalow: a bungalow meant only for tourists and authorised officials

GRAMMAR AND USAGE

1. **Had better:** It is used to give suggestion
   Example: You **had better** repeat your dialogue(s) at least ten times to be able to use them naturally.
2. The verb 'mind' is normally followed by '-ing' form
   Example: "Do you mind calling me by my surname instead of first name?"
3. Whom is not often used in informal English we prefer to use 'who' as an object especially in questions. Example: Who did they arrest?
   We use 'whom' in a more formal style, and we must use whom after a preposition.
   Example: Whom did they arrest (formal)? With whom did you attend the party (very formal)?

EXPRESSIONS AND PHRASES FOR PRACTICE (Pair Activity)

1. Excuse me, could I ....?
2. Could you please tell me how ....?
3. Could you tell me where/when/what ....?
4. Please, could you guide me how ....?
5. I'd be grateful if (you could) ....?
6. I'd like (you) to ....?
7. Do you mind if I ....?
8. Where does this road ....?
9. Yes, of course, ...
10. I'm sorry ....

ACTIVITY

1. Imagine you have joined your present institution only a few days back and you have no idea where the library, canteen and Student Council office are located. Write six exchange dialogues between you and your class representative making enquiry about the location of these places. Make use of the expressions as given above (Pair activity).
2. Note down in your practice notebook the words and expressions given above and revise them every day till you can use them comfortably and naturally with correct pronunciation and proper stress and intonation.

7

AT THE RAILWAY RESERVATION COUNTER

READ aloud along with your friend the following conversation:

Himanshu: Could you please reserve me for Hyderabad by Hyderabad Express on 15th April? I need two berths in AC 2 tier, please.

Reservation clerk: Let me check up the position. Sorry Sir! there's no berth available on this day.

Himanshu: OK. Then tell me when I can get the reservation at the earliest.

Reservation clerk: On 20th April you get clear reservation, and on 19th you'll be waitlisted—number 22 and 23 RAC.

Himanshu: Do you think I **stand a good chance** of getting my RAC numbers cleared, if I book for 19th April?

Reservation clerk: You stand a very good chance, Sir. Based on my experience I can say that all **RAC** numbers upto 50 get easily cleared.

Himanshu: OK then book me for 19th April. How much shall I pay you for two tickets?

Reservation clerk: ₹ 2400/-

Himanshu: Fine! Here is the money!

Reservation clerk: Where is your reservation form?

Himanshu: It's here. I am giving it within 2 minutes after filling in. In the meantime, you can issue me the tickets, please.

Reservation clerk: Have you finished, Sir? Please hurry up. Other passengers are in the queue.

Himanshu: **Here you are!** Where are my tickets please?

Reservation clerk: Here are your tickets, Sir!

Himanshu: Thank you very much for all your help.

Reservation clerk: **You are welcome!**

WORD MEANING

1. **Stand a good chance:** an expression which means that the possibility is great
2. **Here you are!:** an expression used while giving something
3. **You're welcome:** an expression to be used when someone thanks you for something
4. **RAC:** Reservation Against Cancellation

COMPREHENSION

ANSWER the following questions briefly:

1. Where does Himanshu want to go?
2. When does he want to go?
3. How many berths does he need?
4. What does the reservation clerk tell Himanshu regarding his reservation on 15th April?
5. Which alternative date(s) does the clerk suggest to Himanshu?
6. Which date does Himanshu finally decide to travel on?
7. Why does the reservation clerk tell Himanshu to complete the reservation form quickly?

Rehearse the mentioned conversation with your friend 3 times (Pair activity).

EXPRESSIONS AND PHRASES FOR LEARNING

1. Could you please reserve me for Mumbai on 30th Sept. by Rajdhani Express?
2. Do you think I stand a good chance for the desired reservation?
3. Here is the money!
4. How much shall I pay you for AC 2 tier?
5. Thank you very much for all your help!
6. How much baggage is allowed free on one ticket?
7. What time does the train start?
8. What time does the train reach Mumbai?
9. How many stopovers are there between Itarsi and Mumbai Central?
10. What is the route like from Delhi to Mumbai?

EXTENDED VOCABULARY

Look up the following words in a dictionary to know their meanings and pronunciations and use them in appropriate situations.

2 tier/3 tier
Baggage
Book stall
Café
Cafeteria
Carriage
Chair car
Conductor: one who is overall in-charge for a compartment and its passengers
Coupe: a railway compartment meant for two persons only
Dining car
Down trains: trains coming to your station/arrival trains
Escalator
Fast/superfast/express/passenger/goods train
Hawkers
Lavatory/gentlemen/ladies/toilet/WC/washroom/rest room
Luggage room/cloak room
Luggage trolley
Platform ticket
Porters/coolies
Rails
Second AC/first AC
Senior citizen concession: concession given to people above 60 years of age
Sleeper: berth to sleep on
TTE: Train Ticket Examiner
Up trains: trains going away from your station/departure trains

GRAMMAR AND USAGE

1. When a sentence involves both direct and indirect objects, the indirect object (living) precedes the direct object (non-living), e.g.,

   IO DO

   Please buy *me* a kilo of *sugar* from the DDA market.
2. 'Let' can be used to introduce suggestions and orders, when these are not addressed to the hearer/reader. This structure can be considered a kind of imperative.

   For example, we can use: Let us (formal) or let's (informal) to make suggestions or give orders to a group that includes the speaker, e.g., Let's have coffee. OK. Let's all get moving. (This structure is called **first-person plural imperative.**)

   'Let me' is used to give instructions to oneself as well. 'Let me see' and 'Let me think' are very common. This structure is called **first-person singular imperative.**

EXPRESSIONS AND PHRASES FOR PRACTICE (Pair Activity)

1. What time does .... leave ....?
2. What time does this .... Mumbai?
3. How many stopovers .... between ....?
4. Does this train .... attached to it?
5. What are the alternative routes available for....................?
6. How much baggage is .... on one ticket?
7. What's the .... for Mumbai?
8. Does the fare include ....?
9. Where can I get .... from?
10. Is the train no. 202 for Chennai .... ?
11. Can you tell me the .... for journey break?

The given questions and possible answers may be practised in appropriate situations.

ACTIVITY

1. Imagine you want to go to Bangalore on 1st January. Go to some travel agent and book two seats. Write six exchange dialogues between you and the booking assistant.
2. Write down the given words and expressions in your practice notebook and keep revising them till you are able to use them in appropriate situations naturally, with correct pronunciation and proper stress and intonation.

8

BUYING A RAILWAY TICKET AND BOARDING A WRONG TRAIN

READ aloud along with your friend the following conversation:

Rahul: Please give me two tickets for Bhopal.
Booking clerk: Which class?
Rahul: First class!
Booking clerk: I am afraid, there is no seat in the first class. I may, however, give you two seats for 2nd class AC, if you so like.
Rahul: How much does it cost?
Booking clerk: It's five hundred and twenty for one ticket.
Rahul: OK, then give me two tickets for 2nd class AC. **Here is** the money!
Booking clerk: Would you please make the necessary corrections in your reservation form?
Rahul: **Of course**, I'll do it right now. Meanwhile, please issue me the tickets.
Booking clerk: **Would you please** hurry up? There are many people waiting for their turns?
Rahul: **Here you are!** What time does the train leave Delhi for Bhopal, and from which platform number?
Booking clerk: At 2010 hrs. from platform number 4. Everything is written on your ticket. Just **go through** it, please.
Rahul: Thank you very much.

(*Rahul goes to platform no. 4 with his wife and waits for the train. The train arrives and they get into the compartment.*)

Train conductor: Show me your ticket, please.
Rahul: **Here it is**!

Train conductor:	I am afraid, you have **boarded** the wrong train. This train does not stop at Bhopal. It directly goes to Nagpur. Your train will arrive in 10 minutes time from now, after this train has left. Hurry up, please. This train will leave in a few minutes.
Rahul:	Thank you, Sir! You have saved me from a big problem I would have faced if you had not asked me for my ticket.
Train conductor:	Well, it's my duty. Please, hurry up!

(*Rahul gets down with his wife and luggage.*)

WORD MEANING

1. **Here is/here you are:** expressions used while giving something
2. **Of course:** an expression used to agreeing to something
3. **Would you please:** an expression to make a request (a polite way of making a request)
4. **Go through:** read
5. **Boarded the train:** got into the train

COMPREHENSION

ANSWER the following questions:

1. Where does Rahul want to go?
2. Which class does he want to travel?
3. How many tickets does he want to buy?
4. Which class tickets does he finally buy?
5. Why does the booking clerk ask Rahul to hurry up?
6. What information does Rahul want from the booking clerk?
7. What does the train conductor tell Rahul after seeing his tickets?
8. How does the train conductor save Rahul from a big problem he could have faced if he had not seen his tickets?

Rehearse the above conversation with your friend 3 times (Pair activity).

EXPRESSIONS AND PHRASES FOR LEARNING

1. Please get me one first class ticket for Baroda.
2. I want one first class ticket for Baroda, please.
3. How much does it cost?
4. What is the fare like for Baroda by Rajdhani Express?
5. How much time does it take to reach Baroda?
6. What's the departure time of Rajdhani Express from New Delhi Railway Station?

7. What facilities do you provide to passengers going on 'Bharat Darshan'?
8. What are the security arrangements for passengers travelling by Rajdhani Express?
9. Do you have a dining car facility in the Rajdhani Express?

EXTENDED VOCABULARY

LOOK up the following words in a good dictionary/thesaurus to know their meanings and correct pronunciations and use them in your conversation.

AC (air-conditioning)
Book stall
Complaint book
Hawkers
Tea stall
Ticket collector
TTE (train ticket examiner)
Water-cabin
WC Indian style
WC Western style

GRAMMAR AND USAGE

1. The word, 'would like' is used to make a polite request.
2. While speaking, we use "Of course" to indicate our 'agreement' to something said by the speaker. But when we want to contradict it, we say: 'Of course not'.

EXPRESSIONS AND PHRASES FOR PRACTICE (Pair activity)

1. Give me .... for ...., please.
2. I want ...., please.
3. How much does it ....?
4. What's the .... fare from .... by Rajdhani Express?
5. How much time .... to reach .... Agra?
6. What's the departure time .... from .... station?
7. What facilities do you .... on a guided tour?
8. Do you provide .... to all or only to .... it?
9. How much do you charge for ....?

Learn the given expressions and use them in appropriate situations.

ACTIVITY

1. Write six exchange dialogues between two imaginary passengers, each claiming his entitlement to a particular berth in a compartment.
2. Write down the given words and expressions in your practice notebook and keep revising them till they become part of your linguistic attainments. Also use them in appropriate situations as naturally as you possibly can with proper stress and correct pronunciations.

9

AT THE AIRPORT

(*This is Rakesh's first visit to London. He is travelling by Air India flight no. IA 202. He goes to the Air India counter and reports his arrival*)

READ aloud the following conversation between Rakesh and the flight assistant:

Flight assistant: Ticket please.

Rakesh: Here is my ticket. Could you give me a window seat, please?

Flight assistant: Do you want it in the **smoking zone** or non-smoking one?

Rakesh: Non-smoking zone, please, I don't smoke.

Flight assistant: OK. Any baggage?

Rakesh: Yeah. It's over there. Incidentally, how much weight is allowed free on one ticket?

Flight assistant: 25 kg—Well, you have 5.5 kg extra weight. Either you pay for the **excess baggage** or take out a few things from your briefcase. You can keep those things in your handbag, if you so like. You see, we don't weigh a handbag. It's free.

(*Rakesh takes out a few things from the briefcase and keeps them in his handbag*)

Rakesh: Is it all right now?

Flight assistant: Perfectly all right! Here is your boarding pass and ticket. And here is the tag for your handbag. Please tie it on to your bag. It's important. You are not allowed to take your handbag inside the flight without this tag.

Rakesh: OK, I am going to tie it to my handbag right now. What else?

Flight assistant: Well, now you should go to the State Bank to your right and collect your foreign exchange from there. You have already paid your airport tax at the time of buying your ticket.

Rakesh:	Thanks! I am sorry, this being my first air trip I am **bothering** you for one thing or the other. Tell me, if I have to come back to you again after collecting my **foreign exchange**?
Flight assistant:	No, Sir, unless you have a problem.
Rakesh:	By the way, what's our flight position? Is it on time?
Flight assiatant:	No, Sir. Your flight is late by two hours. You can now go for the security check and relax in the passenger lounge till your flight arrives.
Rakesh:	But how will I know that my flight has arrived?
Flight assistant:	Don't worry Sir! There will be an announcement for it. By the way, you are also required to go through the security check and customs and **emigration** clearance, besides identifying your baggage. Have a nice time, Sir! Please make sure that you don't go into the **immigration** section.
Rakesh:	Thanks!
Customs officer:	Please leave your handbag on the board of this x-ray machine. You can collect it at the other end after it passes through this machine.
Rakesh:	Anything else?
Customs officer:	Not exactly. Now you can go to Gate No. 2 for security check.
Rakesh:	Thanks!

(*Rakesh passes through the security check. After collecting his handbag from the x-ray machine he sits on a sofa in the passenger lounge till the announcement for boarding his flight is made.*)

WORD MEANING

1. **Smoking zone:** an area wherein passengers can smoke
2. **Baggage:** luggage
3. **Excess baggage:** extra weight (above the authorised weight) on which one has to pay extra charges to the airlines
4. **Bothering:** troubling
5. **Foreign exchange:** hard currency which is acceptable all over the world as per the conversion rates announced by RBI on day-to-day basis
6. **Emigration:** going out of the country
7. **Immigration:** coming into the country

COMPREHENSION

There are three choices for each question. Tick (✓) the choice you consider to be correct.

1. Where is Rakesh going?
   (a) He's going to Mumbai.

(b) He's going to London.
(c) He's going to Hyderabad.

2. What is Rakesh's request to the flight assistant while reporting his arrival?
(a) He wants a comfortable seat in the front.
(b) He wants a window seat.
(c) He wants a window seat in the non-smoking zone.

3. Why does the flight assistant advise Rakesh to transfer a few things from his briefcase to his handbag?
(a) The briefcase is not closing.
(b) Rakesh will not be required to pay for the excess baggage.
(c) As the handbag is not weighed Rakesh will not be required to pay for the excess baggage.

4. Why does the flight assistant ask Rakesh to tie the tag onto his handbag?
(a) To identify his handbag.
(b) The handbag is not allowed inside the flight without the tag.
(c) If it is lost it can be easily traced out.

5. Why does the flight assistant ask Rakesh to go to the State Bank?
(a) To convert rupees into pounds.
b) To deposit the airport tax.
(c) To collect the foreign exchange.

6. What is Rakesh expected to do before he boards the flight?
(a) He's expected to go through the security check and customs and emigration clearance.
(b) He's expected to identify his baggage.
(c) He's expected to go through the security check and customs and emigration clearance, besides identifying his baggage.

7. What does the customs officer advise Rakesh to do?
(a) To go to the passengers lounge and relax after security check and customs and emigration clearance.
(b) To leave his handbag on the board of the x-ray machine and collect it at its other end.
(c) Not to take any firearm along with him.

Rehearse the conversation with the help of your friend 3 times (Pair activity).

EXPRESSIONS AND PHRASES FOR LEARNING AND PRACTICE

1. Could you give me a window seat, please?
2. Please hang on for a minute. Let me check up my reservation chart.
3. Do you want it in the executive class or the economy class?

4. I want it in the economy class.
5. Could you tell me how much my baggage weighs?
6. It's 35 kg.
7. What're the rates for excess baggage?
8. Where can I find a trolley to carry my baggage?
9. I'm afraid, you're not allowed to carry any firearm inside the flight.
10. Here's your boarding card/ticket!

The given expressions may be learnt and practised with required changes in appropriate situations.

EXTENDED VOCABULARY

LOOK up the following words in a good dictionary to know their meanings and pronunciations. Also use them while travelling by air.

Accompanied baggage vs.
unaccompanied baggage
Aerodrome/airport
Aircraft/Boeing/Airbus
Aircrew/crew/airhostess
Air fare
Air pocket
Air schedule
Air ticket
Baggage
Boarding card
Bon voyage
Break journey
Cabin
Check in
Cockpit
Conveyor belt
Customs clearance
Customs duty
Duty-free item
Duty-free shop
Emergency landing
Emigration/immigration
Entry visa/exit visa/transit visa
Excess baggage
Fasten the seat belt
Flight is boarding
Flight is landing
Foggy
Green channel vs. red channel
Hangars
Hijack
Hopping flight
Itinerary
Ladder
Trolley
Non-stop flight
Open ticket
Overhead lockers
Passage
Pilot
Poor visibility
Reception
Re-fuelling
Reporting time
Route
Runway
Safe landing
Seat belt
Souvenir shop
Take-off

GRAMMAR AND USAGE

1. The past form of "can", meaning PERMISSION is always "could", e.g., I could sit wherever I liked (permission granted). However, when we use 'can' to indicate "capacity" or "ability" we use "is/was able to", e.g., I was able to walk 5 kilometres easily, after my operation (capacity or ability to walk).
2. We can use "have" with or without 'do' as 'have to', replacing must. For example,

   (a) Have you to work hard?
   (b) Do you have to work hard?

ANNOUNCEMENTS AT THE AIRPORT

1. Air India announces the arrival of fight AI 203 from Paris.
2. There is a message for Mr Verma. Mr Verma would you please go to the information counter.

EXPRESSIONS AND PHRASES FOR PRACTICE (Pair activity)

1. Could you ...., please?
2. Please .... for a minute.
3. I want the reservation ....
4. What are .... unaccompanied baggage?
5. I am afraid ....
6. Where can I ....?
7. Here is ....
8. Do you ....?
9. Either you .... or ....

ACTIVITY

1. Note down the words and ideas/unit expressions used here in your practice notebook and keep revising them till you are able to use them naturally in your conversation.
2. You want to see Europe during your vacation along with your parents. Write six exchange dialogues between you and the travel agents enquiring about their tour packages announced in the newspaper.

10

TRAVELLING BY STATE BUS

READ aloud along with your friend the following conversation between Sumit and the bus conductor:

Sumit:	(*Boarding the bus*) Excuse me, does this bus go to Akshar Dham temple?
Bus conductor:	Yes, it does.
Sumit:	Could you please drop me just before Akshar Dham temple? I'm not able to walk much due to my foot injury.
Bus conductor:	Sorry Sir! We are not allowed to stop the bus at a place other than the bus stop.
Sumit:	**Never mind**! I'll somehow manage to walk. Then give me one ticket for Akshar Dham, please.
Bus conductor:	(*Giving the ticket*) Here you are! Give me 10 rupees, please!
Sumit:	Why are you demanding 10 rupees? I'm told it is only five rupees.
Bus conductor:	It is a deluxe air-conditioned bus, Sir. You pay 5 rupees for an ordinary bus only.
Sumit:	OK (*takes out a 500/- rupee note from his pocket and gives it to the conductor*). I'm sorry, I can't **tender** the exact amount, I don't have a note of lesser denomination.
Bus conductor:	I don't have any change, either. If you like you can wait till I have the required balance to give you. Or else, you can get down at the next bus stop.
Sumit:	I think, I'll prefer to wait. Could I sit beside you to avoid any kind of confusion at my bus stop?
Bus conductor:	Please do, no problem!
Sumit:	Thanks Mr Conductor! I think, you are the first conductor, I have ever come across, who is so generous and helpful to the passengers.

Bus conductor: Thanks for your **kind words**, Sir. It is my duty.

(*The bus conductor gives the balance amount to Sumit in hardly ten minutes time, and Sumit gets down at Akshar Dham stop.*)

WORD MEANING

1. **Never mind:** it is an expression used to show that the speaker does not mind the reply of the other person
2. **Tender:** offer; give
3. **Kind words:** words of praise

COMPREHENSION

There are three choices for each question. Tick (✓) the choice you consider to be correct.

1. Where does Sumit want to go?
   (a) He wants to go to the city centre.
   (b) He wants to go for sight-seeing.
   (c) He wants to go to the Akshar Dham temple.
2. Where does Sumit want to get down?
   (a) Just before the temple
   (b) Near the temple
   (c) One stop before Akshar Dham temple.
3. Why does the bus conductor refuse to accept Sumit's request?
   (a) He doesn't care for passengers' problems.
   (b) He is not allowed to stop the bus at a place other than the bus stop.
   (c) He is in a hurry to reach the bus terminus.
4. Why does the bus conductor demand ₹ 10 from Sumit?
   (a) He wants to keep 5 rupees for himself.
   (b) It is a deluxe air-conditioned bus.
   (c) The fare has gone up.
5. What are the two options that the conductor gives to Sumit?
   (a) He should get down or give him an exact amount.
   (b) He should wait till he has the balance amount to give him or he should get down at the next bus stop.
   (c) He may collect the balance amount from the bus terminus or get down immediately.
6. Sumit felt impressed by the behaviour of the bus conductor because,
   (a) The conductor did not ask him to get down from the bus.
   (b) The conductor allowed him to sit by his side.
   (c) The conductor was polite and helpful to the passengers.

EXPRESSIONS AND PHRASES FOR LEARNING

1. Could you please drop me at the National Museum?
2. Sorry Madam, I was not able to deliver your message to your brother-in-law due to taxi-strike.
3. Never mind, I have another interesting role for you.
4. Why are you insisting on cash payment? I can pay you by draft or pay order.
5. I'm afraid, I can't tender you the exact amount.
6. I'll prefer to go by the next bus than to travel on this crowded bus.
7. Could I sit beside you to get an easy access to the exit gate?
8. Thanks for your kind words, Sir!

EXTENDED VOCABULARY

LOOK up the following words and phrases in a good dictionary to know their meanings and pronunciations. Also use them in similar situations.

Break down
Diversion of route
Footboard travelling
Front gate vs. rear gate
Pickpocket
Seat reserved for ladies/senior citizens/physically challenged
Sit beside
Tender the exact amount

GRAMMAR AND USAGE

Anomalous Finites

1. The 24 anomalous finite verbs (such as do, does, did, can, could, shall, should, will, would, has, have, had, etc.) are used in short answers to questions, e.g., Did you invite him? Yes, I did or No, I didn't.
2. These finites are also used to avoid repetition of a verb in the following coordinate clause, e.g., The baby never cried, and when he 'did', no one paid any attention.
3. These 24 anomalous finite verbs are often used in 'tag' questions, added to statements, e.g.,:

   (a) She left yesterday, didn't she?
   (b) You want to come at 5 p.m., don't you?
   (c) They won't be here long, will they?
   (d) Today is Monday, isn't it?

EXPRESSIONS AND PHRASES FOR PRACTICE (Pair Activity)

1. Yes, it does Vs. No, it doesn't.
2. Could you ....?
3. Sorry, I'm not allowed ....
4. Here you are! Now please ....
5. If you wish/like ....
6. Never mind! I ....
7. Kind words ....
8. Tender ....

ACTIVITY

1. Imagine you want to go to 'Qutab Minar' but you have no idea which route number bus goes there. Write six exchange dialogues between you and some passenger waiting at the bus stop, enquiring about the deluxe air-conditioned route bus numbers which may take you to Qutab Minar.
2. Write down in your practice notebook, the words and expressions given in this unit and keep revising them till you can use them in appropriate situations with ease and correct pronunciations.
3. Write down five questions of your choice that you may like to ask the bus conductor on boarding the bus.

11

GIVING A MESSAGE ON PHONE

READ aloud with the help of your friend the following telephonic conversation:

Neena: Hello, is that 22241623?
Parvi: **Yea**. May I know who is **calling**?
Neena: This is Neena Roy.
Parvi: Hi Neena! What can I do for you?
Neena: Could I speak to Rashi, please?
Parvi: I am afraid, **she isn't in** right now.
Neena: When is she likely to be back?
Parvi: No idea. She didn't tell me where she was going and what time she would return.
Neena: In that case, would you please **pass on** one message to her?
Parvi: Of course, with great pleasure. What's it?
Neena: Please tell her that Dr Swami, our Managing Director would like to see her tomorrow at 11 a.m. in his office.
Parvi: In what connection?
Neena: Well, she has applied for a job in our company. He would like to talk to her in that connection. Please **ensure** that she receives this message when she is back home.
Parvi: Don't worry! I'll definitely pass on the message to her personally. Is there anything else I can do for you?
Neena: No, thanks!
Parvi: You're most welcome! Bye-bye!
Neena: Bye-bye.

WORD MEANING

1. **Yea:** Yes

2. **Calling:** speaking
3. **She isn't in:** she is not at home
4. **Pass on:** give
5. **Ensure:** make sure

COMPREHENSION

ANSWER the following questions:

1. Who has called?
2. Who has answered the phone?
3. What's the surname of the caller?
4. Who does she want to speak to?
5. Why does she want to speak to her?
6. Why can't she speak to her?
7. Why can't Parvi tell Neena the whereabouts of Rashi?
8. What message does Neena want Parvi to deliver to Rashi?
9. How does Parvi greet Neena?
10. What words/expressions do Neena and Parvi use to terminate their conversation?

Rehearse the above conversation with your partner 3 times (Pair activity).

EXPRESSIONS AND PHRASES FOR LEARNING (Pair Activity)

1. Could you ask Rashi to call me back?
2. Hold the line please.
3. Would you please pass on a message to Rashi?
4. May I know who is calling?
5. I'm afraid, she isn't in right now.
6. When is she likely to be back?
7. No idea.
8. Of course, with great pleasure.
9. What can I do for you?

EXTENDED VOCABULARY

LOOK up the following words in a good dictionary to know their meanings and pronunciations. Also use them in your conversation in appropriate situations:

Call box
Call conference
Call forwarding/diverting facility
Call hold

Call transfer
Call waiting
Caller
Caller's ID number
Cell phone/cellular phone
Coin operated kiosk
Collect call
Cordless phone
Cradle
Incoming/outgoing call
Itemised bill
Local call/STD/ISD/overseas call
Long distance call
Pay-in-phone
Reverse charge call
Roaming facility
Sim
SMS (Short Message Service)
Tariff plan
VMS (Voice Mail Service)

GRAMMAR AND USAGE

STUDY the following expressions to be able to use imperatives appropriately.

1. Inform her about this meeting. (giving an order)
2. Would you mind informing her about this meeting? (making a request)
3. Could you inform her about this meeting? (making a request)
4. Perhaps you could inform her about this meeting. (expressing a wish)

Please note that it is impolite to give an order when you can get the work done by making a request or expressing a wish.

EXPRESSIONS AND PHRASES FOR PRACTICE (Pair Activity)

1. Could I speak to ....?
2. Who is ...., please?
3. Could you ask .... to call me back when he gets back?
4. I am just returning your call, (a message on the answering machine) please ....
5. I'll put you through ....
6. I am a colleague from work/I am his/her colleague, could you please ....
7. Would/Could you please pass on a message to ....?
8. Of course, with ....
9. Would you please give a tinkle to ....?
10. Could you answer the phone, please? I'm ....

Write down the given expressions in your practice notebook and keep revising them till you are able to use them naturally in appropriate situations.

ACTIVITY

1. Note down the given words and expressions in your practice notebook and keep revising them everyday till you have mastered them and can use in similar situations naturally and effectively.
2. Construct at least six exchange dialogues between two friends seeking and supplying information about the 'Welcome Day' for the new students of your institution.
3. Talk to your close friend on phone everyday for three minutes discussing about various things of common interests.

12

ATTENDING AN INTERVIEW FOR A JOB

A, B, C and D = Members of the interview board (**interviewers**)
E = Chairperson
Ankur Mittal = Candidate (**interviewee**)

READ aloud the following interview (Group activity):

(*Ankur enters the interview room*)

Ankur Mittal: Good morning, Sirs!

All the members: Good morning Mr Mittal !

Chairperson: Please be seated, Mr Mittal. You seem to have a literary name, Mr Mittal. What's the meaning of the word 'Ankur'?

Ankur: **'Sprout'**. My mother is a writer. She has given me this name.

Chairperson: Good! Mr Mittal, as per your **CV** you have changed four jobs in just two years. What's the matter? Do you think your decisions went wrong or the selection committees selected a wrong person?

Ankur: I think, I made wrong decisions. In fact, whenever, I **tendered** my resignation the Director of the company concerned would always **insist** on me to reconsider my decision to resign. What prompted me to resign was my desire to acquire a different kind of experience in the field of consumer products.

Chairperson: Does it mean that here too you intend joining this job only to acquire a different kind of experience?

Ankur: Certainly not, Sir. Now I am married. I can't afford changing my job so frequently. Moreover, your company is a company of repute. No one would like to leave it once appointed here.

A: Mr Mittal, you have a brilliant academic record to your credit. Based on your experience of having worked in four different

	companies, tell us what attracts a customer most to a consumer product.
Ankur:	Well, an **affordable** price, its attractive packing, its quality and its wide publicity.
B:	Ankur, if you were the Production Manager of our company how would you ensure the quality and packing of our toothpaste ***Dazzle***?
Ankur:	Through **monitoring** and quality control committees comprising officials and representatives of workers' union. I would also like to introduce an attractive **incentive** scheme to motivate workers to excel in their performance.
C:	Ankur, you don't have the experience of working in any company dealing in toothpaste. How would you manage in case you are appointed here?
Ankur:	No doubt, the experience in a particular area is of great value, the experience in similar areas is in no way less important. It does help a person by providing him/her a useful frame of mind. I am sure, with all my experience with consumer products I can **deal with** confidence any kind of problem related to your product. Don't worry, Sir. I'll come up to your expectations.
D:	Should we decide to appoint you here in this company, what salary would you expect, and how much joining time would you need?
Ankur:	₹ 80000/- p.m., with perks. Regarding joining time, I can join immediately since I am not working anywhere at the moment.
Chairperson:	Fine! We'll let you know about the result of the interview in an hour's time. In the meantime, would you please wait in the visitor's room. Thank you Ankur for being with us.
Ankur:	Thank you! good day to all of you, Sirs!

WORD MEANING

1. **Interviewer:** one who interviews candidates
2. **interviewee:** one who appears for the interview
3. **Sprout:** starting to grow on something
4. **CV: (abbreviation of curriculum vitae)** a written record of your education and experience that you send when you apply for a job. **Résumé** is yet another word used in place of CV
5. **Tendered:** submitted
6. **Insist:** pressurise
7. **Affordable:** easily payable
8. **Monitoring:** watch and check something over a period of time to see its progress
9. **Incentive:** that motivates one to do something
10. **Deal with:** handle

COMPREHENSION

ANSWER the following questions briefly:

1. Who is the interviewee?
2. How many members constitute the interview board?
3. What was the first question that the chairperson asked the candidate?
4. What was the candidate's reply?
5. What justification does the candidate give for his name?

There are three choices for each question. Tick (✓) the choice you consider to be correct.

1. What inference was drawn by the chairperson from the frequent change of jobs by the candidate?
   (a) The selection committees selected a wrong person.
   (b) The candidate made a wrong decision to join the job each time.
   (c) The selection committees selected a wrong person or the candidate took a wrong decision to join those jobs.
2. Why did the candidate change his jobs so frequently?
   (a) He wanted to earn more money.
   (b) He realised his mistake of joining a particular job only after working for some time.
   (c) He wanted to acquire different kinds of experiences in the field of consumer goods.
3. What reason did the candidate give to the chairperson to stay on in this company?
   (a) He is interested in the product, Dazzle.
   (b) He is a married man and cannot afford to be without a job
   (c) He is married and the company's reputation is very good.
4. What strategy would the candidate adopt to ensure the quality and good packing of the toothpaste Dazzle?
   (a) He would take the help of monitoring committee
   (b) He would ensure it through monitoring and quality control committees.
   (c) He would ensure them through the monitoring and quality control committees, besides offering various incentives to the workers.
5. How would the candidate intend compensating his lack of experience of working in a toothpaste producing company?
   (a) By having a useful frame of mind.
   (b) By learning from his colleagues.
   (c) By using his earlier experience in consumer goods.
6. How much salary does the candidate expect?
   (a) As per the prescribed scale of pay.
   (b) ₹ 20000/-
   (c) ₹ 80000/- with perks

7. Why did the candidate say that he could join immediately, if appointed?
   (a) He never wanted to take any risk.
   (b) He was not working anywhere.
   (c) He was very keen on acquiring a new kind of experience.

Rehearse the above conversation with your partner 3 times (Pair activity).

EXPRESSIONS AND PHRASES FOR LEARNING

1. What are the duty hours?
2. How many days casual/earned leave during a year am I entitled to?
3. What will be the duration of my probation period?
4. Excellent!
5. How come?
6. How about?
7. What about?
8. I am afraid, (I am sorry)
9. Is it a regular/permanent post?
10. Does your company provide LTC to its employees?
11. Is the post pensionable?
12. Do you give your employees all such facilities as are admissible to the central government employees?
13. My wife is M.A., B.Ed. Is there any possibility of her appointment in your company's public school?
14. What are my chances for getting the company accommodation?
15. Do you have a good health centre in the township?

Write down the given questions and expressions in your practice notebook and keep revising them till you are able to use them naturally in appropriate situations.

EXTENDED VOCABULARY

LOOK up the following words in a good dictionary to know their meanings. Also use them in appropriate situations.

Academic qualifications
Audience
Bond
Briefing
Capability
Card punching system
Casual leave/privilege leave/earned leave/extraordinary leave/half-pay leave
Christian name/ first name/middle name/last name/surname
Co-curricular and extra-curricular activities

CV/Resume/bio-data*
Commuted leave
Compulsory subjects
Conveyance allowance
Corrective measures
CPF/GPF/Pension
Disciplinary action
Dismissal
Emoluments
Entitlements
Family name
First love
Gratuity
Guarantee
Guarantor
Hobbies
Honorarium
Interview

Joining time
LTC facility
Maintenance allowance
Optional subjects
Performance appraisal
Perks
Personal discussion
Probation period
Punctuality
References/referees
Reimbursement facility
Reinstate
Responsibilities handled
Revoke
Subject combination; discipline
Surety
Suspension
Work experience

GRAMMAR AND USAGE

Study the following uses of the verb 'insist'.

1. She insisted on his/him wearing a black suit.
2. He insisted on his innocence (to say something firmly).
3. If you insist, I'll definitely attend your marriage (informal).
4. She insists that I should meet her parents immediately.
5. They insisted upon being given every detail of the case.

Insist on/upon something is also a 'phrasal verb'which means to demand something and refuse to be persuaded to accept anything else.

Some verbs change their meaning when used with a particular preposition or adverb. These verbs + preposition/adverb are considered to be a special type of verb, called **phrasal verb**.

SOME USEFUL TIPS TO SPEAK

1. **Cheerful countenance:** Greet the members of the interview board warmly and smilingly, and maintain it throughout the interaction.
2. **Set the direction of the interview:** Usually, the personal interview starts with a question like: Tell us about yourself, or introduce yourself to the members of this board.

* Avoid using it as it is not yet used by the native speakers.

Such a question is asked by the chairperson of the board to pick up the data or area for purpose of giving a direction to the interview. So this is a wonderful opportunity for a candidate to set the direction of his or her own interview. Highlight only those areas in your introduction in which you feel the strongest and most interested.

3. **Be a patient listener:** Answer the questions posed only after careful listening. Don't be in a hurry to answer them.
4. **Give extra attention to other communication skills:** Besides good listening, pay extra attention to your fluency, correct pronunciation and proper stress and intonation. These skills have a deep impact on the members of the interviewing board while deciding on the selection of the candidate.
5. **Body language:** Body language (movements of hands, shoulders and eyes, etc.) conveys a lot about the candidate being interviewed. Hence, make conscious efforts to develop the proper body language as a part of your communication skills.
6. **Eye contact:** An eye contact with the members of the interview board, especially with the one asking you questions, is very important for a candidate to remember. Looking straight into the eyes of the member tells the interviewer about the self-confidence and honesty of the candidate.
7. **Be honest:** What impresses the members of the interview board most about the candidate is his or her honesty in responding to the question(s) asked. So, if you don't know the answer of a certain question asked you had better tell the members that you don't know it rather than bluffing them.
8. **Be polite and respectful:** Politeness does not reflect any kind of weakness on the part of the candidate. Rather it speaks of his or her strength. Everyone likes to be respected and dealt with politely. So do you.
9. **Be properly dressed:** Dress of a person is his or her first introduction to the outside world. So decide in advance what dress you are going to wear on the date of the interview. Always remember that the dress you choose must be as per the weather and occasion. Since the occasion is interview which is indeed a serious occasion you are expected to wear only a formal dress. Avoid wearing a gaudy coloured dress and loud prints.

EXPRESSIONS AND PHRASES FOR PRACTICE (Pair Activity)

1. What's .... Christian name/first name?
2. What's .... surname/family name?
3. What's .... middle name?

4. What's .... full name?
5. What was .... subject combination?
6. You .... a double M.A., ... you? Which is .... first love?
7. When .... you acquire .... first degree?
8. What's the difference .... a regular student and a non-collegiate ....?
10. Why did .... join humanities/science/commerce stream and why not ....?
11. How much salary .... expect?
12. What perks .... you expect?
13. How much joining time .... need?
14. When can you .... the post?
15. Could you .... two sureties?
16. What remedial measures .... to .... from coming late?
17. How can we encourage .... in the management of the company?
18. What are your spare-time ....?
19. How can meditation .... factory's production?
20. What measures would you .... to ensure the quality of the product?
21. What welfare schemes and incentives .... to ....?

ACTIVITY

1. Imagine you are the head boy/head girl of your school. Your school principal has asked you to select 4 House Captains for your school on the basis of their performance in an interview for the same. Organize this mock interview and select 4 House Captains to head the four Houses of your school.
2. Note down the given words and questions in your practice notebook and use them effectively in appropriate situations.

13

AT THE BANK

READ aloud with your friend the following conversation:

Customer: Good morning, Sir!

Manager: Good morning, gentleman!

Customer: I want to open a savings bank account in your branch. Could you please help me?

Manager: **Of course!** Please go to counter no. 3 and ask for Mr Saxena. He'll guide you. If you still have some problems, please come to me.

Customer: Thanks!

(*Customer goes to counter no. 3 and asks for Mr Saxena*)

Customer: Are you Mr Saxena?

Saxena: Yes, I am Saxena. What can I do for you?

Customer: The manager has directed me to contact you in connection with the opening of my savings bank account. Could you help me, please?

Sexena: Of course! It's my duty to help my customers. Tell me, do you want to open a joint account or a single one?

Customer: I think I should **go in for** a joint account. I would like it to be jointly operated by me and my wife. Is it all right?

Saxena: Fine! Wait a minute, please. Let me take out a set of forms to be filled in by you…. (*giving the form*). Here it is!

Customer: Thank you! By the way, could you fill in this form for me? I am not very **good at** filling of forms. I'll sign wherever you want me to.

Saxena: OK, would you please sit just opposite me and give me the required information as I fill in your form.

Customer: No problem.

Saxena: Your name, please; your father's name; permanent address in Delhi; telephone numbers; profession.

Customer: (*Supplies the required information*)

Saxena: Fine, now you can sign at the places marked.

Customer:	Anything else am I expected to do towards opening of the savings bank account?
Saxena:	Yes, just two more things. First you have to get yourself introduced by someone having an account in this branch, or else you have to show me your identity card and submit a photocopy thereof. Don't worry! I myself will attest it. Secondly, your wife also has to sign these set of forms since she is the joint account holder. Where is she?
Customer:	I'm sorry, I don't know any of your customers maintaining their account here. But I can definitely show you my identity card and submit its photocopy. As for my wife, she is sitting in the car outside. She'll be here in no time.
Saxena:	OK. Show me your identity card please. Fine, please get it photocopied now. There's a photocopier just outside this branch.
Customer:	Here is a photocopy of my identity card! My wife is also here to sign the form. Please tell her where to sign.
Saxena:	Just at the marked places, please. (*Gets it done*)
Customer:	Here is the set of forms duly signed by me and my wife! We are indeed grateful to you for all your help. Can we go now?
Saxena:	Oh yes! But wait a minute please! Have you deposited ₹ 1000/- towards the opening of your account and for availing the cheque book facility?
Customer:	Sorry Sir, I just forgot to deposit it. I am going to do it right now. Anything else?
Saxena:	No thanks! You can collect your pay-in-slip and the **personalised cheque-book** in an hour's time. If you like you can wait here.
Customer:	No thanks! We'll be back in an hour to collect the pay-in-slip and the cheque book. Thank you Mr Saxena for all your cooperation!
Saxena:	You are most welcome!

WORD MEANING

1. **Of course:** an expression used to convey agreement to something said or asked
2. **Go in for:** opt for
3. **Good at:** proficient in something
4. **Personalised cheque-book:** a cheque-book with the name of the account holder printed on each cheque leaf

COMPREHENSION

There are three choices for every question given below. Tick (✓) the choice you consider to be correct:

1. Why does the customer go to the bank?
   (a) He goes to the bank to deposit money in his account.

(b) He goes there to withdraw money from his account.
(c) He goes there to open a savings bank account.

2. What does the Bank Manager advise the customer?
(a) The Bank Manager advises the customer to meet Mr Saxena at counter no. 3.
(b) The Bank Manager advises the customer to meet him the next day.
(c) The Bank Manager advises the customer to wait.
3. The customer wants to open,
(a) A single SB Account.
(b) A joint SB Account.
(c) A joint SB Account to be jointly operated by him and his wife.
4. Why does the customer ask Mr Saxena to fill in the set of forms for him?
(a) The customer doesn't know how to read or write.
(b) The customer is not good at filling up the forms.
(c) The customer doesn't have a pen to fill in those forms.
5. What does Mr Saxena ask the customer to do towards the opening of the account?
(a) Mr Saxena asks him to a give a surety for the opening of the account.
(b) Mr Saxena asks him to get himself introduced by someone maintaining an account with that branch of the bank or else submit a photocopy of his identity card.
(c) Mr Saxena asks him to submit a photocopy of his ration card.
6. Why does Mr Saxena want the customer's wife to sign those forms along with his signature?
(a) She is a joint accountholder.
(b) He wants her to sign as a witness.
(c) He wants her to act as a surety.
7. How much money was the customer asked to deposit towards the opening of the account and availing of the cheque book facility?
(a) ₹ 500/-
(b) ₹ 250/-
(c) ₹ 1000/-

Rehearse the above conversation with your partner 3 times (Pair activity).

EXPRESSIONS AND PHRASES FOR LEARNING

1. I would like to open a savings bank account in your branch.
2. Excuse me, are you Mr Sinha?
3. I think, I should go in for a current account.
4. By the way, what are the banking hours?
5. Here is the photocopy of my passport.

6. Since it's a high value cheque, could it be credited to my account today?
7. No thanks, I have had coffee just now.
8. Oh yes, I would like to avail of the credit card facility.
9. Do I have to come to the branch personally to get the draft made?
10. I'm afraid, I don't know any of your bank employees or customers.

EXTENDED VOCABULARY

LOOK up the following words in a good dictionary to know their meanings and pronunciations and use them while banking.

Account payee cheque/bearer cheque/ cross cheque
Accrue
Assets
ATM facility
Authority for payment
Bank advice
Banking hours
Bouncing of cheque/cheque dishonour
Capital gain account/current account/ SB account
Computerised account
Computerised branch
Counterfoil
Credit/debit
Credit card/debit card
Customers/clients
Dealing assistant
Denomination
Deposit slip
Dividend
Double-locking system
Drawee
Drawer
Drawn on
Guarantor
Hiring/surrender of locker
Introduction
Joint operation
Ledger number/ledger folio
Minimum balance
Mode of payment
Online banking
Payee
Pay-in-slip
Post-dated cheque
Specimen signature(s)
Stop payment
Strong-room
Surety
TDS
Teller system
Time-barred cheque

GRAMMAR AND USAGE

When we make negative statements we mostly use no, not, not any, none, etc.

Always remember that a negative verb is usually followed by 'any' (anywhere, anybody, anything). Look at the following examples.

1. (a) There weren't any students in the class.
   (b) There were no students in the class.
2. (a) I called her last night, but perhaps there wasn't anybody in the house.
   (b) I called her last night, but perhaps there was nobody in the house.

EXPRESSIONS AND PHRASES FOR PRACTICE (Pair Activity)

1. What are the conditions for .... (capital gain account/current account)?
2. What documents .... (need for the opening of ....)?
3. What .... (formalities to be completed to .... open/close ....)?
4. What .... (the rate of interest on .... for a period of ....)?
5. What .... (the minimum amount required to open a .... with cheque facility)?
6. How many times a week .... (withdraw money from my .... account)?
7. What .... (difference between a draft and a pay order)?
8. How many days .... (cheque/draft/pay order take for credit into the account)?
9. Do I .... (interest on the cheque amount from the date of its deposit or from the date of its credit)?
10. Who .... (responsible for loss of the cheque in transit—bank or the individual)?
11. How .... (exchange old currency notes for the new ones)?
12. What .... (difference between a credit card and a debit card)?

Drill the given questions and use them in appropriate situations.

ACTIVITY

1. You want to invest ₹ 100,000. Go to the SBI and talk to the bank manager about it. Write six exchange dialogues between you and the bank manager enquiring about the various schemes available for investment of this amount so that you may get the best return of your investment. Use the given expressions and words.
2. Write down the given words and expressions that you find new in your practice notebook and keep revising them in meaningful situations till such time you have learnt them well, and you are able to use them in appropriate situations correctly and naturally, using correct pronunciation and proper stress and intonation.

14

AT THE HOSPITAL

READ aloud with your friend the following conversation:

Patient: Excuse me, could you tell me where will the OPD for ENT take place?

Enquiry: OPD hall no. 3

Patient: What time does it start?

Enquiry: 9 o'clock.

Patient: Who is the doctor in-charge?

Enquiry: Dr Khurana—Prof. and Head, Department of ENT.

Patient: Thank you, sister!

Enquiry: You're welcome!

(*Goes to OPD hall no. 3 and contacts the inquiry*)

Patient: Excuse me sister, I want to contact Dr Khurana. Where can I meet him?

Enquiry: At the OPD. For that, you have to get your name registered here. What's your name please?

Patient: Rama Kant—Rama Kant Gautam

Enquiry: Age?

Patient: 35 years.

Enquiry: What's your **problem**?

Patient: I am suffering from an **acute nasal** problem.

Enquiry: Since when?

Patient: It's a **chronic** problem, for the last 10 years.

Enquiry: Here's your registration card! Please pay ₹ 5/- towards registration fee.

Patient: (*Giving a five-rupee note*) Here you are! By the way, what's my consultation number?

Enquiry: Eighteen

Patient: Thanks!

(*Rama Kant goes to the OPD and meets Dr Khurana*)

Dr Khurana: What's exactly your problem, Mr Rama Kant?

Patient: Well doctor, I keep sneezing all the time, 500–600 times a day. It has badly affected my hearing and vision, besides causing me **embarrassment** and inconvenience to others.

Dr Khurana: How long have you been suffering from this problem?

Patient: For the last 10 years.

Dr Khurana: Can you tell me how it all started?

Patient: Doctor, I was posted to Moscow at that time. For one full year I didn't have any health related problem . In fact, I maintained a very good health despite difficult weather conditions. But soonafter, I developed this problem. It started with cough and cold, with a lot of sneezing. The doctors who treated me for this problem at Moscow told me that I was allergic to cold and I would be all right in a warm climate. But unfortunately, the problem has **persisted** even after 10 years of my coming back to India. Of course, the frequency of sneezing is less now.

Dr Khurana: Don't worry, you will be all right! Can I examine your nose? (*Dr examines the nose*)

Patient: Doctor, what do you find? Is it curable or do you think I will have to live with it throughout my life?

Dr Khurana: There is nothing to worry about. Sinus now is cent per cent curable. Only you will have to be a little patient. You know, it is a chronic case. It also requires surgery.

Patient: How much bed rest do you think I'll need after the operation?

Dr Khurana: About 10 days

Patient: Doctor, in that case please arrange for my operation some time next week. I'll indeed be grateful to you!

Dr Khurana: Fine! Shall I fix next Friday for the operation?

Patient: No problem. Thank you very much, doctor.

Dr Khurana: Mr Rama Kant, would you please deposit Rs 5000/- as an advance towards the operation charges. Also please buy the medicines that I am going to prescribe and take them regularly before we meet on Thursday for your admission for operation. Is it OK?

Patient: OK doctor. I'm going to deposit the advance **right now**. Bye, doctor!

Dr Khurana: Bye, Rama Kant! See you on Thursday!

WORD MEANING

1. **Problem:** medical problem
2. **Acute:** severe
3. **Nasal:** related to nose
4. **Chronic:** old

5. **Embarrassment:** shame, humiliation
6. **Persisted:** continued
7. **Right now:** just now

COMPREHENSION

There are three choices for each question. Tick (✓) the choice you consider to be correct.

1. Who is the doctor-in-charge for ENT OPD?
   (a) Dr Khurana
   (b) Not yet decided
   (c) Some senior doctor from the ENT department.
2. What's Rama Kant's problem?
   (a) He's suffering from throat infection
   (b) He's suffering from acute nasal problem
   (c) He can't hear properly.
3. What kind of nasal problem is Rama Kant suffering from?
   (a) He keeps sneezing most of the time
   (b) He's suffering from cough and cold
   (c) He keeps scratching his nose.
4. Where did this problem start?
   (a) It started when he was working in North East in India.
   (b) It started when he was posted in England
   (c) It started when he was posted in Moscow
5. What did the doctors in Moscow tell Rama Kant about his problem?
   (a) He was allergic to cold
   (b) He was allergic to cold and would be all right in a warm climate
   (c) He would never be cured of his allergy.
6. What does Dr Khurana suggest to Rama Kant?
   (a) He advises him to go in for surgery
   (b) He advises him to keep taking his treatment
   (c) He advises him to be patient and go in for surgery.
7. How many days bed rest is needed for Rama Kant after his operation for sinus?
   (a) 15 days (b) 10 days
   (c) 30 days
8. How much advance money is Rama Kant asked to deposit towards the operation charges?
   (a) ₹ 1000/- (one thousand)
   (b) ₹ 10000/- (ten thousand)
   (c) ₹ 5000/- (five thousand)

Rehearse the above conversation with your friend 3 times (Pair activity).

EXPRESSIONS AND PHRASES FOR LEARNING

1. Excuse me, what time does the doctor come on rounds?
2. How long have you been suffering?
3. What exactly is your problem?
4. Can you tell me how to register my complaint?
5. How much rest do you think I need after the operation?
6. Can I deposit the operation fee tomorrow?
7. Shall I inform you about my condition on the phone?
8. Do you examine patients on Sundays?
9. Here is your registration card!
10. I am suffering from an acute nasal problem.

EXTENDED VOCABULARY

LOOK up the following words in a good dictionary to know their meanings and pronunciations. Also use them in your conversation, if required, while talking about the hospital.

Anaesthesia	Hypertension
Anaesthetist	Insomnia
Appetite	Mortuary
Autopsy	Moving bowels
Biopsy	Obesity
Clinic	Orthodontist
Clinical test	Postmortem
Diagnosis	Prescription
Dietitian	Stethoscope
Gerontologist	Surgery

GRAMMAR AND USAGE

There are two ways to ask questions.

1. By using question words such as: when, what, how, why, who, etc. e.g.,
   (a) Why did you not consult the doctor immediately? or
   Why didn't you consult the doctor immediately?
   (b) When did you meet her last?
   (c) How long have you been learning English?
2. By using auxiliary verbs such as: Do, does, have, can, etc. e.g.,
   (a) Can you tell me when I can discuss my mother's case with you?
   (b) Have you prescribed some energy capsules?
   (c) Do you make your patients walk within hours of their operation?

"Whom": This form has almost disappeared from spoken English. It is now found only in the most formal kind of writing. It is not required in any of the interrogative sentences while speaking. It has been replaced by 'who', e.g., who did you meet at the construction site?

Subject:	Who?	What?	Which?
Object:	Who		
Possessive:	Whose	What (which .... of)?	
Preposition:	Who .... to?	What (which) .... to	

e.g., Who did you meet last night?
Who did you invite to be the chief guest?

EXPRESSIONS AND PHRASES FOR PRACTICE (Pair Activity)

1. Excuse me, where .... Dr .... (find).
2. What time .... the clinic ....? (open)
3. What's exactly ....?
4. Where's ....?
5. Where .... (registration of new patients)?
6. When .... you again? (see)
7. Do you advise me to ....?
8. Here's your ....!
9. I am suffering from ....
10. Do you .... at night? (sound sleep)

Practise the given expressions, using them in appropriate situations.

ACTIVITY (ROLE PLAY)

1. Visit to a Heart Centre.
   (number of characters as per the situation selected)
2. Note down the new words and expressions in your practice notebook and keep revising them till you are able to use them naturally in your conversation.

15

AT THE DEPARTMENTAL STORE

READ aloud along with your friend the following conversation:

Sales girl: Good morning Sir!

Customer: Good morning!

Sales girl: Can I help you?

Customer: No thanks! I am just looking around.

Sales girl: Why don't you go around our newly created ladies corner? There are hundreds of things that ladies of this area have never seen before. I am sure you would find it interesting.

Customer: Thank you very much. I am going there right now.

Sales girl: (*at the ladies corner*) Good morning Sir?

Customer: Good morning. What a lovely corner!

Sales girl: May I help you, Sir?

Customer: Thanks! I'm interested in buying a few **exclusive** lipsticks for my wife. Can you help me?

Sales girl: What brand?

Customer: 'Padmini'.

Sales girl: Never heard of this brand before. Is it a new brand?

Customer: Not so new, my wife has been using it for more than a year now. She says it's **superb**!

Sales girl: Sorry Sir! It's not available with us at the moment. But you'll definitely get it next week. In the meantime, can I show you some other brand lipsticks? I am sure your wife would like them.

Customer: OK then show me whatever you consider best.

Sales girl: (*showing*) Any particular colour and shade, Sir?

Customer: I think dark brown should be all right. It's my wife's favourite colour.

Sales girl: If you don't mind Sir, is your wife very fair?

Customer: Yeah, I think so.

Sales girl: In that case (*showing a lipstick*) this lipstick shade would suit her the most.

Customer: (*looking at the shade of the lipstick on the hand of the sales girl*) I think you are right. This will suit her. How much does it cost?

Sales girl: Very **reasonable** ₹ 120/- only.

Customer: OK please pack it up.

Sales girl: Now would you please go to the cash counter and pay this bill over there. You can also collect your lipstick packet from there.

Customer: Thank you!

Sales girl: You are most welcome! Please visit us again.

(*Customer goes to the cash counter*)

Customer: How much am I to pay for my bill?

Cashier: Rupees one hundred and twenty only

Customer: (*giving two notes of ₹100/- each*) Here you are!

Cashier: (*returning ₹80/-*) Here is your change!

Customer: How about my lipstick pack?

Cashier: Here you are!

Customer: Thank you very much!

Cashier: You're most welcome!

WORD MEANING

1. **Exclusive:** limited to only selected people
2. **Superb:** very good quality
3. **Reasonable:** cheap, affordable

COMPREHENSION

There are three choices for each question. Tick (✓) the choice you consider to be correct.

1. What does the sales girl suggest to the customer?
   (a) To have a look at their newly created 'Ladies Corner'
   (b) To go around their store and select whatever he wants
   (c) To go around their newly created ladies' corner for selection of lipsticks for his wife.
2. How does the customer express his liking for the newly created ladies' corner?
   (a) By saying that he likes it very much
   (b) By saying that it is very beautiful
   (c) By saying 'what a lovely corner'.
3. What's the customer interested in?
   (a) Buying saris for his wife
   (b) Buying lipstick for his wife
   (c) Buying artificial jewellery for his wife.

4. Why couldn't the sales girl give the customer the lipstick of the brand of his choice?
   (a) It was out of stock
   (b) She hadn't heard of this brand before
   (c) The ladies' corner had a limited variety of lipsticks.
5. Why did the sales girl ask the customer about his wife's complexion?
   (a) She wanted to show the customer a befitting colour shade of the lipstick
   (b) She just wanted to know how his wife looked
   (c) She wanted to know about his wife's possible choice of the colour shade of the lipstick.

Rehearse the conversation between the sales girl and the customer with your friend 3 times (Pair activity).

EXPRESSIONS AND PHRASES FOR LEARNING

1. (a) Can I help you?
   (b) What can I do for you?
2. (a) No thanks! I am just looking around.
   (b) Well, let me see things first.
   (c) Just wait, I'll let you know.
3. (a) Never heard of this name before.
   (b) Never heard of this brand before.
   (c) Is it a new brand?
   (d) Has it been recently introduced?
   (e) How old is this brand?
4. (a) Let me see!
   (b) Let me try!
   (c) Let me check up
5. (a) What brand?
   (b) What colour?
   (c) What colour and shade?
6. What a lovely/beautiful piece?
7. (a) What's the price?
   (b) What's the price like?
   (c) What's the price range?
   (d) How much does it cost?
8. (a) How much is the bill?
   (b) What's the bill amount?
   (c) How much am I to pay?
9. (a) What's the guarantee/warranty period?
   (b) Does it carry any guarantee/warranty?

10. (a) Where to make the payment?
    (b) Where can I make the payment?
    (c) Where is the cash counter?
11. (a) Can I make the payment by credit card/debit card?
    (b) Can I make the payment by cheque?
    (c) Can I buy it on credit?
    (d) Can I pay in instalments?
    (e) In how many instalments can I make the payment?
    (f) What will be the terms and conditions for buying a TV on credit?
12. Does it carry any scheme?
13. (a) Which of these two is better?
    (b) Which of these things is the best?
14. Can it be replaced under the warranty period?
15. (a) Is it really so expensive?
    (b) Is it so cheap?
16. What are the main terms of this agreement?
17. Price has gone up and the supply is limited.
18. (a) How does it work?
    (b) How does it taste?
    (c) How does it sound?
    (d) How to assemble it?
19. May I help you.
20. I'm afraid, our terms are cash only.
21. Why don't you show me some exclusive piece?
22. What's the price like?
23. Excuse me, I'm interested in buying an overcoat.
24. Do you have the credit facility?
25. Do you accept payment by a credit card?
26. Shall I show you saris of the latest designs?
27. Could you show me some artificial jewellery?
28. What a lovely table lamp!
29. Here you are!
30. You are most welcome!
31. Have you preference for any particular shade?
32. If you don't mind Sir, we take the payment in advance.
33. How much concession can I get on this deal?

Learn the above expressions and use them in appropriate situations.

EXTENDED VOCABULARY

LOOK up the following words in a good dictionary to know their meanings and pronunciations. Also use them in your conversation while shopping as per your need.

Bloomers
Cash payment
Cashier
Cash-memo
Cosmetics
Customer
Discount
Hosiery
Housecoat
Imported goods
Jacket (coat)
On credit
Public conveniences
Pyjamas
Retail price
Shoeshine
Shorts
Stocking
Toiletries
Trousers (pants)
Trunk
Vest
Waist coat
Warranty

GRAMMAR AND USAGE

The following prepositions are often used in spoken English:
in, on, at, by, around, inside, outside, for, off, up, down, into, onto, above, below, between, before, through, to

Look at the following sentences/expressions:

1. I'll see you in half an hour.
   NOT
2. I'll see you after half an hour.
   The use of "in" is related to the future event, whereas, the use of "after" is related to the past event.
3. I'm looking forward to meeting you.
   NOT
4. I'm looking forward to meet you.
5. With a view to helping him I sold my car.

EXPRESSIONS AND PHRASES FOR PRACTICE (Pair Activity)

1. May I ....?
2. Could you show me a ....?
3. I want to buy a good quality ....
4. Do you have a ....?
5. Can you show me a few .... latest designs?
6. Why don't you ....? I'll show you plenty of latest designs in ....
7. I am afraid, it .... in the stock right now. Shall I show you ....?
8. I am interested in .... Can you ....?
9. Do you deal in ....?
10. How much does it ....?

11. What's the .... like?
12. Excuse me, are you interested in ....?
13. What're your ....?
14. Do you supply on ....?
15. I'm afraid, our terms are .... only.
16. What a lovely ....!
17. What a beautiful ....!
18. Have you ....?
19. Have you got ....?
20. Do you have ....?
21. I am interested in ....
22. I would like to have ....
23. I am looking for ....
24. What about ....?
25. How about ....?

ACTIVITY

1. Write down the words and expressions you find new in your practice notebook and keep revising them till you have mastered them and can use them effectively in appropriate situations.
2. Write six exchange dialogues between you and your school/college canteen manager, enquiring about the food-stuffs of your choice.

16

AT THE CINEMA

READ aloud with your friend the following conversation:

Aman: Give me three tickets for balcony, please.

Booking clerk: I am afraid, the balcony is full. All **sold out**. I can give you tickets for dress circle, if you like.

Aman: No thanks! I am **keen on** the balcony only. By the way, could you give me balcony tickets for tomorrow's show. I don't mind seeing this movie tomorrow.

Booking clerk: Let me check up the reservation chart. Sir, you are really lucky. Only three seats are available in the balcony. So shall I reserve your seats for tomorrow?

Aman: O yes! How much shall I pay you for three tickets?

Booking clerk: ₹ 450/-

Aman: (*giving five notes of ₹ 100 each*) Here's the money.

Booking clerk: (*giving the tickets and the balance amount*) Here you are!

Aman: What time exactly does the show start?

Booking clerk: The show starts at 6.30 p.m. but the actual movie starts at 7.00 p.m. From 6.30–7.00 a documentary film is shown.

Aman: Thank you. Incidentally, how is this movie?

Booking clerk: It's a very good movie, Sir. It's a **crowd puller**. All its shows are heavily booked.

Aman: How about the electricity situation here? Hope there is no power cut when the movie is on.

Booking clerk: Sir, don't worry **on that account**. We have our own generator.

Aman: That's very good. By the way, where can I meet your manager?

Booking clerk: I think he should be available in his office. Usually he is there at this time.

Aman: OK. Thanks a lot!

(*Aman goes to the manager's office to meet him*)

Aman: Good Evening manager sahib. I am Aman from *The Times of India*.

Manager: Good Evening, Mr Aman. What can I do for you?

Aman: I don't need any favour. I just want one information. Can you tell me when you are going to show 'Kabhi Woh, Kabhi Hum' directed by Rahul Dev. There is so much of talk about this film!

Manager: From next Friday. Its premiere show will be held at 6.30 p.m. on that day. You are most welcome to attend it. I can give you a few passes for the same.

Aman: No, thanks! I would like to see the movie only after a week of its release. Let me see its review by our film critic first. Then only I'll **make up my mind**. Anyway, thank you very much for your kind gesture. I must leave you now. I have to meet somebody on the way before I reach home.

Manager: Mr Aman, here's my 'visiting card'. Don't hesitate to ring me up if you change your mind and decide to see the premiere show along with your wife.

Aman: Thank you very much! Bye-bye!

Manager: Bye-bye!

WORD MEANING

1. **Sold out:** no ticket is available
2. **Keen on:** keenly interested in
3. **Crowd puller:** attracting lots of people
4. **On that account:** on that subject
5. **Make up your mind:** decide

COMPREHENSION

There are three choices for each question. Tick (✓) the choice you consider to be correct.

1. Why couldn't Aman get the tickets for balcony for the current show?
   (a) He was too late for the show
   (b) All the balcony tickets had been sold out
   (c) Balcony tickets were available only in black.
2. For which day show did Aman buy the balcony tickets?
   (a) He bought the balcony tickets for the next day show
   (b) He bought the balcony tickets for the next week
   (c) He didn't buy the balcony tickets. He bought the dress circle tickets.
3. How did the booking clerk describe the film?
   (a) It's a very good movie
   (b) It's a crowd puller
   (c) It's a very good movie and a crowd puller.

4. What does the booking clerk tell Aman about the electricity condition?
   (a) There's no power cut
   (b) They have their own generator
   (c) There's hardly any electricity problem.
5. Why does Aman contact the cinema manager?
   (a) To get free passes for his family
   (b) To request for the balcony tickets for the current show
   (c) To know when they're going to show 'Kabhi Woh, Kabhi Hum'.
6. What offer does the cinema manager make to Aman?
   (a) Free passes for his family members
   (b) A few passes for the premiere show of the movie, 'Kabhi Woh, Kabhi Hum'
   (c) To see a film whenever he pleases.
7. Why does Aman want to see the movie only after a week of its release?
   (a) He wants to go through the film review by the film critic of his paper
   (b) There is not much rush in the second week
   (c) The public feedback to the film is available then.

Rehearse the above conversation with your friend 3 times (Pair activity).

EXPRESSIONS AND PHRASES FOR LEARNING

1. I would like to reserve two tickets for balcony for the late night show.
2. Could you tell me what time the movie starts?
3. Where are the eatables available?
4. Where is the ladies' restroom?
5. All tickets are sold out.
6. How has it fared at the box office?
7. How many shows are held everyday?
8. What is the main cast of the film?
9. I'm keen on seeing the premiere of the film to be released.

EXTENDED VOCABULARY

LOOK up the following words in a good dictionary to know their meanings and pronunciations. Also use them while talking about cinema and things connected with it.

Animation
Box office
Cast
Character role
Choreography
Cinematography
Comedy/tragedy/detective/social/religious/mystery

Crowd puller	Hero/villain
Detective	Heroine/vamp
Documentary film	Producer
Feature film/movie	Romantic
Film critic	Star
Film review/viewers' feedback	Superstar
Guest artist	Three-dimensional film
Heavily booked	Thriller

GRAMMAR AND USAGE

The 'how' clauses in sentences: In larger sentences, 'how' clauses are commonly used as the objects of verbs such as ask, tell, wonder or know, which can introduce indirect questions:
e.g.,

1. Tell us how you could convince him.
2. How you convince her is your headache.
3. This is how I have helped her.
4. Spend the money how you like.
5. How you construct your house now is entirely your planning.

EXPRESSIONS AND PHRASES FOR PRACTICE (Pair Activity)

1. I would like to reserve .... for dress circle for the evening show.
2. Can I have .... tickets for tomorrow's show?
3. Could you give me .... balcony tickets for ....?
4. Could you tell me when ....?
5. Where're the public ....?
6. What's the cast ....?
7. What is the film ....?
8. How has it fared at ....?
9. How much shall I ....?
10. All tickets are sold ....

ACTIVITY

1. Note down the given words and expressions in your practice notebook and keep practising them till you have learnt them well, and are able to use them in similar situations with ease.
2. Imagine you want to see a play alongwith your friends at Delhi's most popular theatre. Write at least six exchange dialogues between you and the booking assistant.

17

AT THE PUBLIC LIBRARY

READ aloud with your friend the following conversation:

Student: Where can I find books on English Literature, please?

Librarian: Go to your right and **look for** the bookshelf marked English Literature.

Student: Thank you Madam. How many books can I get issued on my card?

Librarian: You can get 4 books and 2 magazines issued for two weeks. If you need some video cassettes that can also be issued. But for that you will have to deposit ₹ 150/- as a refundable security deposit.

Student: Thank you very much for this information. Madam, how do I know whether a particular book or a video cassette is available or not?

Librarian: For that, computer will help you. Just log on to ***www.libstock.com*** and print the title of the required book or video cassette along with the writer's name etc. The computer monitor will **display** 'Available Shelf No.' or 'Not Available'. If the required title is not available, the monitor will also display the date when it will be available.

Student: Thank you very much indeed for all your help. By the way, I don't know how to **operate** the computer. Will there be anybody to help me out?

Librarian: O, yes. One man is there all the time till the library is closed.

Student: Hope you won't mind my asking you one more question, Madam.

Librarian: Certainly not. Tell me what you want to know.

Student: Well, this is regarding the issuance of books. Can I get the books or video cassette issued in my name re-issued on the **expiry of the date** of return?

Librarian: Yes, you can always do so, provided it is not required by somebody else. The books can be got re-issued only once, even on phone. But **I am afraid**, the video cassette can't be re-issued. They are like hot cakes always in demand.

Student:	When does the library remain closed?
Librarian:	Every Friday. Any more questions, please?
Student:	No, thanks! I'm indeed grateful to you for answering all my questions so patiently. Good bye, Madam!
Librarian:	Good bye!

WORD MEANING

1. **Look for:** search for; try to find
2. **Display:** show
3. **Operate:** use
4. **Expiry of the date:** when the date is over
5. **I'm afraid:** I'm sorry

COMPREHENSION

There are three choices for each question. Tick (✓) the choice you consider to be correct.

1. What subject books is the student looking for?
   (a) General books
   (b) Books on English Literature
   (c) Novels and stories.
2. How many books and magazines can be issued on one card?
   (a) Two books and two magazines
   (b) One book and three magazines
   (c) Four books and two magazines.
3. How much refundable security is a member required to deposit to borrow a video cassette?
   (a) No security.
   (b) ₹ 150/-
   (c) ₹ 100/-
4. For how many days can the books be issued?
   (a) For 10 days
   (b) For one week
   (c) For two weeks.
5. How many times can a book be re-issued after the expiry of the date of return?
   (a) It cannot be re-issued twice
   (b) It can be re-issued only once
   (c) It can be re-issued only once when it is not required by anybody else.
6. Why can't a video cassette be re-issued?
   (a) It is a costly item
   (b) It is always in demand
   (c) It may be needed for various programmes to be organised by the library.

7. When does the library remain closed?
   (a) On Sundays
   (b) On Saturdays
   (c) On Fridays.
8. How can a person know whether a particular book is available or not?
   (a) The librarian is there to tell him or her about it
   (b) The computer displays the required information on its monitor
   (c) A person has been appointed especially for this purpose.
9. What does the student thank the librarian for ?
   (a) For being courteous to him
   (b) For enabling him to borrow books and magazines
   (c) For answering all his questions patiently.

Rehearse the above conversation with your friend 3 times (Pair activity).

EXPRESSIONS AND PHRASES FOR LEARNING

1. (a) How can I get the library membership?
   (b) How can I be the member of the library?
   (c) How can I obtain the library membership?
2. (a) How can I locate a particular book?
   (b) How to refer to the library catalogue?
3. How do I know whether the desired book is available or not?
4. How many books can I borrow at a time?
5. How long can I retain the books issued?
6. (a) Can the books be re-issued?
   (b) What's the procedure for re-issuance of the books?
7. How much is the fine for late return of the books?
8. Where's the reading room/teachers corner?
9. Do you have duplicating/photocopying facility in the library?
10. How much is the membership fee?
11. Do you allow personal belongings to be brought in the library?
12. What time does the library open?
13. What time does the library close?
14. Does the library remain open on Sundays and other public holidays?
15. Could you provide me with necessary help to operate the computer?
16. How can a person know about the new arrivals?
17. How do you display the information about the new arrivals?
18. Have you got in your library a vending machine for hot or cold drinks?

EXTENDED VOCABULARY

LOOK up the following words in a good dictionary to know their meanings and pronunciations. Also use them in your conversation with your librarian or teacher-in-charge for the library.

Book accession number
Bookshelf
Borrow books
Catalogue
Custody
Dailies
Disfiguring the book
Half-yearly
In demand
Issuance
Journals
Maintain silence
Membership fee
Monthly
New arrivals
'Not to be issued'
On demand
Open-shelf system
Periodicals
Personal belongings
Publication year
Quarterly
Refundable security deposit
Requisition
Requisition slip
Reserved
Responsibility
Security deposit
Tearing off pages
Title
Weeklies
Write off

Look up the above words in a good dictionary using phonetic symbols for their correct pronunciations and pronounce them correctly (5 times). If you have a facility to record them it will be of great use to learn their correct pronunciations.

GRAMMAR AND USAGE

We use 'There' or 'It' as an introducing subject in a sentence. This is why when these words are used, as in the following sentences, they are known as **Empty Words**.

e.g.,

1. *There* lived a painter in Rome.
2. *It* is an interesting book.
3. *It* rained heavily last night.
4. *There* was a teacher who taught her pupils after the school was over without charging any tuition fees from them.

EXPRESSIONS AND PHRASES FOR PRACTICE (Pair Activity)

1. How can I ....?
2. How do I know ....?

3. How much ....?
4. How many ....?
5. How about ....?
6. How long .... on Sundays?
7. Do you .... the library?
8. Tell me how to ....?
9. Do you .... at the reduced rates?
10. Where can I ....?

ACTIVITY

1. Imagine you have recently joined a new school or college. You have no idea of the location of the various departments and the students' canteen. Go to the school receptionist and enquire about them.
2. Go to the science laboratory and collect all relevant information about the lab to be able to use it effectively. First write the dialogues and then present them with the help of your friend to the rest of the students of your class.

18

AT THE BOOKSHOP

READ aloud with your friend the following conversation:

Himanshu: Excuse me, do you have English Pronouncing Dictionary by Daniel Jones?

Bookseller: Yeah.

Himanshu: I am interested in its latest edition. Do you have it?

Bookseller: Yes Sir, we have the latest edition. Would you like to see it?

Himanshu: If you don't mind, please.

Bookseller: (*calling his assistant*) Get the latest edition of English Pronouncing Dictionary by Daniel Jones. Be quick!

Assistant: (*giving the book*) Here you are!

Himanshu: (*verifies the details of the publication*) Fine! How much does it cost?

Bookseller: ₹ 640/- for the hardbound edition and ₹ 450/- for the paperback edition.

Himanshu: What's the difference between the two ?

Bookseller: There is **absolutely** no difference in the contents of the two editions. The difference in price is only due to the quality of their paper and their binding. The hardbound or the cloth-bound edition is mostly used in libraries due to its durability.

Himanshu: Well, then please give me the paperback edition—why to pay unnecessarily extra when there is no difference in the contents.

Bookseller: OK Sir. Would you like to see the books that we have recently imported from England. They are the bestsellers and are quite reasonably priced.

Himanshu: I would love to see them. Where are they displayed?

Bookseller: Right in front of you Sir, in the bookshelf marked New Arrivals.

Himanshu: Thank you. By the way, how much discount do you give on the purchase of books.

Bookseller:	We give 10% discount on the printed price of the popular titles and 15% on the rest. Don't worry about the discount, Sir! You just select the books, we'll give you the maximum possible discount.
Himanshu:	(*selects 5 books*) Well these are the five books I would like to buy. Now let me know how much discount you would give me.
Bookseller:	10% on the English Pronouncing Dictionary and 15% on the rest of the books.
Himanshu:	Fine, prepare the bill in the name of CCHRD and pack these books properly. Also please put them in a strong **paper carrier** so that I can conveniently carry them.
Bookseller:	No problem, Sir. We'll pack them as desired. Kindly pay the bill at the cash counter. The packet of books can also be collected from there.
Himanshu:	Thank you very much.
Bookseller:	Thanks a lot for your kind visit. Please **do visit** us again. We keep importing books **from abroad** every month.
Himanshu:	By the way, do you have the home delivery system?
Bookseller:	Not yet, Sir. But we are planning to introduce it shortly. Please leave your visiting card with us. As soon as we decide on introducing it, I'll inform you on your mobile.

(*Himanshu gives his visiting card and goes to the cash counter to pay the bill and collect his packet of books.*)

Himanshu:	Thanks a lot!
Bookseller:	You are most welcome. It's always a pleasure serving our customers like you. Bye-bye Sir!
Himanshu:	Bye-bye!

WORD MEANING

1. **Absolutely:** completely
2. **Paper carrier:** paper bag used to carry things
3. **Do visit:** using 'do' before a verb is to emphasise something, e.g., please do read the advertisement
4. **From abroad:** from foreign countries/overseas

COMPREHENSION

There are three choices for each question. Tick (✓) the choice you consider to be correct.

1. Why does Himanshu go to the bookshop?
   (a) To buy stationery items
   (b) To buy English Pronouncing Dictionary by Daniel Jones
   (c) To find out what discount they give on books purchased.

2. What's the difference between a cloth-bound edition and a paperback edition?
   (a) There is absolutely no difference between the two editions.
   (b) There is no difference in the contents of the two editions, except in the quality of their paper and binding.
   (c) The difference lies in their quality of paper, binding and also in price.
3. Why does Himanshu decide to buy the paperback edition?
   (a) It was light weight.
   (b) He wanted to save money.
   (c) He didn't have enough money to buy the cloth-bound edition.
4. How much discount does Himanshu get on his five books purchased?
   (a) 15%
   (b) 10%
   (c) 10% on English Pronouncing Dictionary by Daniel Jones and 15% on the remaining books.
5. Does the bookshop provide home delivery facilities?
   (a) Yes, they do.
   (b) They don't provide it at present, but they are thinking of introducing it shortly.
   (c) They don't provide it at present, nor do they have any plan for introducing it in future.

Rehearse the above conversation with your partner 3 times (Pair activity).

EXPRESSIONS AND PHRASES FOR LEARNING

1. Excuse me, do you have a complete kit for MBA Entrance Examination by Verma and Gangal?
2. Could I see a few good books on Spoken English?
3. How much does it cost?
4. What's the difference between a paperback edition of a book and a cloth-bound library edition of a book?
5. How much discount do you allow on the books purchased for the library?
6. Do you allow purchase of books on the credit card?
7. Do you deal in old and rare books?
8. Do you have a catalogue of foreign publications?
9. By the way, do you have the home delivery system?
10. Would you permit me to have a look at the books you have imported from England?

EXTENDED VOCABULARY

LOOK up the following words in a good dictionary to know their meanings and pronunciations. Also use them in your conversation about a bookshop.

Accountant
Bill
Binding
Book list
Book rack
Bookshelf
Cash counter
Cashier
Cloth-bound edition
Hardbound
Home delivery
Library attendant
Library discount
Low priced edition
New arrivals
New/latest edition
On approval
On credit
On loan
Packing
Paperback edition
Popular

GRAMMAR AND USAGE

When we talk about people we can address/name them in four ways:

1. By using first name
   e.g., Where is Archana?
   This is informal and is used to talk about our friends, relatives and children.
2. By using first name and surname
   e.g., Isn't she Sharmila Tagore, the actor?
   This style is neutral—it is neither formal nor informal.
3. By using title (Mr, Mrs, Ms) and surname,
   e.g., Can I talk to Mrs Verma?
   Ask Mr Upadhyay to see me.
   This is more formal and is used to talk about people we don't know or when we want to show respect for them.
4. By using surname only
   e.g., I don't think Rao was a very good Congress President.
   We use this style to talk about public figures—politicians, sportsmen and sportswomen, film actors and social workers at the national level.

Please note that 'Ms' is pronounced as |Miz|.

EXPRESSIONS AND PHRASES FOR PRACTICE (Pair Activity)

1. Excuse me, do you have ....?
2. Could I ....it?
3. How much does it ....?
4. How much discount do you give on ....?
5. What's the difference between the old and ....?
6. Do you have the home delivery ....?
7. How much do you charge ....?
8. Do you have a catalogue of books published ....?

9. What're your terms and conditions for ....?
10. Do you allow purchase of books on ....?

ACTIVITY

1. Copy the given questions and words in your practice notebook and learn them till you can use them confidently and naturally in similar situations.
2. Pronounce the given words correctly.
3. Present a role play with the help of your friends and group members displaying a 'Meeting of the School Library Development Committee'.

19

AT THE DINING TABLE

Shashank:	Host
Rashmi:	Shashank's wife (hostess/host)
Rajesh:	Guest
Ragini:	Guest (Rajesh's wife)
Sushi:	Shashank's daughter (studying in class VIII)
Amit:	Shashank's son (studying in class XI)

READ aloud with your friend the following conversation:

Shashank: What a pleasure to have you Rajesh with your wife for dinner this evening!

Rajesh: We are equally happy to meet you and your family. For me it's a **dream come true**.

Rashmi: My husband often talks about you and your family. So I was really **excited** to meet you and your wife, what's her name?

Rajesh: Ragini, although before our marriage she was called Rita. My parents named her Ragini after marriage as she would always keep **humming** film **tunes** whether she was in the kitchen or in the bathroom.

Rashmi: Then we'll have a musical evening today. Won't we?

Rajesh: Oh yes, I am sure my wife won't disappoint you.

Rashmi: Now let me introduce my children to you. First, meet my son, Amit. He is a student of class XI.

Amit: Hi Aunty!

Ragini: Hi young man!

Rashmi: And she is my daughter, Sushi. She is in class VIII this year.

Sushi: Hi Aunty!

Ragini: Hi young lady!

Ragini:	Rashmi, we are indeed very happy to meet your children. They are really very smart and so well-behaved. Which school do they go to?
Rashmi:	J.K. International School.
Ragini:	I think it's a very expensive school, isn't it?
Rashmi:	Well, it is little more expensive than the Modern School or the DPS. Since the school is fully air-conditioned and the teacher–pupil ratio is quite reasonable they charge ₹ 200/- p.m. extra in the name of 'facility fund'. Personal attention is paid to every child. It's indeed a good school. You won't believe that without our efforts or any other external help our children are doing extremely well at school. Their personality is developing in the right direction.
Ragini:	I am so happy to hear that. What's their procedure for admission?
Rashmi:	They admit children on merit basis. The thing I like most about admissions of this school is that there is no place for a **capitation fee** or recommendation.
Ragini:	Well, my son goes to Vivek International Day Boarding School. It's equally a good school. But it is rather expensive.
Rashmi:	In which class is he studying?
Ragini:	Class X. Another two years before he finishes his school education. Somehow, I am quite happy about his education.
Rashmi:	Your husband says you are a very good singer, aren't you?
Ragini:	Well, he is a husband and so he has every right to say whatever he likes. How can I **contradict** him? But this is a fact that music is my weakness. If I had not married Rajesh I would have married 'Music'. You know what I mean!
Rashmi:	Then you are definitely good at music. We would love to hear a song after you have finished your dinner. Hope you **won't mind** it.
Shashank:	Rashmi, wouldn't you allow bhabhiji to eat? I think you **had better** ask her what she would like to eat rather than keeping her busy talking about other things.
Rashmi:	You are right Shashank. I am really sorry to have completely forgotten about it. Thank you very much for reminding me (*turning to Ragini*). It appears you didn't like the food. You are not eating anything.
Ragini:	Don't say that Rashmi. It's really very delicious, particularly the 'stuffed tomatoes'. I would like to note down its recipe before we leave this place.
Shashank:	Rajesh, do you still eat 'Parathe' with fresh butter?
Rajesh:	Well, in a way, 'yes'. Though my wife doesn't like me to eat it as per the doctor's advice, I somehow manage to have it at least once a week.
Shashank:	Rajesh, you are one of those few friends of my student life who have made a permanent place in my heart. Hardly a day goes when I don't miss you. To me friendship and Rajesh are **synonyms**.

Rajesh:	Thank you very much for all your love for me. I equally feel attached with you. Now that by God's grace we are re-united we should continue to meet at least once a month. Do you agree Shashank?
Shashank:	It's a wonderful idea. Let's seriously implement it.
Rajesh:	Shashank, though we would love to stay here for some more time, we must leave your place immediately as our son must be waiting for us. He never sleeps without having a story from me or his mom. Besides, he is leaving for Ajanta and Ellora on an educational tour tomorrow. Some preparations are to be made before he sleeps. Bye, Shashank! Bye, Bhabhiji! Bye children! It was indeed a wonderful evening we have had after ages. Thank you for all this.
Shashank:	Bye, Rajesh; bye, bhabhiji.

WORD MEANING

1. **Dream come true:** a wish or desire comes true/happens
2. **Excited:** thrilled
3. **Humming the tune:** keep singing the tune slowly with lips closed
4. **Capitation fee:** a fixed one time amount charged at the time of admission of the child
5. **Contradict:** say something in against
6. **Won't mind:** will not feel (will not take otherwise)
7. **Had better:** an expression used to suggest something
8. **Synonyms:** words with similar meanings

COMPREHENSION

ANSWER the following questions briefly:

1. Who are the hosts?
2. Who are the guests?
3. Why was Rashmi so excited to meet Shashank and his wife?
4. Why did Rajesh's father change the name of Rajesh's wife after their marriage?
5. What does Rashmi tell Ragini about her children's personality development at school?
6. Which school does Shashank's children go to?
7. How does Rashmi justify charging of 'facility fund' from the parents by her children's school?
8. How does Rashmi prove that J.K. International is a good school?
9. What, according to Rashmi, is the best thing about the admission system of J.K. International School?
10. Which school does Ragini's son go to?

11. What expression does Ragini use to indicate that she is satisfied with the education of her son?
12. How do you know that Ragini is keenly interested in music?
13. What suggestion does Rajesh make to Shashank to strengthen their old ties of friendship?
14. Why does Rajesh want to leave immediately without asking his wife Ragini to sing a song?

Rehearse the above conversation with your partner 3 times (Pair activity).

EXPRESSIONS AND PHRASES FOR LEARNING

1. What a pleasure to have you this evening for dinner!
2. I'm sure, you won't disappoint me.
3. Let me introduce my children to you—meet my eldest son, Rahul. He is an IAS officer.
4. We are indeed very happy to meet your wife and children.
5. It's rather expensive, but it is worth.
6. It's very delicious.
7. It's a wonderful idea. Let's implement it.
8. By God's grace, everything went off well.
9. To me, service of humanity is the service of God.
10. Hardly a day goes when I don't miss you in one or the other context.

EXTENDED VOCABULARY

LOOK up the following words in a good dictionary to know their meanings and pronunciations. Also use them in your conversation with your guest at the dining table.

Courses:	a starter (e.g., soup), appetizer, a main course, dessert, second helping
Describing food:	delicious, tasty, tasteless, bland, sweet, hot/spicy, salty, tender, tough, fatty, lean, fresh, gravy, soup, fattening
Fruit:	apple, orange, pear, banana, grapes, pineapple, cherry, peach, strawberry, melons, mango.
Salad:	lettuce, tomato, cucumber, vinegar, salad leaf, green chillies, ginger, lemon, radish
Vegetables:	potato, mash potato, beans, peas, carrot, cauliflower, cabbage, mushrooms, aubergine (brinjals)
Ways of cooking:	boil, fry, deep-fry, grill, roast, bake, raw

GRAMMAR AND USAGE

Exclamations are often constructed with 'how' and 'what' or with 'so' and 'such', e.g.,

(a) How cold it is!
(b) How beautifully you sing!
(c) What a rude answer!
(d) What lovely flowers!
(e) You are so kind!
(f) She is such a nice girl!

EXPRESSIONS AND PHRASES FOR PRACTICE (Pair Activity)

1. What a pleasure ....!
2. It is a dream ....
3. I am sure ....
4. Let me have the pleasure of ....
5. Let me introduce my ....
6. It's rather ....
7. I am pleased to ....
8. I am so pleased to know ....
9. I am so sad to know that ....
10. There is no place for ....
11. She is good at ....
12. Thank you very much for all your ....
13. You'd better try for ....
14. Please pass me ....
15. Would you care for a ....?
16. I have'd ....
17. I am a bit slow eater/fast scorer ....
18. It was indeed a .... we ever had!

ACTIVITY

1. Prepare and present with the help of your close friends a role play on 'Alumni Meet'.
2. Note down all the new words and expressions in your practice notebook and drill them till you are able to use them in similar situations naturally and confidently.

20

AT THE HOTEL

READ aloud with your friend the following conversation:

Mukesh:	Excuse me, can I get a room here?
Manager:	Yes, of course! Do you want a single bedroom or double bedroom? And do you want a room with AC or without it?
Mukesh:	I want a double bedroom with AC. My wife is also with me.
Manager:	Just a minute, please. Let me check up.... Sir, at the moment we have only one double bedroom without AC. It's on the fourth floor. But don't worry, it's a good room. No disturbance, it being on the top floor. Moreover, you won't feel the absence of AC. You get natural air all the time.
Mukesh:	But I still want a double bedroom with AC, preferably on the first floor. How can you help me?
Manager:	Sir, **if you don't mind**, you can occupy the room available on the fourth floor now. I'll definitely shift you to the room of your choice in the evening. The lady, occupying it, is checking out in the evening.
Mukesh:	That's excellent. Thank you very much! What's the **tariff** like?
Manager:	₹ 2000/- per day for the double bedroom without AC and ₹ 3000/- per day for the room with AC.
Mukesh:	What about other facilities like food, entertainment, STD/ISD facility?
Manager:	You don't have to worry about it, Sir. We take special care of our patrons and customers like you.
Mukesh:	Do you provide the room service?
Manager:	Yeah. But we don't supply meals in the room. We only give tea or coffee with snacks.
Mukesh:	What other facilities do you provide to the tourists staying in your hotel?

Manager:	Well, we organize **conducted tours** twice a week to show them the places of interest in and around the city. We also help them exchange their **hard currency** into rupee at the bank rate in the hotel itself. Besides we have a **souvenir** shop here in the hotel from where they can buy souvenirs and small gifts of their choice.
Mukesh:	Do you hold cultural programmes for entertainment of the tourists?
Manager:	Yes, we do. We organize cultural programmes every evening.
Mukesh:	**Wow**! Please tell me my room number and give me the room key. Would you please also ask your man to take my **baggage** to the room?
Manager:	Here's your key, Sir. Room 404. But first could you please fill in this register?
Mukesh:	Yes, of course (*fills in the register*)
Manager:	Thank you, Sir. Could I have Rs 1000/- towards room advance?
Mukesh:	Yes, of course. Here you are! Now, could you please immediately send some coffee with snacks to us, we are a bit tired.
Manager:	I am sending it within five minutes, Sir.
Mukesh:	OK! **See you** later.
Manager:	Have a comfortable stay, Sir!

WORD MEANING

1. **If you don't mind:** an expression used to mean: Please don't misunderstand
2. **Tariff:** rent
3. **Conducted tours:** tours specially organized, with the facility of guides
4. **Hard currency:** currencies like Pound, Dollar, Yen, Mark and Euro which are universally acceptable and exchangeable at different daily exchange rates. (Indian rupee is not yet a hard currency)
5. **Souvenir:** something you buy or keep to help you remember some special event
6. **Wow:** exclamation used to express a feeling of great joy
7. **Baggage:** luggage
8. **See you:** meet

NOTE: Could/Would is used to make a polite request.

COMPREHENSION

ANSWER the following questions briefly:

1. What kind of room does Mukesh want to hire?
2. What kind of room does the Manager offer to Mukesh?
3. Where is that room situated?

4. What justification does the manager give to Mukesh in support of the room without AC?
5. What promise does the manager make to Mukesh regarding allotment of a double bed room with AC?
6. How much does the double bedroom with AC cost?
7. What kind of room service is provided by the hotel?
8. What facilities are provided to the tourists by the hotel?
9. What formality is Mukesh required to complete before he occupies the room allotted to him?
10. What does Mukesh want the hotel manager to send to his room?

EXPRESSIONS AND PHRASES FOR LEARNING

1. That's excellent!
2. It's very kind of you!
3. See you!
4. Yes, of course!
5. Just a minute, please!
6. What's the tariff like?
7. Do you have room service?
8. Wow! Please book me for tomorrow's guided tour.
9. What facilities do you provide to the tourists?
10. What formalities am I supposed to complete before I occupy the room?
11. I don't mind, it suits me.
12. Could I get a room here?
13. Could you give me a single bedroom/double bedroom, please?
14. Do you permit eatables to be brought in from outside?
15. Could you provide me with one extra bed?
16. Do you have an intercom facility in the room?
17. Do you have a cable TV internet?
18. Do you have a close circuit television in your hotel?
19. What extra amenities do you provide to your customers/to the tourists?
20. Do you organize cultural programmes for the people staying in your hotel?
21. Do you organize guided tours for sightseeing?
22. Do you provide STD/ISD/conference facility to your customers?
23. What's the menu like for lunch/dinner?
24. How far is the railway station/airport from here?
25. Is the taxi/cab available late at night?
26. Is there any branch of State Bank of India nearby?
27. What's the tariff like for a single/double bedroom with AC and without AC?
28. Would you please ask your man to take my baggage to my room?
29. Can I carry the room key along with me while going out or have I to leave it at the reception?

30. Could you give me an east-facing room?
31. Has the bathroom been provided with 24 hrs hot and cold water?
32. Could you please get the geyser repaired? It's not working?
33. Could I deposit the advance in two parts—50% today and the remaining 50% tomorrow?
34. Would you please send my final bill for payment?
35. Where can I buy the souvenirs from?
36. Do you provide exchange facility in your hotel?
37. Would you please get my reservation confirmed?
38. Could/Would you please arrange reservation for my onward journey/return journey to Mumbai by AC II class in Rajdhani Express?
39. Do you have a swimming pool/gym facility here?
40. What are the check in and check out timings?
41. Could I have the railway time table/flight schedule, please?
42. Could I use your telephone, please?
43. Do you show any feature film on your closed circuit TV?
44. Here you are!
45. Here it is!

EXTENDED VOCABULARY

LOOK up the following words in a good dictionary/thesaurus to know their meanings and pronunciations. You may also use them in your conversation while staying at a hotel.

Accommodation	Exchange facility/conversion facility
Amenities	Guest-house
Baggage	Guided tour
Bearer	Hot and cold
Bed and breakfast	Keyboard
Board and lodging	Latch
Book a room/cab/taxi	Linen
Cable internet	Lobby
Cafeteria	Lodger
Cereal	Lounge/lobby
Check in time	Meal
Check out time	Menu card/menu
Closed circuit TV	Motel
Credit	Payment in cash/by cheque/by credit card
Dessert/sweet dish	Places of interest
Dinner/supper	Reception
Double bed	Room service
Double bedroom	Second helping
Entrance hall	

Service charges
Sightsee
Tariff/room rent
Telephone facility—ISD, STD, PCO
Terms cash
Toilet/washroom/rest room/gentlemen, ladies
Turn on/turn off
Veg/non-veg

The questions and possible answers just mentioned may be noted down in the practice notebook and practised and drilled in appropriate situations.

GRAMMAR AND USAGE

Infinitives

1. Infinitives are forms such as: (to) attract; (to) invite; (to) receive.
2. Infinitives are generally used with 'to' to express a person's purpose.
   e.g.,
   (a) He went to the airport *to receive* his aunt.
   (b) She went to Moscow *to participate* in the 'Hindi-Diwas' activities.
3. Infinitives are also used as object or complement of a verb, noun or adjective.
   e.g.,
   (a) She is anxious *to contact* you regarding the arrangements for the marriage.
   (b) You have every right *to reject* his proposal.
4. Besides infinitives with 'to' we also have infinitives *without 'to'*.
   e.g.,
   (a) I made him laugh
   (b) Help her fill the form

EXPRESSIONS AND PHRASES FOR PRACTICE (Pair Activity)

1. Excuse me, can ....?
2. If you don't mind, please, can I ....?
3. Of course, ...
4. I am afraid, you can't ....
5. You are indeed ....!
6. Don't worry, we ....!
7. Quality, service and customer's satisfaction are ....
8. They say, we are .... in the town.
9. Could you book me a .... please?

Rehearse the expressions in the conversation with your partner 3 times (Pair activity).

ACTIVITY

1. Imagine you are a tourist and want to stay in some guest-house. What type of questions would you like to ask the administrator of the guest-house. Write those questions using short sentences.
2. Note down the words and phrases or expressions practised in your practice notebook and keep revising them till you are able to use them naturally in your conversation.

21

ASKING FOR INFORMATION

READ aloud with your friend the following conversation to know how to seek information:

(*Amit telephones his son's school to get information about new admissions to be made by the school. Let's see how he asks for the required information from the* ***receptionist***).

Amit:	Good morning Ma'm. I am Amit Bhatia, General Secretary, **Resident Welfare Association**, Sarojini Nagar. Could you please give me some information about new admissions in your school?
Receptionist:	Yes, Mr Bhatia, tell me what you want to know.
Amit:	When do you start registration for new admissions?
Receptionist:	On the second of April.
Amit:	How long will this **registration** go on?
Receptionist:	For one week, from second of April to sixth of April.
Amit:	What're the classes wherein the **vacancies** exist?
Receptionist:	Two, four, six, nine and eleven.
Amit:	**On what basis** do you select children for admission?
Receptionist:	**Category of the parent** and the child's performance in the admission test.
Amit:	What are the subjects to be tested for the admission test?
Receptionist:	English, Hindi and Environmental Studies for primary classes, and English, Maths and General Knowledge for all other classes upto X. As for the eleventh class only English and Knowledge of **current affairs** will be tested.
Amit:	Is this admission test a **qualifying test** or a competitive one?
Receptionist:	Well, it's a **competitive test** for children in a particular category of parents.
Amit:	Why is a parent's category so important? After all, it is not the parents but the child who is going to be admitted.

Receptionist:	**Of course**, the school admits children only. But as the education of children is closely linked with the postings and transfers of a parent, the parent's category becomes equally important.
Amit:	Madam, one last **query**. Do you have any **reservation** for **socially disadvantaged children** like SC and ST?
Receptionist:	Oh yes, we strictly follow the government's rules **in this regard**.
Amit:	**Incidentally**, what are the visiting hours for parents and others?
Receptionist:	Ten to eleven in the morning and from three to four in the afternoon.
Amit:	Thank you, Ma'm.
Receptionist:	You are welcome, Mr Bhatia.

WORD MEANING

1. **Receptionist:** an official of a company/organisation who provides information to its visitors about various matters related to the company and its affairs on demand
2. **Resident Welfare Association (RWA):** a registered association of the residents of a society formed to look after their welfare and interests
3. **Registration:** registration of child's name seeking admission
4. **Vacancies:** seats available for admission
5. **On what basis:** considerations for admission
6. **Category of the parent:** category of the parent such as central government employee/state government employee/employee of an autonomous body/businessman/retired/unemployed, etc.
7. **Current affairs:** knowledge of current important matters related to national and international events, economy and social issues and all other such issues
8. **Qualifying test:** a test that requires a minimum percentage of marks/grade for a child to be eligible for admission to a particular class
9. **Competitive test:** a competitive test unlike a qualifying test is given to children seeking admission in order to distinguish each one of them from the others. A person getting more marks than the other is preferred
10. **Of course:** an expression used to agree to something said or expressed
11. **Query:** question
12. **Reservation:** reservation of seats (against which only children from a particular class can be admitted)
13. **Socially disadvantaged children:** children belonging to the classes like scheduled castes, scheduled tribes, etc. (so-called lower caste children) who are economically weak and inferior to the children of rich classes or so-called higher castes
14. **In this regard:** in this connection
15. **Incidentally:** by the way; casually; not intentionally

COMPREHENSION

There are three choices for an answer to a question. Tick (✓) the choice you consider to be correct.

1. Why does Amit contact his son's school?
   (a) To seek permission to meet his son's classteacher
   (b) To get information about new admissions to be made by the school
   (c) To attend the parent–teacher meet.
2. What're the classes wherein new admissions can be made by the school?
   (a) In all classes
   (b) Only in classes 2, 4, 6, 9 and 11
   (c) No admission to any classes.
3. What criteria has the school adopted for selection of children for admission?
   (a) Child's merit
   (b) Parent's social status
   (c) Parent's category and the child's performance in the admission test.
4. What's the school's policy for admission of children of SC/ST categories?
   (a) The school follows the government's policy in this regard
   (b) The school has no reservation for SC/ST students
   (c) The school selects them on the basis of their performance in the admission test.
5. What are the subjects for the admission test for class XI?
   (a) English, Maths and General Knowledge
   (b) English and Knowledge of Current Affairs
   (c) English, Maths and Environmental Studies.

Rehearse the given conversation with your partner 3 times (Pair activity).

EXPRESSIONS AND PHRASES FOR LEARNING

1. When do you start registration for admission?
2. How long will the registration go on?
3. What criteria do you adopt to select children for admission?
4. What subjects do you test for admission purpose?
5. What's the eligibility criterion for the student's fee concession?
6. What time can the parents meet the principal?
7. How can the parents discuss their child's progress with the teachers concerned?

EXTENDED VOCABULARY

LOOK up the following words in a good dictionary to know their meanings and pronunciations. Also note down these words in your practice notebook for their future use.

Chalk board/blackboard
Child's performance
Demonstration
Detention
Discrimination
Extra-coaching
Free-studentship
Grace marks
Grading system
Information
In group
In pair
In queue
In the corner
In the front
In twos/threes
Knowledge
Leisure
Merit
Pass marks
Passed with distinction
Progress report
Rapport
Stationery items

GRAMMAR AND USAGE

Remember we always use simple present tense after words such as: never, always, often, usually, sometimes,
e.g.,

1. She *always calls* on Saturdays.
2. He *never goes* to his office before 10.00.
3. Our grandpa *often forgets* our names.
4. He *usually returns* from his office late.
5. She *sometimes invites* her childhood friends to her birthday party.

EXPRESSIONS AND PHRASES FOR PRACTICE (Pair Activity)

1. Excuse me, what time ....?
2. We start at .... in the morning from Monday to Friday.
3. Could you please tell me ....?
4. When will you display ....?
5. What's the last date for ....?
6. It's ....
7. Do you provide .... concession in fee?
8. We allow ....
9. Excuse me, can you explain to me how ....?
10. Well, it's very simple. You can ....

ACTIVITY

1. Present a role play on 'The First Day at School after Summer Vacation'.
2. Note down the new words/phrases and expressions used in your practice notebook and keep revising them till you are able to use them naturally in your conversation.

22

MAKING A REQUEST

READ aloud with your friend the following conversation and see how a request is made:

Neha:	**Excuse me**, Madam. I am Neha. I am a new student. I would like to attend your class on spoken English. Could I attend it?
Teacher:	Can I see your admission receipt, please?
Neha:	Sure Madam! **Here you are!**
Teacher:	**I am afraid**, you can't attend the spoken English class. You haven't paid yet the special fee of ₹ 100/- for this class.
Neha:	Madam, could you allow me to attend this class today? I'll pay you ₹ 100/- tomorrow.
Teacher:	**All right**, you can attend the class today, But please make sure you deposit ₹ 100/- with your classteacher by tomorrow. **Look**! I have nothing to do with the collection of fee for spoken English class. Your class teacher collects it.
Neha:	Madam, I'll definitely deposit the special fee by tomorrow. And thank you very much indeed for permitting me to attend your class today.
Teacher:	Not at all! This is the least I could do.

WORD MEANING

1. **Excuse me/look:** an expression used to attract the attention of someone
2. **Here you are:** an expression used to mean, here it is
3. **I am afraid:** an expression used to mean, I am sorry
4. **All right:** an expression to mean, OK

COMPREHENSION

ANSWER the following questions briefly:

1. What does Neha request her teacher for?

2. Why does the teacher tell Neha that she is not allowed to attend the spoken English class?
3. On what condition does the teacher permit Neha to attend the spoken English class?
4. Who collects the special fee?
5. How much is the fee for the spoken English class?

Rehearse the above conversation with your partner 3 times (Pair activity).

EXPRESSIONS AND PHRASES FOR LEARNING

1. (a) Could I borrow your pen, please?
   (b) Have it, please!
2. (a) Sure. Please wait for a while.
3. (a) Madam, could I meet you in the eighth period, please?
   (b) I am afraid, I am busy. You can meet me after the sixth period. I am free then.
4. (a) Would you please guide me how to prepare for the unit test?
   (b) With great pleasure.
   (c) Of course, I will.
5. (a) Would you mind allowing me to leave your class early today?
   (b) Certainly. You can go whenever you please.
6. (a) Dad, may I invite all my classmates for my birthday party?
   (b) Go ahead. You can invite as many friends of yours as you like.
7. (a) Would you mind if I call you late at night?
   (b) Certainly not. You can ring up whenever you please.

The given questions and their possible answers may be practised till you are able to use them naturally in parallel situations.

EXTENDED VOCABULARY

Allow
Call
Call on
Grant
Grateful/gratefulness
Obliged
Permit/permission
Reinforce
Revaluate/revaluation
Submit

GRAMMAR AND USAGE

It may be noted that the word 'kindly' is not the exact synonym of the word 'please'. So it needs to be used very carefully. For example, the sentence, 'Would you kindly open the door' is not a request, it is an order, which means: Open the door. To make it a request we should say 'Please open the door'.

EXPRESSIONS AND PHRASES FOR PRACTICE (Pair Activity)

1. Please ....
2. Kindly ....
3. Would you please ....?
4. Could you/Could you please ....?
5. Would you mind ....
6. I would be grateful ....
7. I would feel obliged ....
8. Do you mind if I ....
9. May I ....

ACTIVITY

1. You are Rahul/Rita. Write four exchange dialogues between you and your classteacher requesting her for your exemption from attending the extra class in English to be held on Sunday due to your pre-engagement. Use as many polite expressions as you possibly can to get the desired exemption.
2. Note down the new words/phrases and expressions in your practice notebook and keep revising them till you are able to use them naturally in your conversation.

23

TAKING LEAVE OF SOMEBODY

READ aloud with your friend the following conversation to see what people normally say at the time of taking leave:

(*Rakhi and Aman are friends. They have been talking to each other for more than two hours. Now Aman wants to take leave of her.*)

Aman: **Well,** Rakhi, do you know we have been talking for a little more than two hours. I must leave now, otherwise I'll be in trouble.

Rakhi: **Trouble**! What's the problem?

Aman: **Absolutely** no problem as such! The matter is that I have an appointment with Prof. Dixit at half-past eleven. I'll **miss it** if I don't leave right now.

Rakhi: OK. It was indeed nice talking to you. But when are we going to meet again?

Aman: I think tomorrow, during the lunch in the canteen. Hope it **suits** you.

Rakhi: I have no other engagement then. I'll be there in time. Shall I get you some cheese sandwiches from home?

Aman: No, thanks! You needn't bring anything from home. Just come, please.

Rakhi: OK Aman, see you!

Aman: Bye Rakhi!

WORD MEANING

1. **Well:** an expression used to begin saying something—it has no meaning
2. **Trouble:** problem
3. **Absolutely:** an expression used for agreeing to something said
4. **Miss it:** go without it
5. **Suits:** convenient

COMPREHENSION

ANSWER the following questions briefly:

1. Who are Aman and Rakhi?
2. How long have they been talking?
3. Why does Aman want to leave?
4. When are Aman and Rakhi going to meet again?
5. Where do they decide to meet?

Rehearse the above conversation with your partner 3 times (Pair activity).

EXPRESSIONS AND PHRASES FOR LEARNING

1. Would like to take leave of you
2. Nice meeting.
3. Nice talking.
4. It was indeed a very pleasant meeting!
5. It was really wonderful to have met you!
6. Bye; Bye-bye; Goodbye; Goodbye until we meet again.
7. See you!
8. Have a nice time!
9. Look after yourself!
10. Take care!

GRAMMAR AND USAGE

1. 'Shall' as a modal verb is used to make some suggestion, e.g., shall we go for a picnic?
2. 'Must' as a modal verb shows compulsion on oneself, e.g. I must leave right now, otherwise I'll miss the flight.

EXPRESSIONS AND PHRASES FOR PRACTICE (Pair Activity)

1. I must leave now. I have an ....
2. I think I must go now. I am ....
3. Goodbye! See you ....
4. It was indeed very nice ....
5. I should go now. My parents will ....
6. Thank you very much for .... I must hurry up. It's ....
7. Shall I take leave ....?
8. It's getting dark. I must reach home before ....

9. OK, goodbye until ....
10. It was one of the most wonderful evenings I ....

The given expressions and sentences may be noted in your practice notebook and practised till you are able to use them in your conversation confidently and naturally.

ACTIVITY

1. Imagine today is the last day of your 'Friendship Camp'. During the camp you had a wonderful opportunity of making many new friends with whom you now intend maintaining relations. Present a role play taking leave of your new friends in a befitting way. Use appropriate expressions to suit the occasion.
2. Note down the words/phrases and expressions used in your practice notebook and keep revising them till you are able to use them naturally in your conversation.

24

MAKING AN APPOINTMENT

READ aloud with your friend the following conversation to see how an appointment is made:

Rakesh:	I am Rakesh Ahuja. I'd like to meet Dr Bhargave. **Could** I have an appointment with him, please?
Receptionist:	When do you want it?
Rakesh:	Tomorrow morning please.
Receptionist:	I'm afraid, he is not available in the morning. If you like I can fix your appointment in the afternoon.
Rakesh:	I'm sorry, I can't come in the afternoon. **I'm terribly busy** then. Could you give me an appointment on Friday, please?
Receptionist:	Let me see. Yes, you can come on Friday morning. **Shall I** fix your appointment at 11 o'clock?
Rakesh:	Yes, please do. I'll be there **on time**. Thanks.

WORD MEANING

1. **Could I:** a polite form of making a request
2. **I'm terribly busy:** I'm extremely busy
3. **Shall I:** an expression used to make some suggestion
4. **On time:** exact time, neither before nor after the time fixed

COMPREHENSION

ANSWER the following questions briefly:

1. Who wants an appointment with Dr Bhargave?
2. When does he want to have this appointment?

3. Why does Rakesh refuse to have the afternoon apointment?
4. For which day is the appointment finally fixed?
5. What time can Rakesh see Dr Bhargave on this day?

Rehearse the above conversation with your partner 3 times (Pair activity).

EXPRESSIONS AND PHRASES FOR LEARNING

1. How soon could I have an appointment?
2. Is there any possibility of shifting the appointment from morning to afternoon?
3. Could you give me time in the morning on Thursday?
4. How about Saturday evening?
5. I have another appointment at 6.30 in the evening. Can I come a little later?
6. Can you make it 2 o'clock in the afternoon, please?
7. I would like to come in the morning instead of afternoon, please.
8. I think, afternoon would suit me.
9. Could I possibly meet him on Sunday morning, please?
10. Is there any other time available for this proposed meeting?

The given questions and their varied answers may be learnt and practised in appropriate situations.

EXTENDED VOCABULARY

LOOK up the following words in a good dictionary to know their meanings and pronunciations. Also note down these words in your practice notebook for their future use.

At leisure/leisurely
Busy hours
Busy schedule
Leisure hours
On priority
Prior engagement
Round the month/year
Spare-time
Wee hours
Week-end

GRAMMAR AND USAGE

If a question doesn't need an answer, we use a short answer.
For example:

Q.1 Where is your Principal?
Ans. I don't know.
Q.2 When did you buy your shoes?
Ans. I don't remember.

Q.3 Where did you buy your new mobile from?
Ans. At Madhu Vihar.

While answering questions, prefer using short sentences.
Compare the following sentences:

Q.1 Why did you refuse to accept the invitation?
Ans. (a) Because she was doing a formality. (Short answer)
(b) I refused to accept the invitation because she was doing just a formality. (Long answer)

Q.2 What time did she call last night?
Ans. (a) I don't know. (Short answer)
(b) I don't know what time she called. (Long answer)

EXPRESSIONS AND PHRASES FOR PRACTICE (Pair Activity)

1. Could you give me an appointment with .... tomorrow afternoon, please?
2. Can I have an appointment with the ...., please?
3. Can you give me an appointment on ...., please?
4. I would like to make an appointment with .... Could you please tell me when ....
5. Could you please change my appointment with Dr Rao from 10 o'clock .... in the morning on Saturday?
6. Which day or date will be ....?
7. Can you make it .... instead of ....?
8. Can you give me sometime around ....?
9. Which time would suit you ....?
10. I think .... would suit me.

ACTIVITY

1. Your younger sister doesn't want to go to school any more for no explicit reason(s). Call her classteacher and seek an appointment with her to discuss the matter urgently. Write at least six exchange dialogues seeking an appointment fixed.
2. Note down the words and expressions used here in your practice notebook, and keep revising them till you are able to use them confidentally in your conversation.

25

ACCEPTING AN INVITATION

READ aloud with your friend the following conversation and see how an invitation is accepted:

(*Pradeep invites his colleague, Raju to his birthday party. Raju gladly accepts this invitation.*)

Pradeep: Hi Raju. I have been looking for you since morning. Where were you?

Raju: I have been here right in the office all the time. You know, I'm not an officer like you. I've to go wherever the boss asks me to. Anyway, what's the matter?

Pradeep: Do you remember, tomorrow is my birthday? I have arranged a small **stag party** for my close friends, like you, on this occasion. So please do come.

Raju: What time is the party?

Pradeep: Eight o'clock in the evening.

Raju: Thank you for your kind invitation. I would be there punctually. If you, however, want me to help you in the arrangements of the party I can come even earlier.

Pradeep: No thanks! I have already made all the arrangements for the party. You just come.

Raju: Fine, I'll be there. Thank you once again! Bye, Pradeep.

Pradeep: Bye Raju.

WORD MEANING

Stag party: party for singles (without partner)

EXPRESSIONS AND PHRASES FOR LEARNING

1. I've been looking for you since morning.
2. I've been here right in the library all the time.
3. What time is the cultural programme?
4. When are you giving us a treat for the award?
5. Do you remember that tomorrow is our teacher's birthday?
6. What's the problem?
7. No thanks! I've completed my project.
8. Where had you been hiding all these days?

For accepting the invitation

9. (a) Thank you very much for your kind invitation. I'll certainly come.
   (b) I'll be delighted to attend the function.
10. Thanks for inviting me to the party.
11. Thanks, I'd love to attend the function.
12. Rest assured, I'll come for the party.

GRAMMAR AND USAGE

We use the Present Perfect Progressive tense by using has/have been + the verb in the 'ing' form, and for/since to indicate the duration of the action. We use 'for' to indicate the period of time and 'since' to denote the point of time.

For example:

1. She has been learning Indian Classical music for four years (tells about period of time).
2. I have been working on computer since morning (tells about point of time).

EXPRESSIONS AND PHRASES FOR PRACTICE (Pair Activity)

1. Hi Rashmi, I .... for you for the last two days.
2. Well, I have .... wherever my parents ....
3. What time ....?
4. Thanks for ....
5. No thanks! I ....
6. Do you remember ....?
7. What's ....?
8. Where .... all these days?

ACTIVITY

1. You have been invited by your friend to visit him during your summer vacation. Write exchange dialogues accepting the invitation.
2. Note down the words and expressions used here in your practice notebook, and keep revising them till you are able to use them naturally in your conversation.

26

DECLINING AN INVITATION

READ aloud with your friend the following conversation to see how an invitation is declined:

(*Rashmi invites her friend Ranjana to her son's marriage, but she is unable to attend it. See how she excuses herself*.)

Rashmi: (*on the phone*) Hello Ranjana, Rashmi this side.

Ranjana: Hi, Rashmi, **calling** at this odd hour! Hope everything is all right at your end.

Rashmi: I am really sorry to have called you at these **odd hours**. But as I am leaving for Mumbai tomorrow by early morning flight, I thought I could take this liberty with you. Do you mind it?

Ranjana: Of course, not. What is the matter? Please tell me. I am really getting worried.

Rashmi: Ranjana, there is nothing to be worried about. In fact, I am going to give you a good news.

Ranjana: What's that? Tell me.

Rashmi: You know my son, Rahul is getting married.

Ranjana: When is actually the marriage to take place?

Rashmi: On 21st of Sept.

Ranjana: Congratulations! But you never told me about his marriage negotiations.

Rashmi: Ranjana, you won't believe it that everything regarding Rahul's marriage was settled in such a haste that we hardly had any time to consult anybody. We couldn't consult even our in-laws. Sorry about that, Ranjana,

Ranjana: Never mind. It happens like this many times.

Rashmi: To cut short, I have called you to invite you to Rahul's marriage. I know, I should have come to invite you personally, but just couldn't manage. Anyway, we'll be very happy if you please attend this marriage.

Ranjana: Well Rashmi thank you very much for your kind invitation. But I'm afraid, I'll not be able to make it. I'm really very sorry about it.

Rashmi: Why? Are you **cross** with me?

Ranjana: Rubbish! How can you think like that? Have you forgotten that on 21st Sept. my mother is coming from New York? Her flight arrives at 8 o'clock in the evening, and I being the only one here have to receive her at the airport. Hope you'll **appreciate** my **limitation** and forgive me for not being able to attend the marriage.

Rashmi: I do appreciate your problem. But I'll **miss** you every minute in Rahul's marriage.

Ranjana: So will I… Anyway, please do convey my congratulations to Rahul and your husband. I'll definitely come to your house to see your daughter-in-law after they have returned from their honeymoon.

Rashmi: OK Ranjana. Sorry once again for disturbing you at these odd hours. Good night!

Ranjana: Good night, Rashmi.

WORD MEANING

1. **Calling:** telephoning
2. **Odd hours:** late hours (not normal hours)
3. **Cross:** angry
4. **Appreciate:** understand
5. **Limitation:** weak point/helplessness
6. **Miss:** remember

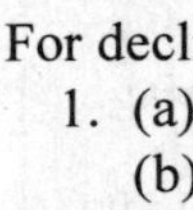

Rehearse the above conversation with your partner 3 times (Pair activity).

EXPRESSIONS AND PHRASES FOR LEARNING

For declining the invitation

1. (a) I'm afraid, I can't make it.
   (b) I'm really very sorry, I can't make it.
   (c) I'm not in town.
2. (a) I'm awfully sorry, I just can't make it.
   (b) I have a pressing engagement.
3. I'm indeed grateful to you for having invited me, but sorry, due to prior engagement I won't be able to attend the programme.
4. Please forgive me for not being able to attend the function.

The given sentences and expressions may be learnt and practised in pair in appropriate situations.

EXTENDED VOCABULARY

LOOK up the following words in a good dictionary to know their meanings and pronunciations. Also note down these words in your practice notebook for their future use.

After working hours
At all hours
Betrothal ceremony
Emergency
Engagement
Exigency
Hour-after-hour
Ring ceremony
Somebody's hour of need
Widow/Widower

GRAMMAR AND USAGE

Modal Verbs

A **modal verb** is a verb that is used before another verb to express ability, permission, possibility, necessity or advice.

The modal verbs are: *can*, *could*, *may*, *might*, *will*, *would*, *shall*, *should*, *must*, *ought to*. Sometimes, *need*, *dare*, *used to* and *had better* are also used like modal verbs besides being used as ordinary verbs.

A modal verb is usually followed by an infinitive without to (exception: ought to). It does not take 's' as the third person singular. It is also not used in the Future, Perfect or Continuous tenses.

Examples:

1. She must report for duty immediately (necessity).
2. She can dance normally after the operation (ability).
3. Could you help me learn English (ability).
4. How dare you call me a liar (ability)?

EXPRESSIONS AND PHRASES FOR PRACTICE (Pair Activity)

1. I'm awfully sorry ....
2. I'm afraid, ...
3. I'm indeed grateful to you for your kind invitation but ....
4. Thank you very much indeed for the offer but ....
5. I would love to .... but ....
6. I'm delighted to .... but ....
7. Please forgive me for ....

ACTIVITY

1. You have been invited by your friend to visit him during your summer vacation. Write exchange dialogues declining the invitation. Justify your decline of the invitation.
2. Note down the words and expressions used here in your practice notebook and keep revising them till you are able to use them confidentally in your conversation.

27

APOLOGISING

READ aloud with your friend the following conversation to know how people apologise when they go wrong:

(*Sumit and Raghav are classmates. One day Sumit speaks to Raghav very rudely. Later on he realises his mistake. So he calls Raghav to apologise for his impoliteness.*)

Sumit: Hello, is that 22241623?

Raghav: Yeah.

Sumit: May I speak to Raghav, please.

Raghav: Speaking.

Sumit: Raghav, this is Sumit. I am extremely sorry about the way I talked to you this morning. Please forgive me for my rudeness. I was little upset due to personal reasons, which, unfortunately, made me talk to you so rudely.

Raghav: Sumit, why are you so apologetic? After all we are close friends. No doubt, I felt bad when you talked to me like that. But soon I forgot about it.

Sumit: Hope you don't have any ill feelings against me.

Raghav: Not at all. How can I have such feelings about you? Sumit, please don't insult me by asking for **apology**. You are still my best friend.

Sumit: Thank you Raghav. You have relieved me of my mental tension. Why don't you come down to my place and have a cup of tea with me this evening?

Raghav: Done. I am reaching there at 6 o'clock. Hope it suits you.

Sumit: Very much. I'll be waiting for you. Until then Goodbye!

Raghav: Goodbye, Sumit!

WORD MEANING

1. **Rude:** impolite
2. **Apology:** forgiveness (apologetic: adj. seeking forgiveness)

COMPREHENSION

ANSWER the following questions briefly:

1. Why does Sumit ring Raghav?
2. Why does Raghav tell Sumit: 'don't insult me'?
3. Why does Sumit invite Raghav to his house over a cup of tea?
4. How does Raghav react to Sumit's invitation to tea?
5. What word or expression does Raghav use to indicate that he has accepted Sumit's invitation?

Rehearse the above conversation with your partner 3 times (Pair activity).

EXPRESSIONS AND PHRASES FOR LEARNING

1. My sincere apology.
2. Sorry about that.
3. Hope you won't mind it.
4. Please forgive me for my rudeness.
5. I'm really ashamed that I behaved so rudely.
6. Please forgive me for this impolite behaviour.
7. I'm awfully sorry for disappointing you.
8. I sincerely apologise for my rude behaviour.
9. Sorry about that. I won't repeat it in future.

EXTENDED VOCABULARY

Accusations and charges
Betrayal
Betraying the confidence
Create a scene
Disclosing the secret
Getting late
My apology
My sincere apology
Not telling the truth
Unparliamentary language

GRAMMAR AND USAGE

'Good' is always used as an adjective. So never use 'good' to answer a question requiring answer about wellness. Use 'well' instead.

e.g.,

They worked well together.

NOT

They worked good together.

'Very' qualifies Present Participle and 'much' Past Participle.
e.g.,

She is very charming.
He is much confused about the new evaluation scheme of CBSE.
But we say:
very pleased, very tired, very surprised, very grieved.
'Too' means more than enough, i.e., more than what is desirable.
For example:
She is too old to marry. (has crossed the marriageable age)
'Too' is used before an adjective or adverb in the positive degree to convey some negative meaning,
e.g.,

He is too weak to walk.
However, to convey some positive meaning, use 'enough', NOT 'too'.
e.g.,

She is old enough to marry. (has reached the marriageable age)

EXPRESSIONS AND PHRASES FOR PRACTICE (Pair Activity)

1. I really apologise for ....
2. I am really sorry that ....
3. I am terribly sorry. This is entirely ....
4. I would like to apologise for ....
5. Sorry about that. Hope ....
6. I'm really very sorry, I ....
7. My sincere apology for ....
8. I'm awfully sorry for ....
9. Please forgive me for all that ....
10. I'm really ashamed of .... Please forgive me for that.

The given questions and possible answers may be practised in parallel situations.

ACTIVITY

Last evening, you made some sarcastic remarks about your friend's father in the presence of your classmates, which greatly embarrassed your friend. You didn't realise the damage you had caused to the reputation of your friend at that moment. But when you realised it, it was too late. Dial your friend's number and tender a sincere apology for all that. Also tell him or her what had caused you to behave so irresponsibly. Write at least six exchange dialogues.

28

APPRECIATING SOMETHING

READ aloud with your friend the following conversation to learn how to appreciate/express liking for something:

Nandita:	Hi Rashmi. I must **appreciate** your colour sense. Your dress is really beautiful.
Rashmi:	Thank you Nandita. You look equally **gorgeous** in the dress you are wearing. By the way, where did you buy it from?
Nandita:	Well, it's not so beautiful as yours. Anyway, thanks for your compliments. Well I bought this dress from The Rainbow, South Extension.
Rashmi:	Do you remember, how much did it **cost** you?
Nandita:	I don't remember the exact price. But I think it cost me around ₹ 400/-.
Rashmi:	Fantastic! Such a beautiful dress, and so **reasonably priced!**
Nandita:	You know, Rashmi, The Rainbow is known for both quality and reasonable price. In fact, my mother always buys clothes for me and my younger sister from them only.
Rashmi:	Nandita, could you request your mother to take me and my mother along with her when she goes to the Rainbow next time. I would like to buy a few dresses for me from that shop.
Nandita:	No problem! I'll definitely tell my mother about it.
Rashmi:	Thanks Nandita.
Nandita:	You are welcome!

WORD MEANING

1. **Appreciate:** praise/express liking for something/someone
2. **Gorgeous:** pretty; lovely

3. **Cost:** price
4. **Reasonably priced:** economically priced

COMPREHENSION

ANSWER the following questions briefly:

1. Who are the people talking to each other?
2. What motivates Nandita to talk to Rashmi?
3. What two things does Rashmi want to know from Nandita?
4. What reply does Nandita give?
5. What request does Rashmi make to Nandita?

Rehearse the above conversation with your partner 3 times (Pair activity).

EXPRESSIONS AND PHRASES FOR LEARNING (Pair Activity)

1. What a nice shirt!
2. What a beautiful voice!
3. It sounds so well/musical.
4. That shirt/jacket really looks nice on you.
5. It's a wonderful idea.
6. It's so interesting/refreshing/bewitching.
7. You mustn't miss this movie/deal. It's one of its kind.
8. It's simply marvellous.
9. It's an institution with difference.
10. I really admire it/him/her/I really appreciate it/her/him.
11. What a beauty!
12. What a figure!
13. What a height!

The given expressions and phrases may be practised and drilled to perfection with the help of your friends in appropriate situations.

EXTENDED VOCABULARY

LOOK up the following words in a good dictionary/thesaurus to know their meanings and pronunciations. Also use them in your conversation in parallel situations.

Aesthetic sense/artistic sense	Appreciation
Affordable price	Approximately

Compliments
Exaggerate
Exclusive
Gorgeous/fantastic/superb/smashing
Pleasing
Sense of beauty

GRAMMAR AND USAGE

Exclamations with:

(a) 'What a —! take countables singular.
(b) What —! take plural, and uncountables.

For example:

(a) What a good idea!
(b) What a beautiful dress!
(c) What grand ideas you have!
(d) What lovely eyes she has!
(e) What beautiful music they are playing!

EXPRESSIONS AND PHRASES FOR PRACTICE (Pair Activity)

1. How nice ....!
2. How beautiful it ....!
3. This colour really ....
4. It's a wonderful ....
5. I really like it. It's simply ....
6. You look very .... in this dress.
7. You are so ....
8. I must really appreciate .... It's so unique.
9. You have such a .... I never knew it.
10. That's a splendid .
11. What a ....!

ACTIVITY

1. Your friend has thrown a party to all your classmates on the occasion of his election as the House Captain. He/She has also got a suit stitched specially for the occasion. Go and appreciate his/her suit and the party arrangements, including the menu of the party. Use as many new expressions as you possibly can to express your appreciation.
2. Note down all the words and expressions that you find new for practice in appropriate parallel situations.

29

EXPRESSING DISAPPROVAL

READ aloud with your friend the following conversation to know how people express their disapproval for the things they don't like:

(*Pradeep and Raju are close friends. One day they go to see a movie titled 'Kaun Apna aur Kaun Paraya'. On return they discuss the movie.*)

Pradeep: Well Raju, what would you like to say about the movie we have just seen?

Raju: Shall I give you my honest opinion?

Pradeep: Yeah.

Raju: I am afraid, I didn't like it. **But for** your company I didn't come out of the cinema hall in the very first half of the film.

Pradeep: Why? What was wrong with the movie?

Raju: There was hardly any story. Dialogues put in the mouth of the hero and heroine were dreadful. As regards its music, it was highly disappointing to the lovers of music. In fact, there was hardly anything good in this movie. I don't think we should have gone for this movie.

Pradeep: Raju, you know, I don't consider anything worthless. Yet I have the same opinion as yours about this movie. Consider the title of the movie. Don't you think, it is philosophical in nature? To make a film on a philosophical topic is not an easy job. Only a director with philosophical bent of mind and actors and actresses having full faith in that philosophy can do justice. From that point of view I don't think the movie can be called a very good attempt.

Raju: Pradeep, I am sure, if you look at this movie like a film critic you'll find many more things to say against it. But we are not professional critics, you know.

Pradeep:	Raju, now we've got late. Our parents must be getting worried about us. So we'll discuss this movie **at length** at some other time when we are rather free from all other thoughts. OK. Let's move then. Bye, Raju!
Raju:	Bye, Pradeep!

WORD MEANING

1. **But for:** except
2. **At length:** in detail
3. **Rather free:** not very busy

COMPREHENSION

ANSWER the following questions briefly:

1. What are Pradeep and Raju discussing?
2. What does Raju tell Pradeep about the movie?
3. Who can successfully make films on philosophical topics according to Pradeep?
4. Why do they suddenly stop discussing the movie?
5. When would they like to discuss the movie at length?

Rehearse the above conversation with your friend 3 times (Pair activity).

EXPRESSIONS AND PHRASES FOR LEARNING

1. It's absolutely disgusting.
2. I'm afraid, I don't like it.
3. I wish we hadn't gone for this movie.
4. I don't consider it entirely worthless.
5. I haven't seen such a poor film.
6. I can't stand it.
7. The director has made a mess of everything.
8. What would you like to say about the movie?
9. How do you rate this movie?
10. Dialogues were dreadful and music highly disappointing.

EXTENDED VOCABULARY

Look up the following words and phrases in a good dictionary/thesaurus to know their meaning and pronunciations. Also use them appropriately in your discussion on films and cultural programmes.

Box office
Cast
Choreography
Dialogues
Dubbing
Film critic
Film review
Script
Theme
Vamp/villain

GRAMMAR AND USAGE

But for: (preposition/conjunction) is used to convey the meaning of 'except', e.g., I would have fallen into the ditch but for your timely warning.

Yet: (conjunction) is used to connect two sentences showing contrasting situations.

EXPRESSIONS AND PHRASES FOR PRACTICE (Pair Activity)

1. It's absolutely ....
2. I can't .... it/I can't .... it!
3. I'm afraid, I .... it.
4. I have never seen ....
5. It's terrible, ...?
6. I don't like the way ....
7. I wish you hadn't ....
8. It doesn't sound .... to me.
9. I don't think it is ....
10. She has made a .... of it.

The given questions and possible answers may be drilled and practised in appropriate situations.

ACTIVITY

You were entrusted with the responsibility of selecting a good play to be presented by the dramatic club of your school or college on the occasion of the School/College Annual Day, which you did with the help of some of your friends. Now discuss the strengths and weaknesses of the play through a group discussion to find out its suitability for presentation.

30

MEETING A SCHOOL FRIEND AFTER A LONG TIME

READ aloud with your friend the following conversation:

Rohan: Hi Reema! What a pleasant surprise! Seeing you **after ages**! Where have you been all these days?

Reema: I am equally excited to meet you Rohan after such a long time. I think we are meeting after two **decades**. Now I am a green card holder and settled in USA.

Rohan: Which city?

Reema: Los Angeles. We have our business over there.

Rohan: Have you come here to meet your parents?

Reema: No Rohan, I have come here to attend the marriage of my brother-in-law. My in-laws stay in Delhi.

Rohan: How are your parents? Hope they are keeping good health!

Reema: Rohan, my parents are no more. They died in a plane crash ten years ago.

Rohan: Reema, I am very sorry to learn all about your parents. How did it all happen?

Reema: Rohan, do you remember when we were appearing at the +2 examination of CBSE, I had told you that my father had applied for a work visa in USA?

Rohan: Yes, I do. Then what happened?

Reema: My father got the work visa and my parents moved to Los Angeles **in search of fortune**. There I spent the happiest days of my life for about ten years, and then fell the **bolt from the blue**. Both my father and mother died in a plane crash while flying from Los Angeles to London, leaving behind me and my younger brother, Raju.

Rohan: What a grim tragedy! What did you do then? I am sure you must have felt highly miserable, besides feeling lonely.

Reema: Yes Rohan, it was the most trying period of my life. I felt completely shattered. Though I wanted to marry the person who loved me so passionately I couldn't think of my marriage till Raju completed his education and settled in life. He was in the final year of the computer engineering then.

Rohan: So where is Raju now? Hope he has happily settled in life!

Reema: Yes, very happily. He is now a well-known computer engineer, with a beautiful wife and two lovely children. His wife also works with him.

Rohan: I am happy to know about Raju. But how about you? Hope your married life is equally happy!

Reema: Very happy. My husband is really a jewel. He loves me so much that I needn't tell him anything. He knows what I want and when.

Rohan: I am so happy to hear all this. May God bless you with all sorts of happiness in life!

Reema: Rohan, you must have also got married by now, haven't you?

Rohan: Yes, I am married, too. I have two children—one son and one daughter. Both of them go to a good primary school in Delhi.

Reema: Rohan, wouldn't you care to tell me how life treated you after I saw you last?

Rohan: Why not? You are my friend and I don't feel shy talking about it. But do you have time to listen to my story of pain and suffering?

Reema: Don't insult me Rohan! We have been very good friends in our student life sharing our joys and sorrows without any inhibition.

Rohan: Then listen. My mother died of cancer some ten years ago. In fact, we never knew that she was suffering from cancer till the doctors told us that she was at the last stage of cancer.

Reema: Didn't you take her to Rajeev Gandhi Cancer Hospital for operation and treatment of cancer?

Rohan: Yes, we did. But the doctors said that we had brought her too late. Nothing could have been done at that stage. Anyway, after my mother's death another problem shook me **through and through**. It was my father's decision to go in for the second marriage.

Reema: So then did he really marry?

Rohan: He not only married much against the wishes of one and all, but also allowed my step-mother to **unleash the hell** on to me.

Reema: Is it? Tell me in detail, Rohan?

Rohan: My new mother would insult me for petty things. At times, she wouldn't give me food for days together on one or the other pretext, and then I had to live on the mercy of my neighbours. When I would complain all about this to my father he would refuse to listen to anything against my new mother. So one day in **sheer disgust** I left my house forever without informing them.

Reema: Rohan, I can't believe it. Do you mean a woman can be so cruel and the man so helpless as not to utter even a single word in favour of his own child?

Rohan: Reema, believe it or not, every word of my story is true. Well, after leaving the house I had to take up a private job at a very low salary. After all I had to survive.

Reema: How long did you carry on with that job?

Rohan: For as many as five years. Then one day while shopping I met a girl who changed the **course of my life**. Do you know who that girl was? She is my wife.

Reema: How did she change your life, Rohan?

Rohan: Well, she was the daughter of the owner of that departmental store where I was shopping. After marriage my father-in-law made me a partner in his business. And now I am a **businessman of repute**.

Reema: I am very happy to know about it. Do you know 'all's well that ends well' is an old saying?

Rohan: Yes Reema. Now that we have met after such a long period, why should we not plan to have a get-together for our families who are still strangers to each other?

Reema: I think it would be a wonderful idea. Please give me your visiting card. I'll contact you over the phone and fix up the date for this proposed get-together with your help. I must leave now, as I am getting late and my in-laws must be getting worried. See you! Bye, Rohan!

Rohan: Bye, Reema!

WORD MEANING

1. **After ages:** after a long time
2. **Decade:** one decade means 10 years
3. **In search of fortune:** to make money
4. **Bolt from the blue:** meeting with unexpected tragedy
5. **Through and through:** completely
6. **Unleash the hell:** put to various kinds of torture
7. **Sheer disgust:** in frustration
8. **Course of life:** direction of life
9. **Businessman of repute:** well-known businessman

COMPREHENSION

There are three choices for each question. Tick (✓) the choice you consider to be correct.

1. After how much time have the two friends met?
   (a) After a very long time.
   (b) After 10 years.
   (c) After two decades.
2. Where has Reema settled?
   (a) In USA.

(b) In UK.
(c) In Russia.

3. Why has Reema come to Delhi?
(a) To meet her friends and relatives.
(b) To meet her parents-in-law.
(c) To attend the marriage of her brother-in-law.

4. What does Reema tell Rohan about her parents?
(a) They are perfectly all right.
(b) They are no more.
(c) They are staying with her brother, Raju.

5. How did Reema's parents die?
(a) In a road accident while travelling .
(b) In a plane crash while travelling from Los Angles to London.
(c) Died of old age.

6. What sacrifice did Reema make to settle her brother in life?
(a) She dropped the idea of her marriage with her fiancé till Raju finished his education and settled in life.
(b) She helped him by giving him a lot of money.
(c) She worked overtime to earn extra money needed for Raju's education.

7. How did Rohan's mother die?
(a) She died of a heart attack.
(b) She died of cancer.
(c) She committed suicide.

8. Why couldn't Rohan's mother be saved?
(a) She was at the last stage of her illness.
(b) She refused to be treated for her illness.
(c) Her doctors mishandled her case.

9. Why did Rohan run away from his house?
(a) His father married again after his mother's death?
(b) His step mother ill-treated him.
(c) His step mother ill-treated him and at times did not give him food for days together.

10. What did Rohan do after running away from his house?
(a) He joined a private company at a very low salary.
(b) He loitered here and there like a vagabond.
(c) He took up a job in a departmental store.

11. How did Rohan's wife change the course of his life?
(a) Both of them worked hard to earn their living.
(b) Rohan's father-in-law was a big businessman who made Rohan his business partner.
(c) Both of them had a very good understanding.

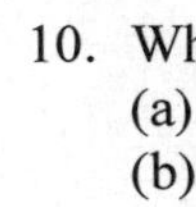

Rehearse the above conversation with your partner 3 times (Pair activity).

EXPRESSIONS AND PHRASES FOR LEARNING

1. What a pleasant surprise!
2. Haven't seen you for ages.
3. How is life?
4. We all miss you a lot, especially my mom.
5. Believe me!
6. I'm sorry I lost track of all my childhood friends.
7. I fail to understand why he acted so foolishly!
8. How often do you go to the theatre?
9. Let's celebrate our re-union!
10. How do you spend your Sundays?
11. What do you do?
12. What's the source of your livelihood?
13. What's the size of your family?
14. How big is your family?
15. Who all are there in your family?
16. How often do you go out on pleasure trips?
17. How do you spend your evenings?
18. How about the education of your children?
19. What's the performance like of your children at school/college?
20. What are your future plans?
21. What have you planned for your future?
22. Any project in the offing?
23. Let's celebrate our meeting/this day.
24. Let's toast to our friendship!

EXTENDED VOCABULARY

LOOK up the following words in a good dictionary/thesaurus to know their meanings and pronunciations. Also use them while conversing with your old friend after a long time.

A jocular comment
Bolt from the blue
Bright career
Brilliant academic record
Bunk the class
Caricature
Carry on
Course of life
Educational trip
Episode
Excursion
For good/forever
Foster parents
Get-together
Get worried
Give regards
Grim tragedy
Inhibition
In search of
Long interval
Long silence
Miserable

Mishap
Miss
Pastime
Pay compliments
Re-live the past
Truancy
Truant

SOME USEFUL TIPS TO SPEAK

1. In a situation dominated by emotions, like the one in the given conversation, use plenty of exclamatory sentences.
2. Make proper use of stress and intonation to make your communication effective.
3. Exclamation is something you say or shout suddenly because of surprise, fear, sorrow, or pleasure, etc.

EXPRESSIONS AND PHRASES FOR PRACTICE (Pair Activity)

1. (a) What a pleasant ....!
   (b) I can't believe my ....!
   (c) Is it ....?
   (d) What a ....!
2. (a) Haven't seen you for ....!
   (b) Where have/had you been all ....?
   (c) Where have/had you been hiding ....?
3. (a) How is life ....?
   (b) How did life treat ....?
   (c) What all happened to ....?
4. (a) I .... a lot!
   (b) I very often ....!
   (c) I wish I were ....!
5. (a) I am sorry I lost track ....!
   (b) I am sorry I didn't know ....
6. (a) Believe it or not ....!
   (b) I know you won't believe but it ....
7. (a) What's your profession ....?
8. (a) I fail to understand why ....
   (b) It's beyond my comprehension why ....
   (c) I can't imagine why ....
9. (a) Do you remember ....?
   (b) Do you recall that incident when ....?

The given sentences/expressions may be drilled with suitable modifications in appropriate situations.

ACTIVITY

Imagine you revisiting your primary school after a gap of 6–8 years and happen to meet the teacher who first taught you how to read and write English. Present a role play with the help of your friend(s) depicting the given situation.

31

AT THE PARENT–TEACHER MEETING

READ aloud with your friend the following conversation:

Parent: Good morning Madam!

Teacher: Good morning Mrs Sharma!

Parent: How is my daughter, Neena, **doing at school**?

Teacher: **Pretty well**. She can, however, do still better.

Parent: What's her position like in the class?

Teacher: Well, she is in the first five students of the class in studies. As regards her performance in **co-curricular activities** she is at the top. She is a very-well behaved child. We are really proud of her!

Parent: Could you tell me her subject-wise performance?

Teacher: Of course. She is A+ in Maths, A+ in Science, A in Social Studies, A+ in English and B+ in Hindi. She is, however, capable of getting A+ in all the subjects.

Parent: How can I, as a parent, help her improve her performance in Social Studies and Hindi?

Teacher: Well, the first thing that you can do is to boost her morale. Impress upon her that she is equally good in all the subjects. Only she needs a little extra work in these subjects. Her Hindi is fairly good. What she needs is to concentrate on the subject matter only. For Hindi you can also provide her some extra coaching at home. At school, we will also try to help her as much as we can. After all she is a promising student of our school. As regards Social Studies, encourage her to make use of the Internet.

Parent: Thank you very much Madam for all your assured help. Could you suggest the name of some good teacher who can coach my daughter after the school hours?

Teacher: Since your daughter is a bright student she needs a bright teacher. I think Miss Sunita Pandey will be most suitable for her. But for this you will have to take permission of the Principal. You see, we teachers are not allowed to give tuition without her permission. Private coaching without Principal's permission is against the Code of Conduct for teachers.

Parent: Thank you Madam. Where can I find the Principal at the moment?

Teacher: She's in her office right now. You can meet her if you so like.

Parent: Thank you Madam. Bye-bye!

Teacher: Bye-bye!

Parent: Could I see the Principal please?

Private Secretary: In what connection?

Parent: It's regarding her permission for private tuition to my daughter by Miss Pandey.

P.S.: I'm afraid, she is busy right now. In a few minutes from now she is going to the auditorium to address the parents' meeting. You can see her after the meet if you please.

Parent: OK. I'll meet her after the parents' meeting. Kindly fix my appointment.

(*The Principal highlights the purpose of the parent–teacher meeting in her address to the parents. She also invites questions from the parents.*)

Parent 'A': How do you ensure that the classroom teaching **caters to** the needs of both the below-average and above-average students, besides looking after the needs of the average child?

Principal: Through interactive participatory approach that we follow in teaching all the subjects.

Parent 'B': What system has the school adopted for personality enrichment of the child?

Principal: All the children of the school have been divided into four houses named after the names of great leaders of India. All the co-curricular activities of the school are conducted on **inter-** and **intra-house** basis. At primary level, particularly in classes I and II, these activities are conducted at the class level. All the programmes that the school organises are **value-based**.

Parent 'C': How do you help the weak students of the board classes in each subject?

Principal: We have allocated one period per week for remedial teaching in each subject. In addition to this, we have also introduced a special time-table for subjects like Maths,

	Science and English for the weak students. This time-table is to be followed during the morning assembly.
Parent 'D':	(*Secretary to P.T.A*) Madam, we are indeed grateful to you for providing a quality education to our children. We are confident that our children are in safe hands. On behalf of the parents of this school I congratulate you and your staff for raising this school to the present heights. I also wish you and your team all success in all your future educational **ventures**.
Principal:	Thank you very much indeed for all your cooperation and help in managing this school. Hope you would continue to extend this help in future, too. All the best!

WORD MEANING

1. **Doing at school:** performance at school
2. **Pretty well:** very well
3. **Co-curricular activities:** literary and cultural activities organised by a school for personality development of the child.
4. **Caters to:** serves
5. **Inter-house:** between two or more houses
6. **Intra-house:** within the house
7. **Value-based:** a programme meant to develop useful values in the child's life
8. **Ventures:** new activities

COMPREHENSION

ANSWER the following questions briefly:

1. Who goes to attend the parent–teacher meeting?
2. What according to her classteacher is the overall performance of Neena?
3. What are rather weak subjects of Neera?
4. What suggestion does the classteacher give to Neena's parent for improvement of her performance in Social Studies?
5. Why does the classteacher recommend the name of Miss Sunita Pandey for giving private tuition to Neena?
6. Why does the classteacher ask the parent to obtain the Principal's permission for private coaching to her daughter?
7. Why is the parent not allowed to meet the Principal immediately?
8. How does the school cater to the educational needs of both the below-average and above-average students in all subjects?
9. How does the school organise the co-curricular activities to ensure participation in these activities by all children?

10. What kind of programme does the school have for the weak students of the board classes?

Rehearse the above conversation with your partner 3 times (Pair activity).

EXPRESSIONS AND PHRASES FOR LEARNING

1. What's my child's performance like?
2. How is he/she performing at the co-curricular activities?
3. How about her performance in English and Maths?
4. He/she is rather careless, but he/she is not dull.
5. Could I know his/her subject-wise performance?
6. What's the new grading system you have recently introduced?
7. What's CCE (Continuous Comprehensive Evaluation)?
8. Thanks a lot.
9. Thank you very much indeed for having given me such a comprehensive evaluation of my child.

EXTENDED VOCABULARY

LOOK up the following words in a good dictionary-cum-thesaurus to know their meanings and pronunciations. Also use them appropriately while attending a parent–teacher meet or talking about the school activities.

Above average; average; below average/bright child

Academic
Activity-based teaching
Affective domain; cognitive domain
All-round development
Arrogance
Assembly
Attitude
Capitation fee
Centenary
Centennial
Chalk-board/green-board/white-board
Chalk-stick/marker
Class library/school library
Class test/unit test
Class time-table
Club activities
Club-master; bulbul flock leader

Co-curricular activities
Community service/social service
Conduct/behaviour
Cooperation
Corporal punishment
Correction; correction symbols
Creativity
Cultural activities
Curricular activities/extra-curricular/co-curricular activities
Curriculum; syllabus/syllabi/syllabuses (plural forms)
Debate/elocution
Debut
Deficiency
Diagnostic test
Donation

Entrance test; admission test
Evaluation; assessment
Extempore speech/elocution
Faculty/staff/teachers
Grace marks
Hobbies
Home-teacher/classteacher
Homework
Impertinent
Incentives; awards
Infrastructure
Innovation
Inspiration
Institutional planning
Inter-house
Intra-house
Investiture ceremony
Journals
Joyful learning
Laboratory
Language laboratory
Late-payment fine
Learning material
Literary activities
Magazines
Mass PT
Merit
Monitoring
Monthly test
Motivation
NCC
Non-teaching staff; ancillary staff
Notes of lesson; lesson planning
Participation
Performance test
Periodicals
Personality
Personality enrichment activities
Personality enrichment programme
Personality traits
Progress report/Performance report
Project work
Proposals
Psycho-motor domain
PTA/PTF
Punctuality
Quality education
Remedial teaching/remove classes
Rows
Scouting and guiding
Scoutmaster; guide captain
Session-ending examination/annual examination
Sports
Sports material
Stationery
Streaming
Student calendar/student diary
Subject teacher
Substitution period/arrangement period
Teaching aids
Time-table
Truancy
Truant
Tuck shop
Value-based education
Wholesome education

GRAMMAR AND USAGE

Some Formal Expressions

1. May I offer any assistance to the school?
2. Shall I leave now?
3. Sorry, I don't understand what you mean!
4. Would you mind elaborating it, please?
5. I'll let you know about the change in my child's behaviour in our next meeting.

6. I will be in touch with you to know all about my child.
7. I hope (that) I didn't disturb you much.
8. I'm looking forward to meeting you soon.
9. I sincerely apologise for my child's behaviour.
10. I regret to inform you that I shall not be able to attend the PTA meating.

Some Informal Expressions

1. Let's go.
2. Sorry, I couldn't meet you earlier.
3. See you soon perhaps next week.
4. Hang on a minute! I tell you the background story.
5. Don't worry! I'll be in touch.

SOME USEFUL TIPS TO SPEAK

1. Always remember that a PTA/PTF is a forum to find out a practicable solution to the problems of the students jointly. It should never be used as a means to find fault with the school and its management.
2. Parents attending the PTA meeting must be polite and respectful to the teachers and the Principal of the school. The suggestions that they make to improve the academic standard of the school must be given in such a language that they are not misunderstood.
3. While discussing the progress of their child they should specifically enquire how the school is going to help their child and what the school expects them to do to solve the problem jointly.

EXPRESSIONS AND PHRASES FOR PRACTICE (Pair Activity)

1. What is .... son's/daughter's performance like?
2. How is he/she faring at ....?
3. Could you tell me .... subject-wise ....?
4. Would you please tell me in detail about ....?
5. May I know about .... progress?
6. Thank you very much for ....
7. What is ....?

ACTIVITY

Present a role play with the help of your friends on 'Parent–Teacher Day' you recently attended.

32

INTERVIEW FOR CHILD'S ADMISSION IN SCHOOL

READ aloud with your friend the following conversation:

Receptionist: (speaking loudly) Nandini's parents

Nandini's Mother: We are here, Madam.

Receptionist: Madam, it's your turn now. Please go into the Principal's office along with Nandini for an interview.

Mother: OK. Thank you!

(*They enter the Principal's office as instructed by the Receptionist*)

Father: Good morning, Sir.

Principal: Good morning, Mr and Mrs Verma. Please sit down.

Father: We are Nandini's parents and we are here to request you to admit her to class I

Principal: What do you do Mr Verma?

Father: I am one of the Directors in a multinational company located in Noida

Principal: Good! Do you also work Mrs Verma?

Mother: No, Sir, I am a **housewife** now. Earlier I was a teacher in DPS, Dadri.

Principal: Why did you leave that job? Were you not happy as a teacher?

Mother: I was quite happy as a teacher but I had to resign the job to **look after** Nandini who was too small to manage on her own then. Now that Nandini is going to join the school I am also planning to join some good public school as a teacher.

Principal: What are your qualifications?

Mother: I'm M.Sc., B.Ed. I am a Maths teacher.

Principal: **Wonderful**! If you are really serious about your job as a teacher we can definitely consider you for the post of T.G.T. (Maths). **But for that** we can talk later. At the moment, I have a few questions regarding your daughter's admission in this school. Hope you won't mind answering them.

Mother: Certainly not. What are your questions, Sir?

Principal: Who teaches Nandini at home?

Mother: Both of us.

Principal: How much time do you spend with your daughter everyday?

Mother: At least one hour. My husband also spends about half an hour talking to her about various things **that interest her**.

Principal: It's very good indeed. Do you think you will be able to spend the same time even after your taking up a job?

Mother: Perhaps more than that. As we are going to have a full-time **domestic help** from the first of the next month, I will have **plenty** of spare time at my disposal.

Principal: Mr Verma, can you tell me what is the subject you mostly talk about while working with Nandini?

Father: I usually narrate **value-based stories** to inculcate in her certain good values. At times, we talk about birds and animals, which Nandini often finds fascinating.

Principal: I am really very happy to know that both of you are doing well to educate Nandini at home. Now, the last question. Why do you want to admit your daughter in this school?

Mother: This school enjoys a very good reputation and is said to be the best school in this locality. Moreover, our house is close by. It takes just 5 minutes to walk down the distance.

Principal: It was indeed nice talking to you. (*Turning to the child*) What's your name child?

Nandini: Nandini Verma.

Principal: And what's your daddy's name?

Nandini: Mr Abhishek Verma.

Principal: Good! and your mummy's name?

Nandini: Mrs Anita Verma.

Principal: What is your surname?

Nandini: Verma.

Principal: Where do you live?

Nandini: At Ramakrishna Vihar, Patparganj

Principal: How many friends do you have?

Nandini: Many.

Principal: Can you count them?

Nandini: Yes, (she counts) 10.

Principal: Who is your best friend?

Nandini: Babita

Principal: Why?

Nandini: She always gives me chocolate. She also gives me her colours and pencils.

Principal: How many colours are there in the sunlight?

Nandini: 7—violet, indigo, blue, green, yellow, orange and red.

Principal: **Excellent!** Who told you about it?

Nandini: My daddy.

Principal: Can you spell the word 'yellow'?

Nandini: Yes. (*she spells correctly*)

Principal: Why do you want to join this school?

Nandini: I like your school uniform very much.

Principal: OK and now the last question (*Pointing to the office clock*) what is the time now?

Nandini: Half-past ten.

Principal: Very good Nandini (*Turning to Mr and Mrs Verma*), I admit your daughter. Congratulations! You can now deposit the fee and other dues with the school accountant in the office. Here is my permission slip!

Mother: Thank you very much Sir! I will come to you tomorrow regarding my appointment as a Maths teacher in your school. Thank you once again for all your **favour**. Bye-bye.

Principal: Bye-bye.

WORD MEANING

1. **Housewife:** A married woman who does not go out for work (not doing any paid job)
2. **Look after:** bring up
3. **Wonderful:** an expression used to appreciate something
4. **But for that:** about that (on that subject)
5. **That interest her:** matters in which she is interested
6. **Domestic help:** maidservant
7. **Plenty:** a lot
8. **Value-based stories:** stories which deal with socially and religiously acceptable thoughts and practices
9. **Excellent:** an expression used to appreciate something/action
10. **Favour:** help

Rehearse the above conversation with your partner 3 times (Pair activity).

EXPRESSIONS AND PHRASES FOR LEARNING

1. What's the admission criteria?
2. What will be the duration of the admission test?
3. Is it a qualifying or a competitive one?
4. Are there any paid seats available?

5. When are you going to declare the results of the admission test?
6. When's the list of the selected candidates going to be displayed?
7. What's the last date for admission to be sought?
8. Are there any seats reserved for bright children?
9. How many seats are reserved for socially disadvantaged children like SC/ST?
10. What will be the standard of the admission test to be conducted?
11. Will the questions in admission test be text-based or of general nature?
12. Is there any capitation fee for admission in the school?
13. Is the school bus duly escorted by a school teacher?
14. How much is the bus fee?
15. Do you have a swimming pool, with a trainer's services available?
16. What hobby clubs do you have for children of primary/secondary/senior secondary classes?
17. Is it only a day school or a day-boarding?
18. Do you provide RO water or plain tap water to your students?
19. Could you explain your evaluation system?
20. How do you inculcate important values in children?
21. Could you describe your value-education programme?

SOME PARENTS MAY FACE QUESTIONS

1. What do you do?
2. Who teaches your child at home?
3. How much time do you spend with your child at home every day?
4. What is your job profile like?
5. Is your wife a working woman or a housewife?
6. How is it that your child's performance in the admission test is not up to the mark?
7. Why does your child look so depressed?
8. Why is your child so quiet? Is there any problem at home?
9. How much time can you spare to help us organise co-curricular activities in our school?
10. In which other ways can you help this school?

EXTENDED VOCABULARY

Calligraphy
CCE (Continuous Comprehensive Evaluation)
Compatibility
Dramatization
Elocution
Extempore
MLL (Minimum Levels of Learning)
Project work
Promotion vs. demotion
Recitation
Reference skills
Remedial teaching
Role-play
Streaming
Withdrawn vs. start

GRAMMAR AND USAGE

Some of the adverbs do not end in '–ly' e.g., soon, always, ever, away, here, too, fast, straight, hard, etc. It may also be noted that 'hard' is both adjective and adverb. When we use the word hardly it means 'scarcely'. So be careful while using 'hard' as an adverb.

e.g.,

1. He works hard. (hard work)
   NOT
   He works hardly. (scarcely)
2. She hardly visits us on sundays. (scarcely)

EXPRESSIONS AND PHRASES FOR PRACTICE (Pair Activity)

1. Are the admissions on or are they ....?
2. How many seats .... in class ....?
3. What're the subjects .... for admission to class ....?
4. Is there a school bus available for .... or a nearby area?
5. What kind of co-curricular activities do you organize for students at the primary/secondary/senior secondary level?
6. How often do you organize parent–teacher meetings in a term?
7. How many excursions and picnics do you organize for students at the primary/secondary/senior secondary level in an academic year?
8. How do you help the weak students in a particular subject?
9. When are the remedial classes held?
10. How do you cater to the needs of the bright children of a class?
11. How do you promote extra-reading habits in your students?
12. How are the library periods of a class utilized?
13. What percentage of your total school budget do you spend on the developmental activities of the school?
14. What was the last year's board examination result for classes X/XII?
15. Do you have a homework time-table for a class?
16. How do you update your teachers in their respective subjects?
17. What is your plan in bringing the home and the school closer?
18. How often do you organise a medical check-up for your students during a year?
19. How do you encourage creativity in your students?
20. Do you admit autistic children in your school?

ACTIVITY

The given questions and possible answers may be noted down in your practice notebook and drilled till you are able to use them naturally and spontaneously.

33

TELLING THE TIME

READ aloud with your friend the following conversation to know how to ask or tell the time:

Radha: Basu, what's the time by your watch? My watch has stopped.
Basu: It's quarter-past ten.
Radha: Any idea what time is our train for Agra?
Basu: Half-past twelve.
Radha: And what time will our train reach Agra Cantt. ?
Basu: Quarter to four.
Radha: **By the way,** when is our connecting train for Bhopal ?
Basu: I think, there is an express train at ten past five from Agra Cantt, and it reaches Bhopal Jn. at five to eleven.
Radha: Then we have plenty of time. **Shall we** go to the railway canteen and finish our lunch first?
Basu: It's a good idea. After lunch we can also have a short **nap** in the waiting room.
Radha: It is wonderful! I badly need some rest. I am **dead tired**.
Basu: OK. Let's go then and have our lunch quickly.

Rehearse the above conversation with your partner 3 times (Pair activity).

WORD MEANING

1. **By the way:** an expression used to convey the meaning of 'incidentally'
2. **Shall we:** indicates a suggestion for consideration
3. **Nap:** a short sleep, especially during the day
4. **Dead tired:** extremely tired (and need some rest)

COMPREHENSION

ANSWER the following questions very briefly:

1. Which is that word that shows that Basu and Radha are travelling together?
2. Where are they going?
3. What is the route to their destination?
4. What suggestion does Radha make to Basu?

EXPRESSIONS AND PHRASES FOR LEARNING

1. What is the time?
2. It's nine o'clock.
3. It's quarter past two.
4. It's half-past four.
5. It's quarter to five.
6. It's ten o'clock.
7. It's five past seven.
8. It's six minutes past three.
9. It's twelve minutes past eight.

EXTENDED VOCABULARY

LOOK up the following words in a good dictionary-cum-thesaurus to know their meanings and pronunciations. Also use them appropriately when required.

2 tier/3 tier
Down trains
Express train/goods train
Loose shunting
Mail train
Overhead bridge
Passenger train
Reservation chart
Sleeper
Up trains

GRAMMAR AND USAGE

Chart Showing Possibility in Progress

Impossible	Improbable	Probable	Possible	Certain
zero%	(not impossible but possible)	lesser possibility	50% chances	100%
can't	couldn't mightn't	could might	may can	must

When we want to say that something is likely to happen we use modal verbs such as may, might, can, could and must. The selection of the modal verb depends on how much is the possibility of its happening.

Examples:

1. (a) It's cloudy. It may rain tonight. (possible)
   (b) It's cloudy. It might rain tonight. (probable)

To express that something is impossible or nearly impossible we use can't or couldn't or mightn't (can't for impossible, and couldn't or mightn't for nearly impossible happening).

Examples:

1. The news of his selection for IAS can't be true because he didn't appear for all the papers.
2. The rumour that she has married again couldn't be true as she is now 75 (the rumour is almost unbelievable).

EXPRESSIONS AND PHRASES FOR PRACTICE (Pair Activity)

1. (a) Excuse me, what's the time by your watch?
   (b) It's ....
2. (a) Could you tell me the right time?
   (b) Oh yes, it's ....
3. (a) What time is it?
   (b) It's .... (11.00/11.30/11.45/12.15/12.20/12.50)
4. What's the time, please?
5. It's .... (8.00)
6. It's .... (7.15)
7. It's .... (8.30)
8. It's .... (4.45)
9. It's .... (9.05)
10. It's .... (10.07)
11. It's .... (5.54)
12. It's .... (11.09)

The given questions and their possible answers may be learnt and practised in appropriate situations.

ACTIVITY

You have to go to Pachmarhi (a hill station in Madhya Pradesh). Make an enquiry on the phone regarding the timings of the various trains available for Piparia from New Delhi via Itarsi. Please note that Piparia is a station from where you get a bus for Pachmarhi.

34

INTERVIEWING A CELEBRITY ON TELEVISION

[Rendezvous (ˈrɒndɪvu:) with Pradeep]

READ aloud with your friend the following TV interview with Amit Sondhi, a pop star in the programme 'Rendezvous with Pradeep':

Pradeep (Anchor): Amit, today you are a **throb** for every pop-music lover. Can you tell us how you managed to reach this envious position in just 10 years time? But before you tell us all about it, please tell us something about the days when you were struggling to make pop-singing as your career.

Amit Sondhi: For that we'll have to go back to my college days when I would take part in all musical programmes of the college. I was then a young man of 20 years with a dream to be a professional pop-singer. From the awards and **applauses** that I would receive from my friends, I was dead sure that I would soon be a famous pop-singer. But unfortunately nothing of the sort happened. I felt quite depressed not knowing what **fate had in its store** for me. And one day, when I was singing, from the stage of the Alumni Association of the college, the chief guest of the programme approached me, after the show was over, with an unbelievable offer. He asked me if I could sing for his music company. I couldn't believe my ears as for me it was **a dream come true**. And this breakthrough made me a professional pop-singer.

Anchor: Though you have produced a number of albums, which have been received very well by your fans and which ones are your favourite ones?

Amit:	Since all are my babies, I like all of them. Still the albums called 'Baat Pyar Kee'. 'Unse Shikayet Hai' and 'Pyaar Hee Pyaar' are the ones on which I'd worked very hard.
Anchor:	What technique or techniques do you adopt to make your musical rendering rather time resistant?
Amit:	I take the help of **'folk music'** and **'fusion technique'** by which the music I produce stays young for a long time.
Anchor:	How many numbers have you given to your fans so far?
Amit:	About three hundred.
Anchor:	How many of them do you think will remain popular for at least a decade?
Amit:	It's difficult to predict about the number. However, at least a hundred of them will not easily die out. You know, the folk music never dies. It travels from one generation to another.
Anchor:	What's the place of fans in the life of a pop-singer?
Amit:	The relationship between a pop-singer and his or her fans is very close. It's like that of the heart in a human body. The moment the heart stops beating the man dies. So does the singer in the absence of his or her fans and admirers. The singer must sing what their fans want to hear, to remain alive in their hearts.
Anchor:	What's your advice to those who wish to take up singing, particularly pop-singing, as their career?
Amit:	There is no fixed recipe to be a good pop-singer. However, a sensitive heart, a clear vision and hard work go a long way to make a person a successful pop-singer.
Anchor:	Is your wife also a pop-singer?
Amit:	Yeah. She is also my lyricist and has the final say in shooting of my songs.
Anchor:	Although we would love to talk to you about many other things to help our viewers know more about you, time is the greatest constraint. However, before we leave, one last question: If given a choice by the Almighty God what would you like to be born as—a male pop-singer or a female pop-singer, and why?
Amit:	A male pop-singer because my fans are already there to recognise me through my voice. As a female pop-singer I'll have to start afresh (laughs).
Anchor:	Well, before I thank you on behalf of the viewers of our programme please give us the number that had given you a break in your career as a professional pop-singer.
Amit:	(*sings that song*)
Anchor:	Thank you very much indeed for this lovely number and for joining us to talk to us about you and your career. We wish you greater heights of success in life!
Amit:	Thank you Pradeep for all your sweet words and introducing me to my viewers and fans. Bye Pradeep!
Anchor:	Bye, Amit!

WORD MEANING

1. **Rendezvous:** meeting at a particular place and time
2. **Throb:** one who increases heart beating; highly exciting
3. **Applause:** praise
4. **Fate had in its store:** what was destined
5. **A dream come true:** fulfilment of a cherished desire
6. **Folk music:** music that belongs to some social group
7. **Fusion:** mixing

COMPREHENSION

ANSWER the following questions briefly:

1. Who is the celebrity selected for the interview?
2. What's the name of the programme under which the celebrity has been interviewed?
3. Who gave him a break?
4. What was the occasion for this offer?
5. What does Amit say about the importance of fans in the life of a pop-singer?
6. How does Amit's wife help him in his professional work ?
7. If given a chance, what would Amit like to be born as and why?

Rehearse the above conversation with your partner 3 times (Pair activity).

EXPRESSIONS AND PHRASES FOR LEARNING

1. I felt quite depressed not knowing what fate had in its store for me.
2. I couldn't believe my ears/eyes.
3. For me it was a dream come true.
4. Some artistes have to struggle a lot before they get a break.
5. One should know how to sell one's ideas.
6. Which are your favourite numbers/movies?
7. What do you do to stay young?
8. What's the place of 'luck' in the life of an actor/actress/singer?
9. How did you manage to get so much popularity/fame?
10. What's your advice to those who wish to be an actor/singer?
11. Today you are a throb of the youngsters.
12. Please tell us about your early struggle.

Note down the given questions and expressions in your practice notebook and drill them with the help of your friends till you have mastered and can use them appropriately in parallel situations in life.

EXTENDED VOCABULARY

LOOK up the following words in a good dictionary-cum-thesaurus to know their meanings and pronunciations. Also use them while interviewing a celebrity on radio or television.

Break through
Career/profession
Compere/anchor/host/introducer
Debut
Dream comes true
Duplicates
Fans/admirers
God-father/patron
Hobbies/spare time activities
Keep one's eye on
Lead role
Leisure time
Limelight

Lyricist
Maiden speech
Main role
Perseverance
Popularity
Profession
Publicity stunt
Rehearse
Seasoned artist
Sell ideas
Side role; main role
Struggle

GRAMMAR AND USAGE

Zero Article

It means that no article (a/an/the) is used.

In generalisations we use zero article.
Examples:

1. Reading short stories in leisure time is a good entertainment.
2. Student Union elections are financed by political parties.

We also use zero article when we talk about meals: breakfast, lunch, dinner.

Examples:

1. What would you have for dinner?
2. I don’t like tea or coffee at breakfast.

However, when we talk about some formal lunch or dinner we use ‘the’, e.g., We’re having the dinner to welcome our new chairperson.

EXPRESSIONS AND PHRASES FOR PRACTICE (Pair Activity)

1. How many years .... struggle ....?
2. For me it was a dream ....
3. Which are your ....?
4. How did you manage ....?
5. What place does luck ....?
6. One should know how ....
7. I couldn't believe what ....
8. I .... depressed not knowing ....
9. What do .... young and active?
10. What advice .... to your fans?

ACTIVITY

Your principal has recently joined your school on transfer from Nagpur. Prepare a questionnaire covering the different aspects of his or her personality, and interview him or her in the morning assembly of your school for the benefit of the students and the teachers alike.

35

OFFERING CONDOLENCES

READ aloud with your friend the following conversation to know how people express their condolences and sympathy:

(*Manoj expresses his condolences and sympathy on phone to his friend, Amrutha, on the death of her father.*)

Manoj: Amrutha, I'm extremely sorry to hear about your father's sudden death. How did it all happen?

Amrutha: Well Manoj, my father, as you know, was a **chronic** heart **patient**. Yesterday when he was watching the pictures of the railway accident of the **Delhi-bound** Rajdhani Express near Gaya on TV he had a severe heart attack. We rushed him to the nearby hospital. But before the doctors could do anything he was declared 'brought dead'.

Manoj: O my God! Was he so sensitive that he **couldn't stand** those accident pictures?

Amrutha: Sensitive he was. In fact, he was **hypersensitive**. He always found it difficult to control himself at the sufferings of others. He was a well-wisher of all, especially the downtrodden.

Manoj: As far as I'm concerned I'm a big loser in his death. Whenever I visited your house in your absence he spent a lot of time with me discussing all such things that interested me. I always looked upon him as my own father. Please accept my heartfelt **condolences** at this sudden and untimely death. Also please convey my deepest sympathy to your mother.

Amrutha: Manoj, thank you very much for all your concern for me and other members of my family. After talking to you I feel a bit strengthened in this hour of tragedy and grief.

Manoj:	Amrutha, I know that no words can help you recover from this big shock, yet I say that in this hour of your tragedy you're not alone. I'm there with you. You can bank upon me.
Amrutha:	Thank you very much indeed for this support and assurance. I'm really proud of you and of our friendship.
Manoj:	Thanks Amrutha! I'll see you in the afternoon on my way back home from the school. Until then Good bye!
Amrutha:	Good bye, Manoj.

WORD MEANING

1. **Chronic patient:** old patient
2. **Delhi-bound:** going to Delhi
3. **Couldn't stand:** couldn't endure the stress
4. **Hypersensitive:** too sensitive
5. **Condolences:** (usually used in plural) sympathy and feelings of sadness for the family at the death of their near and dear ones

COMPREHENSION

ANSWER the following questions briefly:

1. Why does Manoj ring up Amrutha?
2. How did Amrutha's father die?
3. What was the nature of Amrutha's father?
4. How did Manoj look upon Amrutha's father?
5. How does Amrutha feel after talking to Manoj?
6. What assurance does Manoj give to Amrutha?
7. What does Amrutha feel at Manoj's assurance?

Rehearse the above conversation with your partner 3 times (Pair activity).

EXPRESSIONS AND PHRASES FOR LEARNING

1. I'm very sorry to learn about your mother's/uncle's death.
2. I'm extremely sorry to hear that your father/uncle has expired.
3. I've heard that your brother-in-law has died. My deepest sympathy.
4. Please convey my heartfelt condolences to your father/mother/aunt.
5. Please accept my condolences.
6. I'm very sorry to know about your cousin's death. How did it happen?
7. Shoma, my deepest sympathy on this irreparable loss.

8. I heard about your tragic loss. I'm extremely sorry to know it.
9. I heard your grandmother is no more. I'm very sorry indeed.
10. Please accept my deepest sympathy and condolences on the sudden and untimely death of your sister-in-law. She was such a nice lady! May her soul rest in peace!

The given expressions may be noted and practised in appropriate situations.

EXTENDED VOCABULARY

LOOK up the following words in a good dictionary-cum-thesaurus to know their meanings and pronunciations. Also use them in your conversation in a similar situation:

Breathed his last	Grim tragedy
Compensate the loss	Heavenly abode
Deceased	Irreparable loss
Demise	Tragic end
Feel completely shattered and broken	Vacuum has been created

GRAMMAR AND USAGE

Using Determiners: 'Some' and 'Any'

'Some' is used in the affirmative sentences, i.e., the sentences which are not negative.

e.g., I have made some suggestions for the committee to consider (affirmative sentence).

'Any' is used to refer to a negative meaning sentence. It is also used to express doubt.

Examples:

1. Is there any milk in the bottle? (expressing doubt)
2. You can't find any mistake in his calculations. (negative meaning)

EXPRESSIONS AND PHRASES FOR PRACTICE (PAIR ACTIVITY)

1. I'm extremely sorry to .... (death of grandfather)
2. Please accept my .... (death of cousin)
3. My deepest/heartfelt .... (death of uncle)
4. May her ....! (death of mother-in-law)
5. I heard .... (death of brother-in-law)
6. Please convey my .... (death of grand-mother)
7. I'm sorry to .... (death of nephew)
8. When will the last rites ....?

ACTIVITY

Imagine one of your classmates died in a road accident while coming to school. You being his close friend decide to visit his parents, along with some other students of your class, to convey your condolences. Present a role play depicting the scene at the house of the parents of the deceased.

36

GRADING SYSTEM VS. MARKING SYSTEM

[A Panel Discussion]

READ aloud with your friends the following panel discussion organised by National Board of Secondary Education (NBSE) to know the views of principals, teachers and students on the board's decision to replace the 'marking system' by the 'grading system' for the students of class X. The panel discussion was compered by Mrs Jyoti Gupta, Editor-in-Chief, NBSE.

Anchor: (introductory remarks) Friends, in our system of education, right from the admission tests to the board or university examinations marks obtained by an individual play a crucial role. At times, an individual misses the desired seat or a position by just half a mark difference, causing a lot of frustration to him or her parents. Although marking system is a pretty old system of assessing the performance of an individual, and also comparing him or her with his or her counterparts, its reliability and suitability in the present day context is being questioned from all quarters. In fact, in the recent past various education forums of principals and teachers have strongly opposed it and suggested for its immediate replacement by the 'grading system' like A+, A, B+, B and so on. But as we know there is no system in the world, which may be called foolproof, however perfect it may appear to be. Hence, for this panel discussion NBSE has invited a representative body of principals, teachers and students of class X to discuss the issue of grading system at length. Through this panel discussion an attempt will be made to discuss both the strengths and weaknesses of the grading system vis-à-vis the marking system of evaluating students in the board examination.

Now before we start discussing the **merits** and **demerits** of grading system, vis-à-vis the marking system, I'll request the panelists to introduce themselves.

Participant No. 1: I'm Shah—Arun Shah, Principal, R.K. Public School, Delhi.

Participant No. 2: I'm Dr V.P. Garg, Principal, Kendriya Vidyalaya.

Participant No. 3: I'm Mrs Arti Singh, Principal, Government School No. 2, Moti bagh, New Delhi.

Participant No. 4: I'm Mrs Shashi Gupta, Principal, D.A.V School, Patparganj, Delhi.

Participant No. 5: I'm Ajeet Kaushal, Sr. Teacher, Happy Sr. Secondary School, Lajpat Nagar, New Delhi.

Participant No. 6: I'm Mrs Nivedita Ganguli, Headmistress, Bhartiya Vidya Bhawan, Shahadra, Delhi.

Participant No. 7: I am Somya, a student of class X, Air Force School, Gurgaon, Haryana.

Participant No. 8: I am Vineet, a student of class X, Government School, Malviya Nagar, New Delhi.

Anchor: I am Jyoti Gupta, Editor-in-Chief, NBSE, a quarterly Journal of NBSE and Anchor for today's panel discussion. So off we go!

Anchor: What're your views about the marking system used by schools and NBSE to assess the students' performance in the examination?

Participant No. 1: (Arun Shah) It is highly **subjective, inconsistent, unreliable** and **frustrating**. It's subjective because the marks obtained by an individual do not match the child's ability or abilities. They reflect the examiner's perception, which may not be necessarily right. I call the marking system as inconsistent or unreliable because every time a written manifestation is assessed by the same or different evaluators it is awarded different marks. I also call it frustrating because even half a mark difference may lead to a child's rejection for admission or selection for a particular academic stream.

Anchor: To what extent do you agree with Mr Shah's views on the marking system? (*pointing to participant No. 3*)

Participant No. 3: (Mrs Arti Singh) I quite agree to what Mr Shah has told us about the marking system, with the only difference that the marking system has some positive points as well. For example, it's a strong **driving force** behind the student's competitive spirit. Just as in a war the soldiers fight for every inch of land so do students for every mark while preparing for their examination.

Anchor: Now shall we hear what teachers think on this issue? For this I call upon Mr Kaushal.

Participant No. 5: (Ajeet Kaushal) Well, while mostly agreeing to the views of the earlier participants on the merits and demerits of the marking system of evaluation, I would like to say that a good evaluation system must also **discriminate** between good and less good students. And for this marking system is not only the best but also the safest. It also discourages examinees and their parents from going to court to challenge the teacher's assessment.

Anchor: Now let's hear what Mrs Gupta has to say on this marking system of evaluation. What are your views about it, Mrs Gupta?

Participant No. 4: (Mrs Shashi Gupta) Well, I would like to look at this subject from the viewpoint of both the bright students and the weak students. As far as the bright students are concerned they find the marking system highly **motivating**, though a little straining. It keeps them mentally alert and highly competitive all the time. Even half a mark difference means a lot to them. As regards the weak and the average students they find it frustrating. It **shakes off** their confidence and dubs them as poor performers.

Anchor: And Vineet, what's your view about this marking system?

Participant No. 8: (Vineet) To me marking system means frustration all around—students are unhappy at their poor percentage of marks. Parents and teachers are equally upset because lot of students from the Govt. Schools are slow learners.

Anchor: If we go by the views of the panelists of this group here, I'll say that there's an immediate need for the replacement of the 'marking system' by the 'grading system'. So shall we discuss now the relative merits and demerits of the grading system which is being projected as a panacea for all kinds of ills of evaluation. For this I would like to invite Dr Garg to give his considered views on the grading system. What is grading system, Dr Garg?

Participant No. 2: (Dr V.P. Garg) In the grading system, performance of a student is reflected in terms of grades like A+, A, B+, B, C+, C, and so on and not in terms of marks. As per this system we go by the pre-determined grading bands, e.g., A+ for the students obtaining marks between 90 and 100, or A for the ones scoring between 80 and 89. Thus, **unlike** the marking system the students scoring marks between 90 and 100 are all at par in the grading system. They are said to have no qualitative difference in them, whereas in the marking system the student getting 100 marks in a particular subject is considered qualitatively better than the one scoring 99 marks, and hence given preference.

Anchor: How can the grading system check the elements of subjectivity, unreliability and depressing note of the marking system? Mrs Ganguli, could you enlighten us on this issue.

Participant No. 6: (Mrs Nivedita Ganguli) Our long experience as a teacher tells us that generally subjectivity on the part of an examiner may cause a maximum difference to the extent of 10% in a student's scores. This difference gets nullified in the grading system by giving the same grade to the students scoring within the range of a particular grade. For example, A+ grade is awarded to all those students who score between 90 and 100. As for the element of unreliability a cushion of 10 marks is provided on each band of a particular grade in the grading system. The depressing note in the marking system is also taken care of by reflecting grades instead of marks to the students.

Anchor: Then why do most of the bright students oppose the grading system in spite of its edge over the marking system? This time let's listen to the students' representatives.

Participant No. 7: (Somya) It's so simple. They are opposing it on the ground that the proposed grading system doesn't motivate them to work hard to discriminate themselves from other students. The thrill that a bright student wants to experience at the time of examination results is missing in the grading system.

Anchor: (*Turning to participant no. 1*) What's your suggestion to make the grading system equally acceptable by the bright children?

Participant No 1: (Arun Shah) For that the gap between the two grades may be further reduced. Instead of the present proposed gap of 10 marks it may be reduced to five marks. If possible the top grade of A+ may be made A+* for those whose performance deserves three cheers. In other words, for excellence in education there should be no **tangible limit**. Only sky should be the limit.

Anchor: (*summing up*) Friends, I am afraid, due to paucity of time we'll have to finish our discussion here much against our wishes. Hope the NBSE will take into consideration the suggestions given by the panelists here while deciding on the subject. Ladies and gentlemen, on behalf of the NBSE and on my own I thank you all for having come here and participated in this panel discussion, which is so vital in the present day context of examination reforms. Thank you very much indeed!

WORD MEANING

1. **A panel discussion:** a discussion involving a group of people, selected in advance, to discuss the given subject
2. **Merits:** advantages (strengths)
3. **Demerits:** disadvantages (weaknesses)
4. **Subjective:** based on a personal opinion
5. **Inconsistent:** irregular
6. **Unreliable:** which cannot be depended on—not giving the same results all the time
7. **Frustrating:** which causes disappointment
8. **Driving force:** something that inspires a person to act in the desired direction
9. **Discriminate:** separate; distinguish
10. **Motivating:** encouraging
11. **Shakes off:** weakens
12. **Unlike:** different from
13. **Tangible limit:** a limit that can be clearly seen to exist

COMPREHENSION

There are three choices for each question. Tick (✓) the choice you consider to be correct.

1. What's the subject of the panel discussion?
   (a) Grading system vs. Marking system
   (b) Examinations are necessary evil
   (c) Discarding the examination system.
2. How many persons have participated in this panel discussion?
   (a) Many persons
   (b) Eight persons
   (c) A small number.
3. What's the plus point of the marking system according to participant no. 3, i.e., Mrs Arti Singh?
   (a) It's a driving force behind student's competitive spirit
   (b) Students like marks more than grade
   (c) Teachers find the marking system easier than the grading system.
4. Why does participant no. 5 (Ajeet Kaushal) support the marking system?
   (a) It's safest for teachers
   (b) It discriminates between good and less good students
   (c) It's both discriminative and safest.
5. Why do bright students like marking system?
   (a) Marks thrill them
   (b) It's highly motivating
   (c) It makes them mentally alert and highly competitive.

6. Why does Vineet, participant no. 8, recommend the replacement of marking system by grading system?
   (a) The grading system does not provide for detention
   (b) Lots of students of the government schools are slow learners
   (c) Grading system is a tension-free system of evaluation.

Rehearse the above conversation with your partner 3 times (Group activity).

EXPRESSIONS AND PHRASES FOR LEARNING

1. Yes, you maybe right.
2. Yes, I suppose so.
3. No, I suppose not.
4. Don't you think there's other side of the picture?
5. I don't think you're absolutely right/wrong.
6. I don't think we're going to agree on this point, are we?
7. Wouldn't you agree?
8. I fully agree with you on this point but do you think the management/government will also agree?

The given sentences/phrases may be learnt for use during group/panel discussions.

EXTENDED VOCABULARY

LOOK up the following words in a good dictionary-cum-thesaurus to know their meanings and pronunciations, and use them in your conversation in a similar situation:

Adverse
Challenging
Conclusive
Crucial
Discriminative
Discursive
Distressing
Exclusive
Fruitful
Industrious
Objective vs. subjective
Ornamental
Pleasant
Prestigious
Strenuous
Supervised activity
Systematic
Time-consuming
Vital
Wasteful

GRAMMAR AND USAGE

Conjunctions

Conjunctions (and, but, or, therefore, however, so, nevertheless, because, as, if, when, since, etc.) are joining words. They are used to join words, phrases and sentences.

There are two kinds of conjunctions:

(a) Coordinating conjunctions
(b) Sub-ordinating conjunctions

Coordinating conjunctions

(and, as well as, also, but, yet, only, or, nor, so, therefore, hence).

These conjunctions are used to join two things/thoughts/sentences that are grammatically equal in status in a sentence.

Examples:

1. He has a lot of money *but* he spends it very carefully.
2. She is all right, *only* she feels tired.
3. She misbehaved with her classmate *so* she was suspended from the school/ college.

Sub-ordinating conjunctions

(because, as, since, if, when, that, etc.)

These conjunctions are used to connect clauses to show that one clause is grammatically more important than the other.

Examples:

1. She failed to attend the conference *because* she was ill.
2. I will definitely help you *if* you promise to work hard.

EXPRESSIONS AND PHRASES FOR PRACTICE (Pair Activity)

1. Well, you have a point but .... feasible?
2. Well, maybe what you say .... but ....?
3. I'm afraid, I .... you.
4. I'm not sure if I agree ....
5. I see what you mean, but is it ....?
6. Don't you agree ....?
7. Don't you think ....?

ACTIVITY

Present a panel discussion with the help of your friends on 'Homework is an encroachment on the child's personal time' (time duration: 30 minutes).

37

PLANNING A VACATION

READ aloud with your friend the following conversation:

Anju: Hi Fiza, have you decided which hill station you are going to this summer?

Fiza: Not yet, but most probably we'll be going to Nainital.

Anju: Why Nainital ? Why not Simla or Darjeeling ? I understand, you have never been to Simla or Darjeeling.

Fiza: You are right. I have never been to either Simla or Darjeeling but I **can't help**. As I will be going with my parents and they have been to these hill stations before, they are not interested in Simla or Darjeeling. They want to go to Nainital this time.

Anju: Well, if that is the case there is no choice for you. Nainital is equally good for tourists and lovers of nature. The big lake is the biggest attraction of this hill station. By the way, how many days do you want to spend at Nainital?

Fiza: About 15 days, I think.

Anju: Wonderful! Then you can see and enjoy each and every **spot** of Nainital **leisurely**. But before you leave for Nainital why don't you visit the tourist office of Uttaranchal and **get hold** of a list of places of tourists' interest in Nainital.

Fiza: Thank you very much indeed for this **invaluable** advice. I would definitely ask dad to collect the information **brochure**. But tell me which hill station are you planning to go to?

Anju: Well due to my uncle's death last month we aren't going anywhere this year. We will spend our summer vacation in Delhi itself. Anyway, I'm not sorry about it as at least you're going to spend your vacation at Nainital with your parents. Have a nice vacation, Fiza!

Fiza:	Thanks, you too. I'll tell you all about Nainital when we meet again on re-opening of the school after the vacation. Till then, Bye Anju.
Anju:	Bye Fiza, and all the best!

WORD MEANING

1. **Can't help:** I can't do anything
2. **Spot:** place
3. **Leisurely:** at ease
4. **Get hold:** procure
5. **Invaluable:** precious
6. **Brochure:** information guide

COMPREHENSION

ANSWER the following questions very briefly:

1. Why can't Fiza go to Simla or Darjeeling instead of Nainital during her vacation?
2. Why can't Anju go to any hill station during her vacation?
3. What advice does Anju give to Fiza to enjoy her vacation fruitfully?

EXPRESSIONS AND PHRASES FOR LEARNING

1. You are right but I have no choice of my own.
2. Why don't you go to Srinagar?
3. How about you?
4. Well, we aren't going to any hill station this year, my grandmother is seriously ill.
5. I would love to go to Mussoorie this time.
6. What a wonderful idea!
7. Enjoy yourself!
8. Have a nice time/weekend/vacation!
9. If you don't mind please, could I have your mobile number?
10. Thank you indeed for all your guidance.

EXTENDED VOCABULARY

LOOK up the following words in a good dictionary-cum-thesaurus to know their meanings and pronunciations and use them in your conversation in a similar situation:

Entertainment and recreation	Gorgeous
Flora and fauna	Holiday homes

Holidaying
Nature in bounty
Places of interest
Streamlet
Tourists' resorts
Waterfall
Yachting; boating

GRAMMAR AND USAGE

Preposition—Concept, Function and Classification

- A preposition is a word that shows relation between a noun or pronoun and some other word or phrase acting as a noun/noun phrase in a sentence.
- It is usually placed immediately before a noun or pronoun or other word(s) that it relates to.
- It expresses relationship (between words or phrases) of time, space, instrument, means, purpose, direction, etc.

Classification

Prepositions of positions or space

On, at, in, behind, above, below, under, beside, by, with, between, near, over, into, round, up, through, from, across

Examples:

1. The chief-guest is sitting *between* the chairperson and the Principal of the school.
2. The fan is just *above* your head.
3. The dictionary is lying *on* the dining table.

Prepositions of time

at, in, on, till, until, since, before, after, by, between, from

Examples:

1. He usually returns *between* four and five.
2. Shall we meet *at* 4 o'clock?
3. All banks are closed *till* Sunday.

Prepositions of direction/movement

from, to, into, through, across, off, along, up, down

Example:

She works *from* morning to evening.

EXPRESSIONS AND PHRASES FOR PRACTICE (Pair Activity)

1. You're right but ....
2. Really? ....

3. Why don't you ....?
4. I'd love to go but ....
5. By the way/incidentally/if you don't mind, please ....
6. Hi Madhvi! ....
7. Well, ...
8. Have a nice time/week-end/vacation! ....
9. Enjoy yourself! ....
10. What an idea! ....

ACTIVITY

Plan your winter vacation programme in consultation with your friend. But before you finalise it, discuss some alternative programmes, with their relative advantages and disadvantages.

(Write six exchange dialogues in not more than 100 words.)

38

AT THE GREEN GROCER'S

READ aloud with your friend the following conversation:

Asha:	Hi Sandhya! What a pleasant surprise to see you here in this vegetable market ! Do you come here every week?
Sandhya:	No, not every week. It's only when my husband is on tour I have to do this duty. How about you?
Asha:	Well, I come here every Monday to buy vegetables for the whole week. You see, you can conveniently buy all kinds of quality vegetables at a reasonable price. Don't you think so?
Sandhya:	I fully agree with you. Besides buying vegetables from here you can also buy a **variety** of fruits and things of daily use. By the way, have you finished shopping?
Asha:	Not yet, I have just arrived. Shall we go and finish the **vegetable business** first? We can talk later.
Sandhya:	I think you're right. Let's hurry up.
Asha:	(*to the* ***vendor***) How much are these potatoes?
Vendor:	Ten rupees a kilo.
Asha:	Why ten rupees? Yesterday I bought potatoes for six rupees a kilo in my neighbourhood.
Vendor:	Madam, you must have bought the potatoes which taste sweet. The potatoes I'm giving you are the 'Simla potatoes' which are known for their quality and taste. You can buy these potatoes without any hitch. If you, however, don't like them for any reason, you can return them to me next week. I will return the entire amount you pay me today.
Asha:	OK give me two kg.
Sandhya:	A kilo for me, too

Asha:	**How much do these onions cost?**
Vendor:	Twenty rupees a kilo.
Asha:	Charge fifteen rupees a kilo and give us one kilo each. Sandhya do you need one kilo?
Sandhya:	O yes !
Asha:	How about lemon?
Vendor:	Forty rupees a kilo.
Sandhya:	And ginger?
Vendor:	This is eighty rupees a kilo. Madam, don't worry about the rates. You will find my rates the lowest and the most competitive in the market. Moreover, you are my old customer. How can I charge more from my old customers?
Sandhya:	OK give me 250 gm ginger, half a kilo lemon, 250 gm green chillies, and one kilo of golden apples.
Asha:	For me also the same quantity, please.
Vendor:	Hundred rupees each. (*Asha and Sandhya make the payment*)
Asha:	Sandhya, we must **rush home**. We're already late. My husband must be waiting for me. OK Sandhya. See you!
Sandhya:	Bye Asha. I'll call you at night, I have your telephone number.

WORD MEANING

1. **Variety:** kinds
2. **Vegetables business:** work of buying vegetables
3. **Vendor:** a person who sells things going from place to place
4. **How much do these onions cost?:** what is the price
5. **Rush home:** go home quickly

COMPREHENSION

ANSWER the following questions briefly:

1. Where do the two friends meet ?
2. What expression shows that the two friends are meeting unexpectedly?
3. What makes the two friends buy the vegetables immediately without their further enquiry about the rates?
4. Who comes to the vegetable market regularly—Asha or Sandhya?

EXPRESSIONS AND PHRASES FOR LEARNING

1. What a pleasant surprise!
2. At a reasonable price.
3. I fully/partially agree with you.
4. Don't you think so?

5. I think/I hope you're right.
6. How much does it cost?
7. What's the price like?
8. How much do these tomatoes/potatoes cost?/How much are these?
9. Here you are. (*giving something*)

EXTENDED VOCABULARY

LOOK up the following words in a good dictionary-cum-thesaurus to know their meanings and pronunciations, and use them in your conversation in a similar situation:

FRUITS	VEGETABLES	
Apricot	Bean	Jackfruit
Date	Cabbage	Mint
Guava	Capsicum	Mushroom
Orange	Cauliflower	Okra (lady's finger)
Papaya	Cheese	Onion
Pear	Cucumber	Pumpkin
Pineapple	Garlic	Radish
Pomegranate	Gourd	Spinach

GRAMMAR AND USAGE

If Clause (Conditional Clause)

When a particular situation (described in the main Clause) depends on the happening of another situation we use a Conditional Clause. A Conditional Clause usually begins with 'If' or 'Unless' (for a negative clause).

Examples:

1. *If* you reach the railway station one hour before the scheduled time, you can/will get the reservation under 'Tatkal'.
2. *Unless* you reach the railway station one hour before the scheduled time, you can't/won't get the reservation under 'Tatkal'.
3. Jayanti will finish her project well-in-time *if* she works late in the evening.

Examine the following sentences:

(a) If I *know* when you are coming, I*'ll receive* you at the airport. (refers to future situation—possible)

(b) If I *knew* when you were coming, I *would* receive you at the airport. (refers to the present/imaginary situation—improbable situation)

(c) If I *had known* when you were coming, I *would have* received you at the airport. (refers to the impossible past, i.e. the past which can't be revived. In other words it means that I didn't know when you were coming. So I didn't receive you at the airport)

EXPRESSIONS AND PHRASES FOR PRACTICE (Pair Activity)

1. How about ....?
2. By the way ....
3. By and by ....
4. Known for quality ....
5. Here is your ....
6. Here it is ....
7. You see/You know ....

ACTIVITY

1. Imagine your mother has given you a shopping list for buying various things of daily use, including vegetables and monthly ration. Go to some departmental store and buy the things required, after verifying their rates.
2. Prepare a list of questions that you may like to ask the store-in-charge for ascertaining the quality and rates of the things you need.

39

AT THE POST OFFICE

(*There is a big queue of people standing before the registration counter. But unfortunately, there is no official to attend to them. This agitates the people, and one of them goes to the Postmaster's cabin to complain about it.*)

READ aloud with your friend the following conversation in the Postmaster's cabin:

Client: May I come in Sir?

Postmaster: Just a minute, please

(*The client waits for about ten minutes and then without waiting for the formal permission of the postmaster rushes into his chamber in an angry mood.*)

Client: Excuse me Sir, we have been waiting at the registration counter for more than an hour now. But so far no official has come to attend to us. Why is this **callous attitude**?

Postmaster: Young man, first I request you to calm down and then listen to me with a little patience. Well, I'm quite aware of your problem. It is not because of the callous attitude on the part of the Post Office staff as you think. It is all because of the shortage of the staff. Do you know why I had asked you to wait for a while when you first wanted permission to come in. It was all because I was busy talking to our Head-Office regarding your problem. Perhaps you may not know that we have hardly one third of the sanctioned staff. So every person has to do the job of at least two persons everyday. Unfortunately, the person working at the registration counter had to absent himself all of a sudden on account of his wife's heart attack. This accounts for the absence of an official at the registration counter.

Client: In that case, why don't you **depute** somebody else at the registration counter?

Postmaster:	Well, it is just not possible as each one of them is already busy with one or the other duty.
Client:	Then does it mean that the Post Office will not accept letters for registration till such time you get the required substitute?
Postmaster:	I'm sorry you didn't allow me to complete what I wanted to say. I wanted to tell you that as other officials are already busy only I would have to take this responsibility in **larger interest**. So without further wasting your time I must tell you that I'm reaching the counter in just two minutes time. Please bear with us.
Client:	OK. We are waiting for you there.
Postmaster:	Don't worry, Sir. Before you take your position in the queue I'll be there. Sorry for the inconvenience caused!
Client:	Thank you very much for your cooperation.

WORD MEANING

1. **Callous attitude:** insensitive; lacking compassion; cold feelings
2. **Depute:** put on duty
3. **Larger interest:** public interest

COMPREHENSION

ANSWER the following questions briefly:

1. Why was a big queue before the registration counter?
2. Why did one of the clients go to the postmaster's chamber?
3. What was the condition of that man when he entered the postmaster's chamber?
4. What charge does he level against the Post Office officials?
5. How does the postmaster solve the problem of the people queuing up before the registration counter?

EXPRESSIONS AND PHRASES FOR LEARNING

1. Excuse me.
2. What a callous attitude!
3. I'm disappointed.
4. Bear with us/me.
5. In the larger interest.
6. In public interest.
7. Thick skinned.
8. Depute/allocate/assign.
9. Thanks for your cooperation/compassion.
10. Just a minute, please.

GRAMMAR AND USAGE

Reported Speech

There are two types of questions:

1. Yes/No type questions, i.e., the questions that can be answered in 'yes' or 'no'. For example,
   Do you like coffee?
   Yes, I do.
   or
   No, I don't.
2. 'Wh' questions, i.e., the questions that begin with what, where, why, how, who, etc. For example,
   What is your future plan?
   I intend joining the Army.
   While reporting Yes/No type questions we don't use 'that'. Instead we use 'if' or 'whether'. For example,
   Do you play cricket?
   (Reporting) He asked me *whether* I *played* cricket.
   While reporting 'wh' questions we retain the 'wh' word used by the speaker.
   The word order of a question (Both a Yes/No type question and a 'wh' question) becomes like that of statement, i.e., subject, verb, object (SVO) while reporting.
   The question mark is also dropped.
   For example,
   Who is your favourite author ?
   (Reporting) He asked me who my favourite author was.

EXPRESSIONS AND PHRASES FOR PRACTICE (Pair Activity)

1. We have been waiting at the Reception for more ....
2. Please calm down and ....
3. It's because .... the office.
4. I was busy talking to ....
5. I'm sorry, you didn't .... me to complete what I wanted to tell you.

ACTIVITY

Imagine you have to withdraw some money urgently from your bank account. But unfortunately there is nobody at the counter to serve the clients. Go to the bank manager and discuss the problem to get your work done.

40

LODGING AN FIR WITH POLICE

READ aloud with your friend the following conversation:

(*Abhaya goes to the police station to lodge a complaint against his house owner*)

Abhaya: Excuse me, could I meet the Sub-Inspector of Police?

Cop: What for?

Abhaya: To lodge a complaint of **harassment** against my house owner.

Cop: Well, at the moment SI sahib is busy with some urgent work. He won't be available before two hours. If you like, you can wait for him here, or else you can come afterwards.

Abhaya: OK. I'll be back by 11.30 a.m., by which time he will be free from his urgent work, I hope.

Cop: Hopefully!

(*Abhaya goes away and returns at 11.30 sharp to meet the SI*)

Abhaya: Could I meet the SI now?

Cop: Wait a minute. Let me ask him.

(*Constable goes in and returns after ten minutes*)

Cop: Sorry, he can't meet anyone. He is **awfully busy** with a murder case today.

Abhaya: It's very strange that the police officers have no time to meet the public on one or the other pretext, though they claim to be their friend. OK in that case you can write my complaint.

Cop: Sorry, I can't write any complaint until SI sahib orders me for that.

Abhaya: Well, in that case I must speak to your officer right now.

Cop: I'm afraid, you can't meet him. He is not free.

Abhaya: He being a public servant can't refuse to meet people. I insist on your writing down my **FIR**. If you still refuse I have no alternative except to complain to your Inspector General about the whole matter. You see, I'm a journalist, and I won't leave you till I am heard.

Cop: OK. Tell me what your complaint is.

Abhaya: My name is Abhaya Shrivastava. I work with *Daily Times* as a senior journalist. I had rented the House No. H-183, South Ext., Part II, New Delhi belonging to Sardar Amir Singh six months ago on a monthly rent of ₹ 10000/- It was for a period of 11 months. Now, even before the expiry of the **tenancy period** he has started harassing me and my family. He is also **pinching our mail**. He keeps scolding my children for one or the other reason to force me to vacate the house. He is demanding vacation of his house just after six months. I fear he can do any thing to my family when I'm away. So I request you to take an immediate action against Sardar Amir Singh and protect us against any possible **wilful** injury.

Cop: OK. Now that we have your FIR with us we'll call Sardar Amir Singh to **resolve** your problem. You are also most welcome to meet us to know about our action taken on your complaint.

Abhaya: Thank you very much.

(*Abhaya leaves the police station*)

WORD MEANING

1. **Harassment:** force; intimidation
2. **Awfully busy:** extremely busy
3. **FIR:** First Information Report
4. **Tenancy period:** rental leasehold; period of occupancy
5. **Pinching our mail:** stealing our letters
6. **Wilful:** knowingly
7. **Resolve:** solve

COMPREHENSION

ANSWER the following questions very briefly:

1. Why does Abhaya go to the police station?
2. Why is he not allowed to meet the SI even after his second visit?
3. How does Abhaya ultimately succeed in lodging his complaint?
4. What assurance does the cop give to Abhaya after writing his FIR?

EXPRESSIONS AND PHRASES FOR LEARNING

1. (a) I would like to lodge a complaint. Could I meet the SI?
   (b) I'm afraid, he is n't in. He has gone out for some investigation.
2. (a) Could I have a copy of the FIR?
   (b) Why not? Here you are.
3. (a) Do you need any witness ?
   (b) No, just your complaint would do.

4. (a) Could I talk to you on the phone in case of emergency?
   (b) You're most welcome.
5. (a) Thank you very much for all your help and guidance.
   (b) Not at all. It's a part of my duty. I'm happy you liked our services.
6. Thanks a lot.
7. Wait a minute!

EXTENDED VOCABULARY

LOOK up the following words in a good dictionary-cum-thesaurus to know their meanings and pronunciations, and use them in your conversation in a similar situation:

Abduction	Kidnapping
Assault	Litigation
Case of cheating/forgery	Mutual compromise
Compensation	Reimbursement
Emergency; contingency; exigency	Suicide

GRAMMAR AND USAGE

Active and Passive Voices

Active and Passive Voices are not two different forms of saying one and the same thing. In fact, they convey different messages. So use them appropriately and not mechanically.

When to use a Passive Voice

- When the agent or doer is not known.
  e.g., My train reservation was cancelled at the last moment (don't know who did it).
- In describing processes or procedures.
  e.g., Antecedents of an individual are verified before the passport is issued.
- When our interest lies in the action and not in the person who caused it.
  e.g., The thief was arrested on the spot.
- When the following words are used as subject of the active verbs: people, we, they, someone/somebody, servant.
  e.g., The matter has been solved.
  The use of 'by' before the agent/doer is not always required in the passive voice.

EXPRESSIONS AND PHRASES FOR PRACTICE (Pair Activity)

1. I would like ....
2. Could I have ....?

3. I am afraid ....
4. I fear ....
3. At present, I'm ...., working ....
6. He being ....
7. It's very strange that ....
8. If you .... you can ....
9. What time ....?
10. When do you think ....?
11. How about ....?
12. What's ....?
13. If you still insist ....

ACTIVITY

1. Imagine you have received a packet of torn and soiled hundred rupee notes from the cashier at the cash counter. You want the cashier to change these notes of poor quality. But he is not prepared to change them despite your request. Go to the bank manager and complain against the cashier for his stubborn attitude.
2. Note down in your practice notebook the given sentences/expressions and new words and practise them in appropriate situations till they become a part of your linguistic ability.
3. Present a role play showing the argument between the cashier and the client at the cash counter regarding the replacement of torn and soiled 100 rupee notes.

41

ORDERING A MEAL AT THE HOTEL

READ aloud with your friend the following conversation:

(*Aman and Sarita go to a posh hotel for dinner*)

Bearer: Sir, do you want a big table or a small one?

Aman: A small table.

Bearer: In that case, why don't you occupy that corner table, Sir? It' a **cosy** corner, with the least disturbance to the occupants.

Aman: Thank you. I like that table.

Bearer: Sir, here is the **menu card**. I will be back in two minutes. In the meantime, you can decide what you want to order.

Aman: Sarita, what would you like to eat—veg or non-veg?

Sarita: I'd prefer veg. It's not safe to eat non-veg at hotels these days.

Aman: Fine! then tell me which dish would you like me to order for you?

Sarita: (*Going through the menu card carefully*). *Dal makhani*, *Paneer Tikka*, curd and salad. How about you?

Aman: I don't have liking for any particular dish. I enjoy eating anything and everything as long as it is properly cooked and is **somewhat hot**.

Bearer: (*appears with a writing pad and a pen in his hand*) Yes Sir, could I have your order, please?

Aman: *Dal makhani, Paneer Tikka,* curd and salad.

Bearer: Would you **care for** *Roti* or *Naan* ?

Sarita: Get us four *Naans* but make sure they are hot and **crisp**.

Bearer: OK Madam. But you haven't told me about the **dessert** you would like to have.

Aman: We'll let you know about it later.

Bearer:	Sir, would you care for a drink before the meal?
Aman:	No thanks! We don't drink.
Bearer:	Shall I get you then Pepsi, or some other light drink, Madam ?
Sarita:	Don't you listen to the daily news? People are finding fault with these soft drinks. They are reported to have pesticides.
Bearer:	I know all that, Madam. But it is our duty to ask our patrons for that. Drinking or not drinking is their prerogative.
Aman:	Well, before you go away you may add to our order two 'Vanilla' ice-cream. But please bring it only when we have finished our meals.
Bearer:	OK. Sir.

[*Aman and Sarita enjoy their meal. The finger bowl is brought. Aman and Sarita clean their fingers and pay the bill when brought. They also leave some money (10% of the bill amount) in the plate towards tip to the bearer), and then leave the hotel quietly.*]

Bearer:	Bye, Sir, Bye Madam. Come again!
Aman:	Bye, and thank you very much for your prompt service!

WORD MEANING

1. **Cosy:** warm and comfortable
2. **Menu card:** a card showing the dishes/food items available with their rates
3. **Somewhat hot:** a little spicy
4. **Care for:** would like
5. **Crisp**: brittle, crunchy
6. **Dessert:** sweet dish
7. **Prerogative:** special right
8. **Finger bowl:** A bowl containing hot/lukeworm water with a piece of lemon for cleaning the customer's fingers
9. **Tip:** A small amount of money given to someone who has provided you service, in addition to the payment of the bill amount.

COMPREHENSION

ANSWER the following questions very briefly:

1. Why does Aman decide to occupy the corner table?
2. Why do they not order the non-veg ?
3. What does Sarita tell the bearer about the cola drinks?
4. What instruction does Sarita give to the bearer about 'Naans'?
5. What for do they leave some change in the plate after paying off the bill?

EXPRESSIONS AND PHRASES FOR LEARNING

1. Could we have a big table for six people?
2. No, we don't need a small table. We want a big one. We are eight people.

3. What is your special menu today?
4. Do you undertake home delivery of food items?
5. Would you please pack up the entire leftovers?
6. Do you cater for small parties as per the given menu?
7. Do you have a spacious accommodation for holding kitty parties/birthday parties?
8. How much discount do you offer on the parties organized by individuals in your restaurant?
9. How much advance do you expect for special parties organized by you?
10. How do you ensure that there is no mixing up the non-veg with the veg items?
11. Could you give us a list of the dishes to be provided under your standard menu?

EXTENDED VOCABULARY

Look up the following words in a good dictionary-cum-thesaurus to know their meanings and pronunciations, and use them in your conversation in a similar situation:

A cosy corner
Continental food
Curry
Dessert/sweet dish
Finger bowl
Fish
Gravy
Lamb
Liquor
Meat
Menu card
Mustard
Mutton
Onion and garlic
Pepper and salt
Pork
Recreation programme
Sauce
Soup
Wine

GRAMMAR AND USAGE

'Certainly' and 'Surely'

Certainly means, 'it is definite'.

'Surely' can replace 'certainly', but it is rarely found with this meaning. Coming at the beginning of a sentence it means: 'I firmly believe to be true, though I am not certain it is most likely to happen. For example:

1. Surely, you're not going on a picnic (I should be highly surprised if you did).
2. It's certainly the best movie of the year (There is no doubt about it).

EXPRESSIONS AND PHRASES FOR PRACTICE (Pair Activity)

1. I'd like to reserve .... for dinner.
2. That sounds .... idea.
3. All right. May ....?
4. What would you ....?
5. I'd prefer ....
6. Would you care ....?
7. Get me/us ....
8. No thanks! We ....
9. Well, before you leave ....
10. Well, let you ....

ACTIVITY

Imagine you have thrown a birthday party to your close friends (about 20 heads). Go to some good hotel and fix up the menu and other relevant details about the party to make this event a memorable one for your friends.

42

AT THE BEAUTY PARLOUR

READ aloud with your friend the following conversation:

(*Rashmi is waiting at the beauty parlour for the bridal make-up of her younger sister, Ila who is getting married late in the evening.*)

Rashmi: Excuse me, how much time will you take?

Beautician: Your number is four. I think it will take another two hours before your turn comes. In the meantime, you can go out and finish your work, if you have any.

Rashmi: No thanks! We'd prefer to wait here than going out. It's very hot outside.

Beautician: You're welcome. Would you like to have a cold drink?

Rashmi: No, thanks! By the way, how much do you charge for the complete bridal make-up?

Beautician: Not much. Our charges are very nominal—just ₹ 3000.

Rashmi: Don't you think your rates are very high?

Beautician: Madam, what're you saying? Our rates are very reasonable, and probably the lowest in the market. Others are charging between ₹ 4000 and ₹ 5000 for this work. I wonder if you know that we use only herbal **cosmetics**, which are so expensive these days. In fact, other beauty **parlours** are using all kinds of cheap cosmetics which damage your skin.

Rashmi : OK. By the way, what does the complete bridal make-up include?

Beautician: Well, it includes shampooing and hair-setting, facial, eyebrow and eye-lashes, usual make-up, **pedicure**, **manicure**, cutting and colouring of hair. *Alta*, *mahavar*, *henna* and many other things that are normally used to beautify the bride. We also provide artificial jewellery, though we charge separately for it.

Rashmi: Do you also provide flowers for the bride?

Beautician:	Yes, we do. Sorry, I forgot to mention about it.
Rashmi:	Could you tell me how much time does a complete make-up need?
Beautician:	About three hours.
Rashmi:	In that case, could you oblige us by starting my sister's bridal make-up right now? My family members will get worried if we fail to reach home by 7 o'clock.
Beautician:	Well, we serve people strictly according to their turn. You are, however, most welcome to request any lady before you to help you by giving her number to you.

(*Rashmi explains her problem to the lady before her and requests her for help, to which she agrees*)

Rashmi:	I'm indeed grateful to you, Madam for this favour. Really, you have saved us from a big problem.
Lady:	(one who gave her turn to Ila) I'm happy I could give you this happiness. Hearty congratulations and good wishes for a very happy and prosperous married life.
Rashmi and Ila:	(together) Thank you very much!

(*Both Rashmi and Ila leave the beauty parlour happily after the bridal make-up was over.*)

WORD MEANING

1. **Cosmetics:** make-up material
2. **Parlour:** lounge
3. **Pedicure:** cleanliness and treatment of feet
4. **Manicure:** cleanliness and treatment of hands

COMPREHENSION

ANSWER the following questions very briefly:

1. What is the occasion when the two sisters go to the beauty parlour?
2. What is their waiting number for the make-up?
3. Why does Rashmi request the beautician to do her sister's make-up out of turn?
4. How does Rashmi succeed to get it done?
5. How does the beautician justify her rates for the bridal make-up?
6. How much minimum time does the complete bridal make-up need?

EXPRESSIONS AND PHRASES FOR LEARNING

1. Excuse me, could you oblige me by doing my sister's bridal make-up out of turn?
2. What are your charges for the complete bridal make-up?

3. What does the complete bridal make-up include?
4. Do you undertake the complete body massage?
5. Would you mind giving me your turn?
6. I would love to wait here at the reception.
7. I would prefer to wait than coming tomorrow.
8. By the way, are you working on all the seven days of the week?
9. Do you think, I should start dyeing/colouring my hair now, or should I wait for some more time?
10. You're most welcome to fix the appointment on the phone.

EXTENDED VOCABULARY

LOOK up the following words in a good dictionary-cum-thesaurus to know their meanings and pronunciations, and use them in your conversation in a similar situation:

Bleaching
Dyeing/colouring
Eyebrow setting
Hair dressing
Head massage
Head wash
Manicure
Pedicure
Trimming
Waxing

GRAMMAR AND USAGE

What?

When you have not heard what someone has said and you want them* to repeat it, you can say: 'What?', but this is not polite. It is better to say: Sorry? or Pardon?

e.g., "The function is tomorrow".
"Sorry?"/Pardon
I said the function is tomorrow.

EXPRESSIONS AND PHRASES FOR PRACTICE (Pair Activity)

1. Excuse me ....
2. How much do you charge .... (haircut/pedicure/manicure/massage/hair dye)?
3. Do you undertake .... (manicure/pedicure/body massage)?
4. I would prefer to ....
5. You are most welcome .... (time/day).
6. Would you like to ....?
7. I would love to ....

*them = him/her

8. No thanks, I ....
9. By the way, ...
10. Do you think ....? Don't you think ....?
11. I wonder if ....
12. I'm indeed grateful ....

ACTIVITY

1. Imagine today is the last day for the payment of the electricity bill. Your father has asked you to pay it while going to your school/college. But when you reach there you find a big queue of people waiting to pay their bills. So you approach a lady with a request to pay your bill along with hers. Make a request justifying it.
2. Present a role play with the help of your friends, showing a conversation between you and the lady concerned. Also include the dialogues of other people in the queue objecting to your request to the lady.

43

LIFE IN METROPOLIS

READ aloud with your friend the following conversation to know how to discuss life styles in urban and rural areas:

Renu: **What's wrong** with you, Neha? You seem to be **tensed**, aren't you?

Neha: Yeah. I'm really **sick of** the **metropolitan life**, and I can't do anything about it. **I wish** I could get away into the **country** and live a quiet life!

Renu: My dear friend you will soon get bored of the so-called quiet life.

Neha: Why?

Renu: I don't think you expect me to answer your question in detail. Dear, aren't you aware of the dark lanes, small and uncomfortable houses, dirty surroundings, **unhygienic** conditions and absence of **daily necessities** of life in villages and even in small towns? Believe me, they would **drive you mad** and your dream world would **collapse** once you stay there even for a couple of days.

Neha: I don't think so. **I wonder** if you know that I was born and brought up in a small town in Bihar. So I'm quite **used to** the country life you are so **vehemently** criticizing. The fact is that even now I love it with the same intensity with which I did when I was a child.

Renu: That's all very well for a short stay. But when you have to stay for a longer period your liking for the country life will change into **aversion** for it, especially when you go over there from a metropolitan city. How can you be an **exception** to it? You are crazy!

Neha: Well, this is one way of looking at life. The other way is what I'm going to tell you now. Most people in metropolitan cities are running the **mad race** after the materialistic **pursuit**—from necessities to comforts and from comforts to luxuries. Their life is full of care and have no time to **'stand and stare'**, as the poet rightly says. Believe me, I have no liking for this mad race. I want to stay **far from the madding crowd**.

Renu:	OK. But are you ready for your **intellectual starvation** which you have always been advocating against? You will always have to deal with uneducated people once you **switch over** to the country life.
Neha:	Well. I don't mind dealing and interacting with the so-called uneducated people. In fact, I have always found them **bubbling with** sincerity and honesty, which is the rarest thing in metropolitan cities these days.
Renu:	Well, there is no point in arguing with you on this subject any more as you seem to be highly prejudiced against life in metropolitan cities. However, to conclude our discussion, I would like to say that though the people living in a country are honest and sincere, as you have rightly said, they are deprived of science and its powers in this twenty-first century, which even a common man from a metropolitan city experiences **day in and day out**. Bye Neha! Have a nice time!
Neha:	Bye Renu! Look after yourself!

WORD MEANING

1. **Metropolis:** a very large city, often the most important city in a large area
2. **What is wrong:** what is the problem
3. **Tensed:** nervous and anxious
4. **Sick of:** mentally tired
5. **Metropolitan life:** life in a big city
6. **Country:** village
7. **Unhygienic:** dirty and unclean
8. **Daily necessities:** essential things of daily use
9. **Drive you mad:** make you extremely annoyed
10. **Collapse:** fall down; completely demolished
11. **I wonder:** an expression used to ask oneself
12. **Used to:** to be habitual of something
13. **Vehemently:** severely
14. **Aversion:** hatred; dislike for something
15. **Exception:** someone or something which is not included in a rule
16. **Mad race:** on activity in which people participate without any special reason
17. **Pursuit:** search
18. **Stand and stare:** watch nature's beauty peacefully
19. **Far from the madding crowd:** a situation in which a person is free from all kinds of man-made problems and tensions
20. **Intellectual starvation:** mental deprivation; mental hunger
21. **Switch over:** shift
22. **Bubbling with:** full of
23. **Day in and day out:** all the time
24. **Especially:** particularly
25. **so-called:** thought to be (but not exactly)

COMPREHENSION

ANSWER the following questions briefly:

1. Why is Neha upset?
2. What does Neha wish for?
3. Why is Neha so positive about her happiness in living the country life?
4. What are the reasons that Renu thinks will soon make Neha bored of the so-called quietness of the rural life?
5. What arguments does Neha give in support of the country life?
6. What final remark does Renu make in support of the metropolitan life?

EXPRESSIONS AND PHRASES FOR LEARNING

1. I wonder if everything is all right at her end.
2. I wonder why she is so scared of every stranger.
3. That's very well but that's not the goal of life.
4. She can't be an exception to the well-established social traditions.
5. He is bubbling with lots of creative ideas.
6. Day in and day out she keeps talking about her dream house.
7. Have a nice time!
8. Look after yourself!
9. Believe me, I totally depend on your advice.
10. You are crazy!

EXTENDED VOCABULARY

LEARN the meanings and pronunciations of the following words from a good dictionary-cum-thesaurus and use them appropriately in sentences of your own:

Bourgeois
Business/employment opportunities
Cosmopolitan
Customs and traditions
Elite
Illiterates
Leisure/spare-time activities
Luxuries
Malls
Manners and etiquettes
Multinational
Pastimes
Permissive society
Posh
Precinct
Pubic conveyance
Rural
Shopping centres
Urban
Values

GRAMMAR AND USAGE

Words that go with reaction

- Bring/provoke/produce a reaction
- An adverse/angry/negative reaction

- A favourable/positive reaction
- A lukewarm/warm/mixed reaction
- Knee-jerk reaction
- First/gut/immediate/initial reaction
- Reaction against/towards something

EXPRESSIONS AND PHRASES FOR PRACTICE (Pair Activity)

1. What's wrong ....?
2. I wish ....
3. Believe me ....
4. I wonder ....
5. .... used to ....
6. That's all very well but ....
7. .... mad race for ....
8. Day in and day out ....
9. Have a ....
10. Look after ....

ACTIVITY

1. Write six exchange dialogues between two school teachers on the comparative usefulness of public school education over the government school education in the Indian society.
2. Organize a group/panel discussion on the public school education in the present day scenario.
3. Use the words provided under Extended Vocabulary in sentences of your own creating life-like situations.
4. Also note down these words in your practice notebook and keep revising them till they become a part of your spoken vocabulary.
5. Transcribe these words using phonetic symbols and master them.

44

TALKING ABOUT PEOPLE

READ aloud with your friend the following conversation to know how we describe a person:

Vivek: Antara, we have known each other for more than a year now. But it is a pity that we have not met each other's parents even once.

Antara: You are perfectly right. But before I decide on meeting your parents could you just tell me how they look like and what their nature is. This will facilitate me to understand them before I actually get a chance to meet them to discuss our relationship.

Vivek: Fine, with great pleasure!
Well, my father is a good looking, tall and kind-hearted gentleman. His friendly and compassionate behaviour endears him to one and all. His ever smiling face and jovial nature makes him the centre of attraction wherever he goes. One more important thing I would like to tell you about my dad. He is highly punctual in all his appointments. I have never heard of a time when he was late for anything in life.

Antara: It means he will expect the same punctuality from me when we get married.

Vivek: Perhaps yes perhaps no. Since he himself is very punctual he would like others to value time like him. But as he is highly compassionate and generous he accommodates even those who fail to come up to his expectations in terms of values of life.

Antara: Thanks for this detailed account of your father's personality. I feel a bit relaxed now. But how about your mother? Is she equally generous and punctual like your father?

Vivek: It is indeed difficult to answer your question as no two persons are exactly alike. We all have individual differences, you know. However, for your satisfaction I may tell you that you would equally like her. She is beautiful and attractive even at this age. Like dad, she is also

	very cooperative and kind to all. She is a lady with great self-confidence and every inch honest in all her dealings. All the ladies of our apartment love and respect her for her childlike innocence and affectionate nature.
Antara:	Thanks Vivek for introducing me to your parents through such a picturesque description about them. I will let you know about my parents when we meet tomorrow as the bell is already gone and we have to rush to our classes. Bye Vivek!
Vivek:	Bye Antara!

EXTENDED VOCABULARY

Qualities

Positive traits	**Negative traits**
Cheerful	Miserable
Clever	Stupid
Cooperative	Non-cooperative
Friendly	Unfriendly
Generous	Mean
Hardworking	Lazy
Honest	Dishonest
Imaginative and creative	Orthodox
Kind	Unkind
Optimistic (always thinks positive)	Pessimistic (always thinks negatively)
Pleasant	Unpleasant
Punctual (always on time)	Always late
Relaxed	Tense
Reliable	Unreliable
Self-confident	Shaky
Sociable	Shy
Strong	Weak
Warm (loving)	Cold (indifferent)

Physique

For Man: handsome, good looking, tall, broad shoulder, over-weight, fat, dark, beard, moustache

For Woman: beautiful, good looking, attractive, pretty (*usually for a girl*), gorgeous, smashing, slim, tall, over-weight, fair complexion, plain (not beautiful), ugly, thin, skinny, fat, dark

Hair: straight, curly, wavy, blonde, boy-cut, shoulder cut, wearing plaits

ACTIVITY

1. Go through the given dialogues once again to know which words from the list have been used therein, and which ones have been left out.
2. Write another set of six exchange dialogues describing some other person(s). Use only the unused words from the list in your description of the person(s) selected. (Pair activity)

45

TALKING ABOUT NEWSPAPERS

READ aloud with your friend the following conversation to know how we talk about newspapers:

Shreya: Anjali, which English daily do you like the most?

Anjali: *The Times of India* is my favourite newspaper. How about you?

Shreya: Well, I like *The Hindu*, but also enjoy reading *The Times of India.*

Anjali: Any idea, how much circulation does *The Hindu* have in North India?

Shreya: Sorry, I can't give you the exact figure, but I think it is as popular as *The Times of India* or *The Hindustan Times.* People like to read it not only for its news but also for its views. The articles appearing in this newspaper are of special interest to its readers. The bold editorial is yet another thing for which I have great regards for *The Hindu.*

Anjali: By the way, does it give an exhaustive coverage of sports events ?

Shreya: I think so. In fact, there is hardly any paper that doesn't cover sports news, especially cricket news these days. Many a time they overdo it, don't they?

Anjali: Shreya, do you know why I like *The Times of India*? Let me tell you, I like it because it gives a balanced view of the news besides bold and catchy news headlines. I also like it for its lashes and political punches. Its cartoons are my additional attraction because they are done by one of my friends from Hyderabad, Keshav.

Shreya: I think it's high time we stopped discussing the newspapers. Don't you remember we are getting late for our rehearsals? Let's go to the school auditorium immediately before we get reprimand from the teacher-in-charge.

EXTENDED VOCABULARY

Articles
Back (support)

Bid (an attempt)
Broadsheets (paper of large size)
Business news
Circulation (number of readers)
Cover-page news (news on the first page of the paper)
Critics (persons who write about new films, plays and books, etc.)
Daily (published everyday)
Editorial (a piece of writing in a newspaper that gives the editor's opinion about some important event)
Editor (a person who controls the contents of the paper)
Features (longer articles about important subjects and persons)
Foreign/international news (news about other countries)
Fortnightly (published once in two weeks)
Headlines (headings of news)
Home news (news about our country)
Journalists (people who write for newspapers)
Lash (hit)
Monthly (published once a month)
Political news (news related to politics)
Radio/TV programmes
Reporters (people who report news for the paper)
Reviews (when critics write and give their opinions about new films, plays and books, etc.)
Sports news
Tabloids (small in size)
Talks (discussions)
Weather forecast (telling about the weather in advance)
Weekly (published once a week)
Yearly (published once a year)

ACTIVITY

1. Go through the given dialogues once again to know which words from the list have been used therein and which ones have been left out.
2. Write another set of six exchange dialogues on the same subject, using the unused words from the list.

46

TALKING ABOUT COMPUTERS

READ aloud with your friend the following conversation to know how to talk about computers and their world:

Salman: What percentage of Indians can use a computer effectively?

Rahul: Between 20 and 30%.

Salman: Would you like to reconsider your answer by way of taking the help of public poll, or shall I lock your answer?

Rahul: OK. Tell me what the public poll says on this question:

Salman: 10–15%.

Rahul: In that case, I would like to go with the public.

Salman: Is it final ?

Rahul: Yes, it's final.

Salman: Now let's check up what the computer has to say on this question—Yes, your answer is absolutely correct. You win ₹ 10000/- for your correct answer.

Rahul, could you tell us how intimate are you with the computer?

Rahul: Well, I spend 4–5 hours everyday working on the computer. I think I am quite proficient in handling any type of software. Though not trained as a hardware engineer, I can troubleshoot almost all kinds of hardware problems, including hard disc related problems. Of course, for any major hardware problem we have to call for the hardware engineer for its solution.

Salman: I'm indeed very happy to learn that we have among us people like you who can handle the computer and its related problems independently. On behalf of the organizers of this programme I present to you this memento along with a cash award of ₹ 10000/- that you have won just now in appreciation of your talent.

Wish you a very bright career and greater heights of success, Rahul.

Rahul: Thanks, thanks a lot.

EXTENDED VOCABULARY

A bug (a software problem)
CD-ROMs (compact disc-read only memory)
E-mail (electronic mail)
Floppy disc (meant to record information on it)
Hard disc (inside the computer to record information)
Hardware (machine)
Internet
Key board
Laser printer
Monitor
Mouse (used to click on different icons)
Screen
Software (the program required to work on a computer)
System/network
User-friendly (easy-to-use)
Virus (a software problem)

ACTIVITY

1. Go through the given dialogues once again to know which words from the list have been used therein and which ones have been left out.
2. Write another set of six exchange dialogues on the same subject, using the unused words from the list.

47

TALKING ABOUT TELEVISION

READ aloud with your friend the following conversation to know how we talk about television and its world:

Geeta:	Rashi, do you have cable TV, or as you get the TV programmes through the satellite?
Rashi:	Well, until last month we had cable TV, but recently we have switched over to the satellite programme by subscribing to the Tata Sky. It's really wonderful—much better than your cable TV.
Geeta:	How many channels do you get on your TV?
Rashi:	Plenty of them. To be precise, we get 120 programmes. Of course, some of them are pay channels.
Geeta:	Could you just tell me why you call this Tata Sky arrangement wonderful?
Rashi:	I think, it is because of its digital picture and quality sound, besides its prompt and efficient customers' services. Price-wise also it is much cheaper than what I was paying for the cable TV earlier. It is just ₹ 150 per month.
Geeta:	Thank you Rashi for all this information, especially about Tata Sky. One more question, please! Hope you won't mind answering it.
Rashi:	Which is your favourite TV serial these days, and which chat show you would never like to miss ?
Rashi:	*Aapki Antara*—dealing with the problems of autistic children. Regarding the chat show, I always want to watch *Rendezvous with Simi Garewal.*
Geeta:	Thank you Rashi for your invaluable information!

EXTENDED VOCABULARY

Antenna
Black and white TV/colour TV
Cable TV (when you get TV programmes through cable and not through antenna)
Channel
Chat show (a programme in which a presenter talks to famous people)
Idiot box
Pay channel (when one has to pay extra to get that channel)
Picture
Plug in
Remote (an instrument to operate the TV)
Remote-controlled (operated with a remote)
Satellite dish (used to get a programme)
Snow (when picture is not clear)
Soap opera (a serial dealing with the lives of a group of people—often exciting)
Sound
Tele
Tuning (setting of a channel)
Turn it off (switch off)
Turn it on (switch on)

ACTIVITY

1. Go through the given dialogues once again to know which words from the above list have been used therein and which ones have been left out.
2. Write another set of six exchange dialogues on the same subject, using the above unused words from the list.

48

TALKING ABOUT WEATHER AND TEMPERATURE

READ aloud with your friend the following conversation to know how to talk about weather and temperature:

Swanti: What an icy wind! Any idea what is the temperature like?

Rema: I have no idea about the actual temperature, but I'm freezing. I think it may be around 8–10 degree Celsius.

Swanti: I think, we will soon have a thunderstorm or a heavy snowfall.

Rema: I don't think there was any forecast about such a rough weather by the meteorological department today.

Swanti: Well, it is always difficult to predict about the weather conditions correctly. I know that most of our weather forecasts are proved wrong at the end of the day. Still the meteorological department is required to give the expected temperature and weather conditions daily.

Rema: I don't know why people are so much concerned about the daily weather forecast.

Swanti: It is so simple. Advance knowledge of temperature and weather helps people to prepare themselves to face it boldly. They are not caught unaware.

Rema: However, despite the positive side of daily weather forecast people are always grumbling about weather whatsoever.

Swanti: But before we stop discussing various other aspects of usefulness of weather forecast I would like to point out that the advance warning about things like hurricane, heavy rains and foggy weather greatly helps all of us. Don't you think so?

Rema: Yes I do. Thanks a lot!

EXTENDED VOCABULARY

A strong wind
Boiling
Breeze
Chilly/cold
Cloudy
Foggy
Freezing
Heavy rain
Hot
Humid
Hurricane
Icy
Showery
Spell (period)
Sunny
Thunderstorm
Windy

ACTIVITY

1. Go through the given dialogues once again to know which words from the list have been used therein, and which ones have been left out.
2. Write another set of six exchange dialogues on the same subject, using the unused words from the lists.

49

TALKING ABOUT ART AND MUSIC

READ aloud with your friend the following conversation to know how to talk about various kinds of art and music:

Rachna: Arti, do you regularly watch Boogie Woogie programme?

Arti: O yes. In fact I always wait for it; but why're you asking?

Rachna: Well, it is because I want to know the name of the choreographer whose troupe was honoured with a cash award of ₹ five lakhs in yesterday's episode.

Arti: If I can bank upon my memory, it was Ragni Bhalla—a new entrant in the field.

Rachna: O you have wonderful memory! Thank you very much! By the way, do you also remember the name of the lyricist who composed the accompanying song for this award winning dance. Believe me, I equally liked the song.

Arti: Well, you would be surprised to learn that even the lyricist is a newcomer in the field. I don't think anybody might have heard his name before, yet he is a great artist. His name is Kamal Joshi.

Rachna: Arti, I'm really very happy to know that you too like Boogie Woogie as much as I do. Now we can always discuss this programme from the critic's eye. Thank you once again for the names I was so eager to know.

Arti: It was indeed a great pleasure talking to you after such a long gap, and that too on the subject so close to my heart.

EXTENDED VOCABULARY

Artist
Choreographer (one who designs the steps of a dance)
Choreography (art of designing and arranging the steps and movements in dance)
Classical
Composer
Dance
Lyricist
Lyrics
Opera (a play in which the words are sung)
Orchestra (a large group of musical instruments)
Painter; painting; sculptor; pop music

For meanings and pronunciations of the given words refer to some good dictionary. Also use these words in appropriate situations.

ACTIVITY

1. Go through the given dialogues once again to know which words from the list have been used therein, and which ones have been left out.
2. Write another set of six exchange dialogues on the same subject, using the unused words from the lists.

50

INTERVIEWING A NATIONAL AWARDEE TEACHER

READ aloud with your friend the following interview with Ms Ritu Gupta, a National Awardee teacher of English for broadcast on the FM Channel of All India Radio (the interviewer is Archana):

[The mock interview was taken on the occasion of her getting National Award for teachers. It is a useful guideline for the practising and prospective teachers of English].

Interviewer: Madam, congratulations on your getting the most **prestigious** award for teachers!

Ritu Gupta: Thank you very much!

Interviewer: Madam, I'm Archana Roy from FM Channel of All India Radio, New Delhi. Would you mind answering a few questions for the benefit of our listeners, particularly those who teach English at the Primary and Secondary levels of School Education.

Ritu Gupta: Certainly not. Rather it's a great honour. Tell me what you want to know from me.

Interviewer: Madam, do you mind if I address you by your first name, Ritu?

Ritu Gupta: Certainly not. Go ahead, please.

Interviewer: Rituji, I believe you're the youngest in this **galaxy of teachers** honoured by the nation today. Tell us how you feel at getting this prestigious National Award.

Ritu: Overwhelmed with feelings of joy and pride. I'm also a little worried.

Interviewer: Well, we all can understand your feelings of joy and pride at getting such a great honour at this young age. But tell us what makes you worried at this hour of happiness.

Ritu: Well, although a lady doesn't feel like telling her age, I must tell you that I'm just 38 and I have another 22 years to work before I retire. So my worry is that the expectations of my Principal, parents and students from me will further increase due to this National Award, and I don't know to what extent I'll come up to their expectations.

Interviewer: Now I can better appreciate your feelings on this memorable occasion of your life. Rituji, would you please tell us what according to you makes a good English teacher at the school stage?

Ritu: First, he/she should be **a teacher by choice** and not **by chance**. You know what I mean. Only the person who is genuinely interested in teaching should think of becoming a teacher. Then he/she should be thorough with the latest methods and techniques of teaching English. His or her innovative practices to make learning of English a joyful experience for the students will go a long way to make him or her an effective classroom teacher of English.

Interviewer: What do you mean by innovative practices? Would you please clarify it?

Ritu: The teacher should always remember that there are hundred and one ways of saying or doing a thing. Since every child learns at his or her own pace and in his/her own way the teacher should keep trying new teaching techniques till all the students have acquired the learning point of the unit. Naturally, this will require **interactive participatory approach** to the teaching of English, with an emphasis on creativity on the part of the teacher.

Interviewer: Rituji, although the quality of the prescribed textbooks for a particular class has considerably improved in the recent past, the quality of the product, I mean the students, has not proportionately improved. It is rather poor. What would you suggest to improve the language **competencies** of the students?

Ritu: Activity based and skill-based teaching instead of content-based teaching.

Interviewer: Could you elaborate it for the benefit of our listeners, please?

Ritu: Well, teaching English does not mean teaching the prescribed textbooks. It means developing in the students the language competencies through various activities and projects related to listening, speaking, reading and writing skills. The prescribed textbooks are only a means to an end. They're not the end in themselves.

Interviewer: Rituji, don't you think that the shift of emphasis from content-based teaching to skill-based teaching will make the teaching and learning of English a monotonous activity to both the teacher and the taught?

Ritu: I don't think so. You see, a good teacher never tries to develop these language skills in isolation. He or she does it by creating appropriate life-like situations through an activity-based teaching. The interaction between the teacher and the taught and between the students themselves goes a long way to develop the language skills, besides making the teaching–learning of English a pleasurable experience to both the teacher and the learner.

Interviewer: Do you mean that the teaching of English should be situational besides being interactive and activity based?

Ritu: Exactly!

Interviewer: What else should a good teacher of English do to help the students acquire effective **communication** skills at the school stage?

Ritu: Well. The teacher should regularly expose his or her students to a good listening material. This is because a child learns a language mostly through good listening. In fact, listening activity for 5–10 minutes daily should form the integral part of English teaching.

Interviewer: Rituji, how is it that even after 10 years of English most of our students find it difficult to speak English effectively?

Ritu: It's because of the teacher's over-enthusiasm to correct each and every mistake that a student commits while speaking. By doing such a correction, you see, the child gets demotivated to speak for fear of committing mistakes.

Interviewer: Do you mean to say that a teacher should allow the students to speak incorrect and faulty English?

Ritu: In a way, yes. Instead of correcting the mistake in the student's speech the teacher should provide the right model in his or her own speech by saying it with a little extra force. Thus, looking at the right model in the teacher's speech the student will correct his or her mistake without being asked by the teacher to correct it. Further, this will give a tremendous confidence to the student, which is a must to motivate him/her to open his/her mouth and make the correct utterance.

Interviewer: Rituji, what do you think of the efficacy of the translation method for a learner to be able to speak and write English effectively?

Ritu: Although I may not reject it totally, I think it should be sparingly used and that too with a lot of caution. A translation requires mastery of the concerned two languages on the part of the user, which is not possible at the school stage. Moreover, as English is a unique language in terms of sounds, structures, vocabulary, idioms and grammar, translating from one language into another is rather difficult for the learner.

Interviewer: What are your views on grammar teaching for learning good English?

Ritu: Only the functional grammar should be taught at the school stage and that too in the context. No doubt, the **prescriptive** grammar helps a student to learn certain rules of grammar, it does not help him in applying those rules while speaking or writing English. Further, grammar should be taught through interactive approach only—function and not the form is important for learning good English.

Interviewer: Rituji, as a rich vocabulary is a must for a person to speak or write effectively many teachers suggest that a person desirous of enriching his vocabulary should learn 10–20 words from the dictionary everyday. What are your views on this approach?

Ritu: I don't approve of it, as it's a waste of time on the part of the learner. Since a word conveys a meaning in a situation only, words should never be taught or learnt **in isolation**. Instead, they should be acquired in life-like situations. Further, vocabulary may also be developed through the etymological approach and the thesaurus technique.

Interviewer: Correct pronunciation is a ticklish problem for majority of our students. What's your advice to the teachers of English on this issue?

Ritu: Well, to develop the correct speech sounds among the students the teacher should use phonemic approach instead of alphabetical approach at the primary level. The phonemic approach helps the learners to acquire and produce all the 44 sounds of English language correctly. Further, their familiarization with the phonetic symbols goes a long way to help them know the correct pronunciation of unfamiliar words from a dictionary. However, the knowledge of phonetic symbols is not a must for a learner.

Interviewer: Rituji, What provides musicality to one's speech?

Ritu: Stress and intonation.

Interviewer: Could you explain them for the benefit of our listeners?

Ritu: Depending on the meaning a speaker wants to convey, certain words of a sentence are said with an extra force. This is called **stress.** In English while speaking normally all picture-words like nouns and adjectives are stressed, and when we say a thing at a higher or lower pitch it is called intonation.

Interviewer: Rituji there's so much of talk about value-based education these days. Do you think values can be developed through English as well, or only through subjects like Hindi or Social Studies?

Ritu: Well, for value-based teaching all teaching subjects can be profitably used. English is no exception to it. For developing values at the primary level telling stories loaded with various work or cultural values can be effectively used.

Interviewer: Rituji, what are your views on creativity in language teaching?

Ritu:	Truly speaking, creativity is the **essence** of life. In fact, no language of the world can **afford** to serve its users effectively with fixed expressions and rules of grammar. It's creativity that keeps a language alive and saves it from being extinct. As such an English teacher, from the very beginning must impress upon his/her student's mind the need for expressing their ideas in different ways to make their communication a joyful experience to all.
Interviewer:	Rituji, everything comes to an end and so does this interview. I know our listeners would like to ask you many more questions related to English teaching. But as time is our greatest constraint we have to finish this interview much against our wishes. On behalf of the FM Channel and our listeners I thank you very much for finding time to talk to us in spite of your very busy work schedule. I also wish you greater heights of professional success in life. Bye-bye Rituji.
Ritu:	Bye-bye Archanaji.

WORD MEANING

1. **Prestigious:** very important or of very high quality
2. **Galaxy of teachers:** a group of famous teachers
3. **A teacher by choice:** one who wished to be a teacher
4. **A teacher by chance:** becoming a teacher without any planning or wish for the same
5. **Interactive:** involving the two—both the teacher and the students
6. **Participatory approach:** an approach in which all the students actively participate
7. **Competencies:** skills like listening, speaking, reading and writing
8. **Communication:** a conversation between two persons
9. **Prescriptive:** authoritative, e.g., do this, don't do this, this is right, this is wrong
10. **In isolation:** out of context or without context
11. **Essence:** main thing
12. **Afford:** to be able to do something or manage

Some Important Questions to Ask an Interviewee

1. Would you mind answering a few questions for the benefit of the listeners/readers?
2. Do you mind if I address you by your first name?
3. Could you tell us what made you join this profession?
4. Are you a teacher by choice, or you wanted to do something else in your life?

5. What makes a person effective as a Principal/teacher of a residential school?
6. These days, in most of the public and private schools we find women working as Principals. Does it mean that ladies are better educational administrators than men? Could you give your views on this subject?
7. What, according to you, discipline and self-management mean ?
8. How do you provide academic guidance to your teachers/students?
9. What is your concept of quality education ?
10. What role, do you think does a teacher play an important role in developing and promoting values among students?
11. How can the working women, according to you, contribute to the all round development of their children's personality?
12. Why is a man called an architect of his own destiny?

ACTIVITY

1. Interview the teacher of your school who has been selected by the British Government to teach Hindi to the Indian immigrants at the University of Manchester under their Teacher Exchange programme.
2. Interview the Principal who has recently joined your school on transfer from Mumbai.
3. Interview a writer on her being awarded the *'Gyanpeeth award'* for her novel: **Learning in the Mother's Womb**.
4. Interview the Cricket Captain who couldn't save the school's honour in the inter-school cricket matches of your town.

PART III

ESSENTIALS OF SPOKEN ENGLISH

For excellence only sky is the limit.

1

IDIOMATIC EXPRESSIONS

1. An idiom is a group of words in a fixed order that have a particular meaning that is different from the meanings of each word understood on its own.
2. Mastery over the following idiomatic expressions will help you speak presently and effectively.

A bird's eye view: general view
e.g., *The director gave a bird's eye view of the conference while welcoming the delegates.*

A black sheep: a disloyal person
e.g., *At times a union strike fails due to some black sheep.*

A bolt from the blue: shock, complete surprise
e.g., *His son's decision to contest election against him in the recently conducted assembly elections was a bolt from the blue to him.*

A bone of contention: cause of dispute
e.g., *Their father's will was the bone of contention between them.*

A burning question: a subject of wide interest
e.g., *Whether we should permit rowdism even in assembly or parliament is a burning question of the day.*

A chip of the same (old) block: a person very much like his father in character
e.g., *There is hardly any difference between him and his father as a businessman. After all he is a chip of the same (old) block.*

A fair-weather friend: a person who is your friend only in prosperous days
e.g., *Never depend on a fair-weather friend because he may not even call you his friend in the hour of distress.*

A feather in one's cap: an honour to be proud of
e.g., *Getting 'Param Veer Chakra' for his act of bravery on the Indo-Pak border is a feather in his cap.*

A gone case: something hopeless
e.g., *She is at the last stage of cancer, and so she is a gone case.*
A white elephant: anything which is costly to maintain
e.g., *Keeping both a driver and a full-time domestic help is a white elephant for a middle class person.*
Above board: absolutely fair and open, clean in dealings, nothing underhand
e.g., *To command public respect one has to be above board.*
Accede to: to accept, agree
e.g., *In spite of my best efforts he did not accede to my request for cancelling my transfer order.*
Ad hoc: arranged for a specific purpose
e.g., *Principals of government schools have been permitted to appoint teachers on ad hoc basis till such time they are able to recruit teachers on a regular basis.*
After a person: to resemble
e.g., *She takes after her mother so closely that it causes confusion to people about their identities.*
All along: from the beginning, all the time
e.g., *As a business partner he has tried to cheat me all along.*
All in all: when everything is considered
e.g., *All in all his professional career had been highly successful.*
All over: dead
e.g., *I rushed to see my ailing grandfather but it was all over with him before I reached.*
All and sundry: everyone without exception
e.g., *He invited his classmates to his birthday party all and sundry.*
Allow me: used in Spoken English to offer help politely
e.g., *Ladies and gentlemen, please allow me to introduce the chief guest for today's function.*
Alma mater: a term used for one's college or university
e.g., *How a person behaves in life determines the image of his or her alma mater.*
Anything but: definitely not
e.g., *The programme was anything but entertaining.*
At arm's length: to avoid close association
e.g., *He is a strict officer. He keeps his subordinates at arm's length.*
Bag and baggage: with all your possessions, especially secretly or suddenly
e.g., *Out of fear for the creditors he left one night for an unknown place with his bag and baggage.*
Be in attendance: to be present at a special event
e.g., *Several heads of states were in attendance at the funeral of princess Diana.*
Be up in arms (about/over something): (of a group of people) to be very angry about something and ready to oppose it strongly
e.g., *On the government's decision to sell the Balco Plant, its workers were up in arms to stop the deal.*

Bear in mind: to remember
e.g., *Always bear in mind that courtesy to all always pays.*
Bear with somebody/something: to be patient with somebody/something
e.g., *If you bear with me a little longer I'll clear all your doubts.*
Beat (out) something into something: change the shape of something (metal) by hitting it with a hammer
e.g., *The gold is beaten out into thin strips.*
Beat about the bush: to talk about something for a long time without coming to the main point
e.g., *Please do not beat about the bush and tell me what you want.*
Bed of roses: not easy or a pleasant situation
e.g., *The life of freedom fighters of India was never a bed of roses to them.*
Beggars can't be choosers: when there is no choice and one should be satisfied with what is available
e.g., *The government has allotted one bedroom flats to all those whose monthly income is Rs 1000/- or less. Quality-wise also they are poor. But what to do, beggars can't be choosers.*
Behind bars: in prison
e.g., *He was put behind bars for murdering his political opponent.*
Birds of a feather: persons of similar taste
e.g., *They are birds of a feather as they are both extremely fond of good food and fashionable clothes.*
Black and white: in writing
e.g., *The police will not take any action in your case unless you give your complaint in black and white.*
Blood is thicker than water: family relationships are stronger than any other relations
e.g., *Although the two brothers keep quarrelling with each other, they are always united when a third person tries to criticise either of the two. After all blood is thicker than water.*
By the by/bye: by the way
e.g., *I haven't received my salary for the last six months. By the bye, are you receiving your salary regularly?*
By word of mouth: verbally
e.g., *The management of the school has not given any advertisement for admission in the newly created branch of their school, yet thousands of parents have applied. The entire publicity has gone by word of mouth.*
Bye-bye: good bye
e.g., *When we separate we say bye-bye to each other.*
Climb/jump on the bandwagon: (disapproving) to join others in doing something to become popular or successful
e.g., *Some politicians have no principles of their own in life. They just eagerly wait for an opportunity to jump on the bandwagon of the winning political party. Various political parties declaring their support to Anna Hazare's movement over night.*

Crocodile tears: false grief
e.g., *He'd shed crocodile tears at the death of his worst political enemy.*
Cut out: suited
e.g., *Although he has offered English Literature for his graduation he is not cut out for it.*
Double dealing: duplicity
e.g., *You can't rely on what he says. He believes in double dealing.*
Drag on: to continue something even after its interest is lost
e.g., *Although the entire agenda for the meeting was over, the meeting dragged on.*
Food for thought: something which helps in getting ideas
e.g., *The keynote address by the Chief Guest at the inaugural function of the three-day seminar on Value Education provided a good food for thought for the participants.*
Fool's paradise: hoping for something impossible for fulfilment
e.g., *He has invested all his hard-earned money in the share business, thinking that he could double-treble it in a short time. By thinking like this he is living in a fool's paradise due to the uncertainty of the share market.*
For ages: for a long time
e.g., *They waited for ages before they finally got married.*
From A to Z: from beginning to end
e.g., *(a) He can recite a long poem from A to Z.*
(b) He explained the whole case from A to Z.
From hand to mouth: in poverty
e.g., *He got a small pension on his retirement. As a result he is living from hand to mouth these days.*
From head to foot: all over the body
e.g., *(a) He appeared clad in heavy woollen clothes from head to foot due to cold wave.*
(b) he was alleged to be corrupt from head to foot.
Give somebody a buzz: to telephone somebody
e.g., *I'll give you a buzz tonight.*
Glance over: to read hurriedly/cursorily
e.g., *As I had no time to read his speech thoroughly I just glanced it over.*
Go astray: to become lost; to be stolen
e.g., *(a) Thousands of New Year greetings went astray.*
(b) Parents are usually worried about their children thinking they may go astray in the company of undesirable boys and girls.
Go-between: a person who acts as a middleman between two persons during negotiations (intermediary)
e.g., *A good social worker should be a go-between the government and the public.*
Half the battle: a great part of the difficulty
e.g., *By restoring his self-confidence his doctor has won half the battle.*

Have an axe to grind: to have private reasons to get involved in something or to support a cause

e.g., *He had no axe to grind. He was canvassing for her just out of his concern for the welfare of the residents of the society.*

If the worst comes to the worst: in the event of the worst situation

e.g., *Even if the worst comes to the worst Kashmir will continue to be an integral part of India.*

In a fog: confused

e.g., *The government is in fog how to tackle the problem of terrorism across the country.*

In cold blood: deliberate; pre-thought

e.g., *He killed his political opponent's son in cold blood.*

In due course: at the proper time

e.g., *Don't worry about anything. Everything will be all right in due course.*

In full swing: something at its peak activity

e.g., *This newly started business is in full swing due to the patronage of some politicians.*

In quest of: in search of

e.g., *The forward looking institutions are those which are always in quest of excellence in education.*

In the air: spreading all around

e.g., *The news that Congress is going to change leadership in Maharashtra is in the air.*

In the good books of: to enjoy the favour of somebody

e.g., *He is bound to get promotion to the post of professor this year as he is in the good books of the Director.*

In vain: useless

e.g., *He made all possible efforts to escape from the life-sentence for the murder he had committed. But all his efforts were in vain.*

Let bygones be bygones: to decide to forget about disagreements that happened in the past

e.g., *Let bygones be bygones and start the chapter of our friendship afresh.*

Lion's share: largest share of something

e.g., *Being the youngest child of her parents she enjoyed the lion's share of her father's affection.*

Neck and neck: very close

e.g., *It was neck and neck competition between the two candidates for the Lok Sabha seat and it was difficult to say till the last moment who was going to win.*

Of high order: of a very high quality

e.g., *Amitabh Bachchan's acting in most of his films is of a high order.*

Of one's own accord: willingly

e.g., *He offered to get my brother appointed in his company of his own accord.*

Off the record: unofficially

e.g., *Please don't quote me, I am telling you the inner story off the record.*

On account of: as a result of something
e.g., *He was sacked on account of his misbehaviour with his boss.*
On record: something in writing
e.g., *He has admitted his fault and it is on record.*
On the air: wireless broadcasting
e.g., *Within a few minutes of Rajiv Gandhi's assassination the news of his death was on the air all over the world.*
On the alert: watchful; vigilant
e.g., *Cross-border terrorism unleashed by Pakistan on India keeps the Indian army and the border police on the alert all the time.*
On the one hand: from one point of view
On the other hand: on the contrary
e.g., *On the one hand he is out of job and on the other hand he is extremely extravagant.*
One's good offices: through one's help
e.g., *I could manage to get my visa for USA through the good offices of one of my old friends.*
Open mind: ready to receive new ideas
e.g., *Her parents have an open mind on her decision to have an inter-caste marriage.*
Out of hand: out of control
e.g., *The government took immediate action otherwise terrorist activities in the country would have gone out of hand.*
Part and parcel: an essential part (inseparable)
e.g., *Inculcation of good values in children is part and parcel of quality education.*
Patch work: untidy work
e.g., *His so-called research work is a mere patchwork with hardly any originality in it.*
Queen's/King's English: standard English
e.g., *English as spoken in south-west of England is Queen's English.*
Run amok: to suddenly become very angry and excited and start behaving violently in a public place
e.g., *The elephant leading the procession ran amok and started killing people following it.*
Run down: poor health
e.g., *He has considerably run down after his kidney operation.*
Safe and sound: secure
e.g., *You can stay with me safe and sound till you are able to find out a suitable accommodation for yourself.*
Scot-free: unpunished
e.g., *For want of evidence he was left scot-free in the bank scam.*
The flag at half-mast: indicator of mourning the death of some great personality
e.g., *All the international flags flew at half- mast at the death of Prime Minister Smt. Indira Gandhi.*

The gift of the gab: fluency of speech
e.g., *To be a successful politician one needs the gift of the gab.*
The other day: sometime ago
e.g., *I was shocked to get the news of my friend's death, for only the other day together we were watching the public performance of Shah Rukh Khan.*
The sword of Damocles: constant danger
e.g., *With the government's decision to implement the citizen's charter in all government offices the sword of Damocles is now hanging over the heads of the lower bureaucracy.*
Thick skinned: insensitive
e.g., *Politicians are often thick skinned because they do not care for the sufferings of the people after they get elected.*
Till doomsday: forever
e.g., *Abhishek and Neha make an ideal couple. Their friendship will last till doomsday.*
Time and again: repeatedly
e.g., *Time and again she doubts whether her step-mother really loves her.*
To add insult to injury: to insult a person in addition to harming him
e.g., *By refusing to help his sister in the hour of need and telling her not to bother him again for anything, he added insult to injury.*
To back out: to withdraw
e.g., *Once you have given a word to someone you should never back out.*
To back up: to support
e.g., *Parents always back up their children in the hour of their need. They never desert them.*
To be hand and glove with: to be very intimate
e.g., *The principal and his head clerk have become hand and glove with each other due to the call for a general strike by the staff and the students.*
To be in a fix: to be undecisive
e.g., *In a car accident near Jammu the entire family of my friend was killed on the spot, leaving him and his one-year-old daughter alive. He was in a fix what to do to look after his small daughter.*
To bear somebody/something out: to confirm that somebody is right or that something is true
e.g., (i) *You will bear me out, when I say service of mankind is the service of God.*
(ii) *You will bear out what I say.*
To bear the brunt of: to receive the main force of something unpleasant
e.g., *Whenever petrol prices go up the poor bear the brunt of the rising prices of the necessities of life.*
To begin with: at first
e.g., (i) *I found my job extremely tiring to begin with but I soon got used to it.*
(ii) *To begin with we'll study the whole problem patiently, and only then we'll decide the course of action.*

To blow hot and cold: to change one's opinion about something frequently
e.g., *Never rely on her, she blows hot and cold on the transfer policy of the Management.*

To build castles in the air: to indulge in dreaming or a visionary plan
e.g., *Before getting his job as per his choice, he spent most of the time in building castles in the air.*

To burn fingers: to suffer on account of rashness or meddling
e.g., *I've already burnt my fingers so I am not going to deal in share business in future.*

To change hands: to go into the possession of another person
e.g., *My Maruti car is soon going to change hands.*

To come across: meet by chance
e.g., *While entering the church I came across my childhood friend waving at me.*

To come off age: to become major/well established
e.g., (i) *Now that he has come off his age, his parents are seriously thinking of getting him married.*
(ii) *Now that the cable TV has come off age, the government should come out with a bill in the parliament to stop the cable operators from exploiting their clients.*

To come off with flying colours: to get unbelievable success
e.g., *He not only got selected for IAS but also came off with flying colours on the merit list.*

To come to blows: to fight
e.g., *Many a time people come to blow while discussing politics.*

To come to light: to become known
e.g., *During investigation the corrupt practices of the cashier came to light.*

To compare notes: to compare different views or opinions on a subject
e.g., *The committee members decided to compare notes before submitting their report to the government.*

To cut a sorry figure: to give a poor performance
e.g., *The Indian cricket team cut a sorry figure at the one day matches held at New Zealand recently.*

To die by inches: to die slowly
e.g., *It is better to be killed in one stroke than to die by inches.*

To do away with: to get rid of
e.g., *I have done away with my old fridge and have bought a new one.*

To face the music: to face unpleasant consequences of something done
e.g., *He has been caught red-handed taking bribe and the case has been filed against him. Now he has to face the music.*

To find fault with: to blame
e.g., *He never admits his mistakes. On the contrary, he is in the habit of finding fault with others for his own mistakes.*

To fish in troubled waters: to exploit a difficult situation
e.g., *During Indo-Pak war when there was a shortage of food stuff in the country some businessmen fished in troubled waters.*
To follow in the footsteps of (somebody): to follow the example
e.g., *A boy very often follows the footsteps of his father.*
To get along: to be successful
e.g., *With tips from his father he is getting along in his new business.*
To get hold of: to obtain
e.g., *With all possible efforts on my part I have not been able to get hold of a piano mechanic to repair my old piano.*
To get on: to progress
e.g., *How are you getting on with your new assignment?*
To get through: to pass
e.g., *All the students of class X got through the board examination.*
To gird up one's loins: to prepare oneself for any unexpected happenings
e.g., *We have to gird up our loins to eradicate corruption from our country.*
To give in: to yield/to surrender
e.g., *In spite of barbaric treatment and tortures by the enemy the prisoners of war (POW) did not give in.*
To give vent to: to express
e.g., *It's really difficult to give vent to one's feelings at the time of his transfer from the place where he has served all his life.*
To go: to happen
e.g., *The annual function of the school went off very well.*
To go to the dogs: to be ruined and destroyed
e.g., *With the change in the educational leadership the administration of the school has gone to the dogs.*
To grease the palm of: to bribe
e.g., *In the revenue departments of government, corruption is so much that one can get anything done by greasing the palm of the official concerned.*
To hit below the belt: to take unfair advantage of
e.g., *If you hit somebody below the belt he is bound to retaliate.*
To kill two birds with one stone: to accomplish two purposes in one attempt
e.g., *By going to Mussoorie during the summer vacation he could meet his closest friend of his student life and also enjoy his summer vacation with his family at a hill station. Thus, he tried to kill two birds with one stone in this trip.*
To lend a hand: to help
e.g., *Would you please lend me a hand in decorating this conference room?*
To look after: to care for somebody
e.g., *His father committed suicide because he failed to look after him properly.*
To make a fool of: to make fun of
e.g., *Only those persons make a fool of others who themselves suffer from inferiority complex.*

To make a mountain of a mole hill: to exaggerate
e.g., *It was a small quarrel between two persons of different religions and so to call it a riot is to make a mountain of a mole hill.*
To make both the ends meet: to have income as per the need
e.g., *In the days of everyday rising prices it is indeed extremely difficult for a retired person to make both the ends meet.*
To mend one's ways: to correct one's behaviour
e.g., *I am sure after his social boycott he will definitely mend his ways.*
To open up a new vista: to provide new opportunities
e.g., *Use of computer in daily life of man has opened up new vistas for employment.*
To put into action: to practise
e.g., *The decision of the government to allow its employees to seek premature retirement will be put into action from the next financial year.*
To put one's foot down: to refuse for something firmly
e.g., *The Finance Minister wanted to take away all kinds of subsidies in the new budget but the Prime Minister put his foot down.*
To read between the lines: to understand a writer's hidden meaning
e.g., *One who has learnt to read between the lines can appreciate things well.*
To run down: to criticize somebody bitterly
e.g., *A good friend is one who never runs down his friend publicly for small things.*
To set apart: to reserve
e.g., *My aunt set apart a sum of ₹3,00,000/- for her medical treatment in her old age.*
To set on fire: to ignite
e.g., *The terrorists set on fire the entire village after it was seized by the police.*
To shell out: to pay
e.g., *An employed son should not expect his father to shell out his own hard earned money for him.*
To show off: to make vain display
e.g., *In kitty parties women wear costly saries and ornaments just to show off their richness.*
To take a heavy toll: to cause big loss
e.g., *The earthquake in Gujarat took a heavy toll of life in the Kutch area.*
To take a thing amiss: misunderstand
e.g., *Hope you will not take it amiss if I am not able to attend your son's wedding.*
To take French leave: to be absent from without permission or leave
e.g., *Taking advantage of the absence of the Principal, she takes French leave whenever she pleases.*
To talk shop: to talk about one's own professional affairs
e.g., *One should not talk shop when one goes to listen to religious discourses.*
To think twice: to avoid taking hasty decision
e.g., *Think twice before you commit to somebody for anything. This will help you to avoid any future embarrassment.*

To turn one's back upon: to desert
e.g., *A real friend is one who never turns his back upon his friend in trouble.*
To vie with: to compete
e.g., *On Christmas and Deepawali festivals people vie with one another in decorating and illuminating their houses.*
To wind up: to conclude
e.g., *The chairperson wound up his speech by assuring the members of a favourable decision.*
To wink at: to take no notice of
e.g., *In spite of evidence for Pakistan's involvement in terrorist activities, America has been winking at the terrorist activities of Pakistan.*
Too many cooks spoil the broth: too many workers spoil the work
e.g., *It is always good to distribute the work clearly as too many cooks spoil the broth.*
Tooth and nail: with great energy
e.g., *Gandhiji opposed the Britishers' plan for partition of India tooth and nail but could not succeed.*
Tug of war: hard struggle
e.g., *There is a tug of war between the Congress and the BJP in the forthcoming assembly elections in Rajasthan.*
Up and down: to and fro
e.g., *Going up and down in a new place helps one to know its complete history.*
Well-to-do: prosperous
e.g., *The students of J.K. International School come from well-to-do families.*
Willy-nilly: somehow or the other
e.g., *She carried out my orders willy-nilly.*
With a bang: (informal) very successfully
e.g., *He started his election campaign with a bang.*

Activity

1. Copy out the above idiomatic expressions in your practice book and keep using them in appropriate situations till you are able to use them confidently.
2. Use each of the above idiomatic expressions in sentences of your own and compare them with the sentences produced by your learning partner.

(Pair Activity)

2

WORDS OFTEN MISPRONOUNCED

Note: The phonetic symbols used to provide the pronunciation of the following words are the ones that have been used by Daniel James in his English Pronouncing Dictionary.

A

abbreviation	/əbri:vi'eɪʃən/
abdomen	/'æbdəmən/
ability	/ə'bɪləti/
abolish	/ə'bɒliʃ/
abolition	/æbə'lɪʃən/
absurd	/əb'zɜ:d/
academician	/əkædə'mɪʃən/
accommodation	/əkɒmə'deɪʃən/
across	/ə'krɒs/
address (n)	/'ædres/
address (v)	/ə'dres/
adolescence	/ædə'lesəns/
aegis	/'i:dʒɪs/
against	/ə'genst/
agility	/'ədʒɪliti/
advertisement	/əd'vɜ:tɪzmənt/
agony	/'ægni/
aesthetic	/i:s'θetɪk/
air	/'eə/
air-condition	/'eəkəndɪʃən/
ant	/ænt/

apology	/ə'pɒlədʒi/
appreciation	/ə'pri : ʃieıʃən/
appropriate	/ə'prəʊpriət/
aren't	/ɑ:nt/
August	/'ɔ:gəst/
august	/ɔ:'gʌst/

B

Baggage	/'bægɪdʒ/
balcony	/'bælkəni/
balloon	/bə'lu:n/
bald	/bɔ:ld/
ballet	/'bæleı/
beer (drink)	/bıə/
bear (animal)	/beə/
beginner	/bɪ'ginə/
biology	/baı'lədʒi/
biscuit	/'bɪskɪt/
bizarre	/bɪ'za:/
blasphemy	/'blæs'fimi/
blithe	/blaıð/
blonde	/blɒnd/
board	/bɔ:d/
boarding card	/bɔ:diŋka:d/
bona fides	/'bəʊnə fadi:z/
bowl	/bəʊl/
bridle	/'braıdl/
buoy	/bɔı/
buffe	/bʊfeı/
buyers	/baıəz/

C

cadet	/kə'det/
cantonment	/kæn'tu:ɒnmənt/
canal	/kə'næl/
careful	/'keəfəl/
cassette	/kə'set/
cathedral	/kə'θi:drəl/
cello	/'tʃeləʊ/
chaff	/tʃ*a*:f/
chameleon	/kə'mi:liən/
closet	/'klɒzit/

clear	/'klıə/
colleague	/'kɒli:g/
comb	/'kəʊm/
communiqué	/kə'mju:nikeı/
congratulations	/kən ˌgrætʃʊ'leıʃənz/
cosmopolitan	/kɒzmə'pɒlɪtən/
cosmos	/'kɒzmɒs/
course	/'kɔ:s/
cough	/'kɔ:f/
coup	/ku:/
court	/'kɔ:t/
cupboard	/'kʌb∂əd/
curriculum	/kə'rikjələm/
coward	/'kaʊəd/
cow	/kaʊ/
cypher	/'saıfə/

D

dairy	/'deəri/
dais	/'deıs/
damage	/'dæmɪdʒ/
debacle	/deı'bɑ:kl/
debris	/'deıbrɪ:/
debut	/'deıbju:/
decade	/'dekeıd/
deficiency	/dɪ'fıʃəntsi/
decipher	/dɪ'saıfə/
declamation	/dekl∂'meıʃ∂n/
decrease	/dɪ'kri:s/
dejure (in law, by right)	/deı'dʒʊreı/
delinquent	/dɪ'liŋkwənt/
demeanour	/dɪ'mi:nə/
demonstrate	/'demənstreıt/
democracy	/dɪ'mɒkrəsi/
democrat	/de'məkræt/
denouement	/deınu:ma:/
desert	/'dezət/
dessert (sweet course or fruit served at the end of a meal)	/di'zɜ:t/
despair	/dɪ'speə/
desolate	/'desəlit/
development	/dɪ'velʌpmənt/
devotee	/devə'ti/

director	/dɪ'rektə/
drawers	/drɔ:z/
drought	/draʊt/

E

echo	/'ekəʊ/
ecology	/i:'kɒlədʒi/
ecological	/ˌi:kə'lɒdʒikəl/
economics	/i:kə'nɒmiks/
efficient	/ɪ'fɪʃənt/
elucidate	/ɪ'lu:sideɪt/
elusion	/ɪ'lu:ʒən/
embarrassment	/ɪm'bærəsmənt/
emergency	/ɪ'mɜ:dʒəntsi/
encourage	/ɪn'kʌridʒ/
encroach	/ɪn'krəʊtʃ/
enjoyable	/ɪn'dʒɔɪəbəl/
envelop (v)	/ɪn'veləp/
envelope (n)	/'envələʊp/
errand	/'erənd/
eulogy	/'ju:lədʒi/
extempore	/ɪk'stempəri/
exam	/ɪg'zæm/
exaggeration	/ɪgzædʒə'reɪʃn/
excuse me	/ɪk'skju:z mi/
excuse (n)	/ɪk'skiu:s/
executive	/ɪg'zekjətɪv/
exhibition	/eksɪ'bɪʃn/
exposure	/ɪk'spəʊʒə/

F

facsimile	/ˌfæk'siməli/
famine	/fæmɪn/
fascism	/'fæʃɪzəm/
fascist	/'fæʃɪst/
features	/'fɪ:tʃəz/
fete	/feɪt/
fiance (the man that a woman is engaged to)	/fɪ'ɒnseɪ/
fiancee (the woman that a man is engaged to)	/fɪ'ɒnseɪ/
fidelity	/fɪ'deləti/

files	/faɪlz/
finale	/fɪ'nɑ:li/
flour	/flaʊə/
flower	/flaʊə/
foetus	/fi:təs/
force	/fɔ:s/
forehead	/'fɒrɪd/
furniture	/'fɜ:nɪtʃə/
furthermore	/fɜ:ðə'mɔ:/

G

garage	/'gærɪdʒ/
garbage	/'gɑ:bɪdʒ/
genealogist	/ ˌdʒi:ni'ælədʒist/
gesture	/'dʒestʃə/
geography	/dʒi'ɒgrəfi/
gerund	/'dʒerʌnd/
ghetto	/'getəʊ/
gigantic	/dʒaɪ'gæntɪk/
gorilla	/gə'rɪlə/
government	/'gʌvənmənt/
guardian	/'gɑ:dɪjən/
guns	/gʌnz/
greengrocer	/'gri:ngrəʊsə/
gynaecologist	/gaɪnə'kɒlədʒɪst/

H

h	/eɪtʃ/
hair	/heə/
handsome	/'hænsəm/
haphazard	/hæp'hæzəd/
harmful	/'hɑ:mfəl/
hazard	/'hæzəd/
helpful	/'helpfəl/
holiday	/'hɒlədeɪ/
honest	/'ɒnɪst/
human resources	/hju:mən rizɔ:sɪz/
heinous	/'heɪnəs/
heir	/'eə/
heiress	/'eəres/
heist (n and v)	/'haɪst/
hero	/'hɪərəʊ/

heroine	/'herəʊɪn/
hierarchy	/'haɪərɑ:ki:/
hind	/'haɪnd/
holocaust	/'hɒl∂əkɔ:st/
homage	/'hɒmɪdʒ/
horizon	/hə'raɪzn/
hostage	/'hɒstɪdʒ/
husband	/'hʌzbənd/
hyperbole	/haɪ'pɜːbəli/

I

IATA (Internal Air Transport Association)	/aɪ'ɑ:tə/
ides (15th March, May, July and Oct.)	/'aɪdz/
idiom	/'ɪdɪəm/
idiot	/'ɪdɪət/
idol	/'aɪdl/
illiterate	/ɪ'lɪtərɪt/
image	/'ɪmɪdʒ/
import (n)	/'ɪmpɔ:t/
import (v)	/ɪm'pɔ:t/
increase (n)	/'ɪnkri:s/
increase (v)	/ɪn'kri:s/
innocent	/'ɪnəsənt/
incredulous	/ɪn'krədjʊləs/
indices	/ɪndɪsi:z/
indict	/ɪn'daɪt/
indigestion	/ɪndɪ'dʒestʃən/
indirect	/ɪndɪ'rekt/
indisposition	/ɪndɪspə'zɪʃən/
infallible	/ɪn'fæləbl/
ironing	/aɪənɪŋ/
insatiable	/ɪn'seɪʃəbl/
inter alia (Latin word—among other things)	/ɪntər'eɪlɪə/
internet	/'ɪntənet/
interrogate	/ɪn'terəgeɪt/
introspection	/ɪntrə'spekʃən/
itinerary	/aɪ'tɪn∂rəri/

J

Japan (country)	/dʒə'pæn/
jazz (music)	/'dʒæz/

jeans	/'dʒi:nz/
jewel	/'dʒu:əl/
jewellery	/'dʒu:əlri/

K

kaftan	/'kæftæn/
kaleidoscope	/kə'laɪdəskəʊp/
kangaroo	/kæŋgə'ru:/
karate	/kə'rɑ:ti/
kernel	/'kɜ:nl/
kilogram	/'kiləgræm/
Korea (country)	/kə'rɪə/
Korean (people of Korea)	/kə'rɪən/

L

laboratory	/lə'bɒrətri/
laissez-faire	/leseɪ'feə/
lamb	/læm/
language	/'læŋgwɪdʒ/
laugh	/lɑ:f/
lawyer	/'lɔɪə/
legend	/'ledʒənd/
leopard	/'lepəd/
lettuce	/'letɪs/
library	/'laɪbrəri/
lion	/'laɪn/
live (adj)	/'laɪv/
lively	/'laɪvli/
lounge	/'laʊndʒ/
luggage	/'lʌgɪdʒ/
luxury	/'lʌkʃəri/
luxurious	/lʌg'ʒʊərɪəs/

M

mafia	/mæfɪə/
manage	/'mænɪdʒ/
manoeuvre	/mə'nu:və/
mass	/'mæs/
massage	/mæsɑ:dʒ/
maximum	/'mæksɪməm/
medicine	/'medsən/

memoir	/'memwa:/
menu	/'menju:/
measure	/meʒə/
mechanic	/mə'kænɪk/
memory	/'meməri/
menace	/'menəs/
menstruation	/menstru'eɪʃn/
monarchy	/'mɒnəki/
monotony	/mən'ɒtəni/
monopoly	/'mən'ɒpli/
morale	/'mə'rɑ:l/
mortgage	/'mɔ:gidʒ/
moustache	/'mə'stɑ:ʃ/
Mr.	/'mistə/
Mrs.	/'misiz/
Miss	/'mis/
Ms.	/'məz/, /'mɪz/

N

nadir	/'neɪdıə/
narrator	/'nereıtə/
national	/'næʃənəl/
negotiate	/nɪ'gəʊʃɪeıt/
Nepalese	/nepl'i:z/
nepotism	/'nepətɪzm/
newspaper	/'nju:zpeıpə/
newsreader	/'nju:zri:də/
New Zealand	/nju:'zi:lənd/
Nobel	/nəʊ'bel/
noble	/'nəʊbl/
now	/'naʊ/
numbness	/'nʌmnes/
numerical	/nju:'merɪkl/
numerology	/nju:mər'ɒlədʒi/

O

obscene	/əb'si:n/
obscure	/əb'skjʊə/
occasion	/ə'keıʒən/
oedipus complex	/'i:dɪpəs 'kɒmpleks/
official	/ə'fıʃəl/
onomatopoeia	/ɒnəmætə'pi:ə/

opinion	/ə'pɪnjən/
orator	/'ɒrətə/
orthopaedics	/ɔ:θə'pi:dɪks/
oven	/'ʌvən/
oxymoron	/ɒksɪ'mɔ:rɒn/

P

panacea	/pænə'sıə/
panorama	/pænə'ra:mə/
paparazzo (freelance photographer)	/pæpə'rætsəʊ/
paparazzi (plural)	/pæpərætsi:/
paradigm	/pærədaım/
pear	/peə/
period	/'pıərıəd/
petition	/pɪ'tɪʃən/
phlegm	/flem/
phoenix	/'fı:nɪks/
plenary	/'pli:nəri/
plumber	/'plʌmə/
prerogative	/prɪ'rɒgətɪv/
principal	/'prɪnsɪpl/
propensity	/prə'pensɪti/
prophet	/'prɒfit/
provoke	/prə'vəʊk/

Q

question	/'kwestʃən/
queue	/'kju:/

R

radiate	/'reıdieıt/
raft	/'rɑ:ft/
rapport	/ræ'pɔ:/
rare	/'reə/
rear	/'rıə/
rebel (n)	/'rebl/
rebel (v)	/rɪ'bel/
recipient	/rɪ'sɪpɪənt/
recipe	/'resɪpi/
reciprocal	/'rɪ'siprəkl/

recognise	/'rekəgnɑız/
recollect	/'rekəlekt/
reconcile	/'rekənsaıl/
recreation	/'rekrɪeıʃən/
redeem	/rɪ'di:m/
refrigerator	/rɪ'frɪdʒəreıtə/
refuge	/'refju:dʒ/
relinquish	/rɪ'lɪŋkwɪʃ/
renaissance	/rə'neısəns/
renal	/ri:nəl/
renovate	/'renəveıt/
repute (v)	/rɪ'pju:t/
residue	/'rezidju:/
romance	/rə'mæns/
row (dispute)	/raʊ/

S

Sagittarius	/'sædʒɪteəriəs/
saloon	/sə'lu:n/
salvage	/'sælvɪdʒ/
sans	/sænz/
saturation	/sætʃə'reıʃn/
says	/sez/
sew	/səʊ/
sociology	/səʊʃɪ'ɒlədʒi/
sophistication	/səfisti'keıʃən/
soften	/'sɒfn/
suggestion	/sə'dʒestʃən/
suite	/'swi:t/
syllable	/'sɪləbl/
symbol	/'sɪmbl/
symmetry	/'sɪmətri/

T

tableau	/'tæbləʊ/
target	/'tɑ:git/
tear (n)	/'tɪə/
tear (v)	/'teə/
tempest	/'tempɪst/
tensile	/'tensaıl/
tenure	/'tenjə/
territory	/'terətri/

thank	/'θæŋk/
theoretical	/θɪə'retɪkl/
thesaurus	/θɪ'sɔ:rəs/
they'd (short form of they had or they would)	/ðeɪd/
thumb	/θʌm/
Thursday	/'θɜ:zdeɪ/
thwart	/θwɔ:t/
tilde	/'tɪldə/
tomato	/tə'mɑ:təʊ/
towel	/'taʊəl/
tower	/'taʊə(r)/
transcend	/træn'send/
translate	/træns'leɪt/
trespass	/'trespəs/

U

usage	/'ju:sɪdʒ/
used to (to something)	/'ju:st tə/
usual	/'ju:ʒʊəl/

V

vacilate	/væsəleɪt/
validity	/və'lɪdəti/
valuables	/'væljʊəbəlz/
vantage point	/vɑ:ntɪdʒ pɔɪnt/
various	/'veərɪəs/
vegetarian	/vedʒə'teərɪən/
vehicle	/'vɪ:əkl/
venal	/'vi:nl/
vendetta	/vendetə/
version	/'vɜ:ʃn/
vicar	/'vɪkə/
victuals	/'vɪtlz/
video	/'vɪdɪəʊ/
Virgo	/'vɜ:gəʊ/
vis-à-vis	/vi:zɑ:'vi:/
viva voce	/vaɪvə' vəʊsi/

W

want	/'wɒnt/

war	/'wɔ:/
wash	/'wɒʃ/
water	/'wɔ:tə/
wear	/'weə/
Wednesday	/'wenzdeɪ/
were	/'wə(r)/
what	/'wɒt/
wheel	/'wi:l/
when	/'wen/
where	/'weə(r)/
whet	/'wet/
whip	/'wɪp/
why	/'waɪ/
wilderness	/'wɪldənəs/
workbook	/'wɜ:kbʊk/
writhe	/raɪð/
wrong	/rɒŋ/

3

EXPRESSIONS FOR EFFECTIVE COMMUNICATION

GREETING PEOPLE

- Hi/Hello: (We say hello/hi to our friends or to people we already know)
- Good morning: (Before 12 o'clock)
- Good afternoon: (Between 12 noon and 6 pm)
- Good evening (After 6 pm)

1. "Goodnight" is not used to greet people while meeting them. It is used to say good bye to them.
2. The expression, "how do you do!" is used in a very formal situation, and so it is not often used while meeting people.

SAYING GOODBYE

- Bye: (We usually say 'bye' and NOT 'goodbye' when taking leave during the day)
- Goodbye: (Usually at the end of the evening/when not being able to see each other for quite sometime)
- See you: (Soon/tomorrow/next week/on Monday, etc.)
- Take care
- It was nice meeting you/talking to you
- Goodnight
- I'm afraid, I have to leave now. Goodbye
- Look after yourself

MAKING REQUESTS

- Could you?—Could you wake me up at 4 in the morning?
- Would you mind—(doing something)? Would you mind reminding her of my work?
- Can you—? Can you lend me ₹ 1000/- till Friday?
- Will you—? Will you buy me these medicines from the 'Blessings'?
- I wonder if you would mind—(doing something)? I wonder if you would mind giving this lunch box to my wife in your office.

Saying YES or NO to a Request

YES	NO
• Certainly	Sorry, I am rather busy today
• No problem	I'm afraid, I'm extremely tied up
• Yes, sure	I'm awfully sorry. I'm not going to office today
• OK	
• All right	

SAYING THANK YOU

- Thanks
- Thank you
- Thank you very much (for—): Thank you very much for having looked after my mother in my absence.
- Thank you very much indeed
- Many thanks for—: Many thanks for your kind invitation
- Thanks a lot: Thanks a lot for all your support
- It's/That's very kind of you
- I really appreciate you for—: I really appreciate you for all your efforts to get my brother appointed

What to Say when Someone Thanks You for Something

- You are welcome
- That's OK
- Don't mention it, please
- It was a great pleasure doing all that
- No problem

SAYING SORRY (Apologising)

- Sorry, I'm late for the class/function.
- I'm sorry/really sorry for my impoliteness.
- I apologise for being rude to you.

MAKING A SUGGESTION

- **Let's**
  Let's invite all our old friends on our marriage anniversary this time.
- **Shall we/I**
  Shall we raise funds to help the lepers?
- **What about—? How about?**
  How about going to Nainital this summer?
- **Why don't we/you?**
  Why don't you try for a work visa for Australia? You have all the required qualifications.
- **You could/We could**
  We could invite the girl on Deepawali to know her mind about the proposed marriage.

Replying to a Suggestion

YES/YEAH	NO
• How about having a friends' get-together? Yes, I'm planning	Sorry, I can't. I'm busy with my project.
• **OK/All right/Good idea** Let's establish an Alumni Benevolent Fund	Sorry, many of our friends may not agree to it Good idea. Let's implement it
• **Sure**	
• **That sounds great** I would prefer to (do something) I would rather do (something) I would rather stay back I would prefer to see some play	Sorry, it is not feasible.

OFFERS

- **Do you want me to?**
  Do you want me to drop you at the clinic?
- **Shall I?** (British)
  Shall I drop you at the airport?
- **Should I?** (American)
  Should I drop you at the airport?
- **Would you like me to?**
  Would you like me to drop you at the taxi-stand ?

Saying YES or NO to an Offer

• Yes, please	No, thanks
• Thanks	No, thanks! I can manage myself
• That's very kind of you	That's very kind of you, but I will help myself

ASKING FOR ADVICE

- I don't know whether to accept the offer or turn it down. **What do you suggest I should do?**
- **Do you think I should—?**
  Do you think I should accept her proposal ?
- I'm thinking of getting my head shaved. **What do you say?**

GIVING ADVICE

- **You should/You ought to**
  You should tell her the truth if you want to maintain good relations with her.
- **If I were you**
  If I were you, I would invite her over a cup of tea to tell her the truth.
- **What you should/ought to do is**
  What you should do is get them to pay the house rent in advance.
- **Make sure (that)**
  Make sure (that) you don't repeat such a mistake in future.
- **The best thing is to** learn the poem by heart.

INVITING PEOPLE

- **Would you like to?**
  Would you like to meet your old friends on Sunday?
- **I was wondering if you**
  I was wondering if you would like to have a cup of hot coffee?

Saying YES or NO to the Invitation

YES	NO
• That sounds great.	Sorry, I'm in a hurry. I have to reach the hospital before the visiting hours end.
• I would love to.	No thanks! I'm terribly busy on Sunday.
• Yes, I would like that	Sorry, I can't. I have to attend an interview for my promotion.

SEEKING DIRECTIONS

- **Could you tell me where?**
  Could you tell me where can I meet Prof. Sharma?
- **Is there any?**
  Is there any pathologist nearby?
- **How do I get to?**
  How do I get to the police station?

GIVING DIRECTIONS

- **Turn left/right and then go straight till you hit the taxi stand.**
- **Keep going until you get to the newly constructed mall.**

EXPRESSING OPINION

- **I think (that)**
  I think you must accept this offer without further delay.
- **I believe (that)**
  I believe she is the best teacher of our school.
- **As far as I'm concerned**
  As far as I'm concerned, I look upon him as the most unpredictable person.

ASKING FOR OPINION

- **What do you think about?**
  What do you think about going on a picnic next week?
- **What do you think of?**
  What do you think of our new Principal?

AGREEING

- **Absolutely**
  She should not have joined her duties if she wanted to go abroad.
  Absolutely.
- **Exactly**
  She shouldn't have married him if she loved somebody else.
  Exactly.
- **Yes/Yeah**
- **I agree**
- **I think so**
- **You are right**
- **I know**
- **That's right**
- **You're right**

DISAGREEING

- **I know, but**
  I know, but I find delicate to talk to her on this subject.
- **I take your point, but**
  I take your point, but people may not like it for obvious reasons.
- **Yes, but**
  Yes, but her ego is standing on her way.
- **But don't you think**
  But don't you think that there is another version of this case?
- **I can't accept that**
  I can't accept that a mother can be so cruel
- **I'm not so sure**
- **You must be joking!**

WHILE CONVERSING

- **Anyway**
  Anyway, I finally agreed to her offer.
- **I mean**
  I mean, do you still like him with all his false promises?
- **Pardon**
- **Could you repeat?**
- **Sorry, I didn't quite catch**
- **Sorry to interrupt**
- **Do you know what I mean?**
- **Well**
- **Right**
- **OK**

WHILE TALKING ON THE PHONE

- Can I speak to ...., please?
- May I speak to ...., please?
- Is .... there, please?
- Is that ....?
- This is ....
- It is ....
- Sorry she is ....
- Can I take .... for Sunita?
- Hold on/hang on .... I .... shortly.

MISCELLANEOUS

- Don't mention it, Mr Sharma. I'm always glad to help you.
- I'm on a business tour/on holiday
- I hope, I'm not disturbing you.
- We don't get on very well.
- Where shall I drop you off?
- I'll be back to you on the subject soon.
- He will get over it soon.
- It's now eleven. I wish he'd come.
- All right, but don't take long.
- Things are getting better/worse these days.

4

THE BODY LANGUAGE

NEED

Words and speech are not the only means of communication. Had it been so, small children and people with hearing and speaking problems could never have been able to communicate about what they wanted and how they felt about a particular situation. For example, a baby cries when it feels hungry or pain in some part of its body, drawing the attention of the mother. Similarly, the deaf and dumb people communicate with the help of their hands, eyes, facial expressions, head movements, and their touch behaviour. The trained deaf and dumb people communicate with the help of the sign language evolved to facilitate them. Sometimes, when people are not allowed to speak in certain situations, they try to communicate through their various improvised signs, if communication is a must in that situation. Even silence, at times, speaks more loudly and clearly than the words. During the observance of silence, as recommended by the Vedic tradition of Hinduism, communication takes place through various body signs only. In short, man is not a slave to the language of words and speech alone for the purpose of communication. He uses many other non-verbal techniques to communicate, called the *body language*. So, knowing about the body language and using it appropriately, while speaking, is equally important for effective communication. Both verbal and non-verbal languages need to be matched.

WHAT BODY LANGUAGE CONSISTS OF

The body language comprises the facial expressions and the movement of the eyes, eye-brows, head, nose, shoulders, teeth, lips, hands, feet and legs, etc. of the listener(s)/speaker. The sitting and standing postures of the person at the receiving end also come under the ambit of the body language. In fact, the whole body is used to give various kinds of signals, both positive and negative. Thus, familiarity with each of these signals will help a person working in the area of effective communication understand the extent of the involvement of the listener(s) in the talk/conversation under progress. The following are some of the commonly used signals of the body language that a good speaker must get acquainted with to get the desired results.

Signs of Body Movements

- Listener's leaning forward, as soon as the conversation begins, suggests that he/she wishes to get involved. But when he or she angles, it indicates that he or she is less interested in what the speaker is taking about.

Eye-contact

- The person who is willing to participate in a conversation often looks directly into the eyes of the speaker, whereas an uninterested person avoids eye-contact.

Movement of Head

- Similarly, a frequent movement of the listener's head suggests that he or she is not interested in listening to the speaker for some reason, which a conversationalist/speaker must always try to find out to be received by the person at the receiving end.
- Yawning, dozing off, blank face, looking at the watch every now and then and asking the same question again and again for answer even though it has already been answered by the speaker clearly indicate a lack of interest on the part of the listener.

SOME DOS AND DON'TS FOR AN EFFECTIVE COMMUNICATOR

Don't Move Your Head Too Much

- In conversation, listeners often concentrate on the face and head of the speakers. As such, too much head movement distracts the attention of the listener.

Don't Walk from One Side to Another

- Some people keep moving from their initial position to another while addressing. This practice also needs to be totally shunned as the shunting of the speaker from one direction to another distracts the attention of the audience.

Control of Mannerisms

- The way of speaking and moving which is typical of a particular person is called mannerism. The native speakers of English are taught right from their early childhood to speak without any hand movements. However, in the case of non-native speakers, there are a few people who do not use their hands while addressing a public gathering or when they are engaged in their private conversation. It is perhaps because of their inability to use the right intonation in their speech. The native speakers manage to give the required stress with the help of the right kind of intonation pattern, which is an integral part of their speech right from their early childhood.

Do not Touch the Other Listener

- Some people are in the habit of touching the shoulder or arm of the person they are talking to. The listener may not say anything to the speaker out of regard for him or her, but keeping quiet does not mean they approve of this irritating behaviour. As such, it must be avoided at all cost.

Break Physical Barriers

- While talking, avoid speaking from behind the tables and desks, etc. as it creates some kind of mental barrier in the listener's mind, besides restricting the speaker from reaching out to the listener, which at times may be absolutely necessary to create the desired rapport.

SOME NON-VERBAL BEHAVIOUR AND THEIR UNIVERSAL INTERPRETATIONS

Non- verbal behaviour	*Interpretation*
• Standing erect with hands on hips	confidence, readiness
• Sitting with legs crossed and foot kicking slightly	boredom
• Sitting with legs apart	relaxed
• Arms crossed on chest	defensiveness
• Stroking chin	trying to make a decision
• Rubbing the eyes	showing disbelief
• Biting nail	showing nervousness
• Tilted head	showing interest
• Head resting in hand with eyes downcast	boredom
• Sitting with hands clasped behind head and legs crossed	showing superiority and confidence
• Looking into the listener's eye	speaker's sincerity and confidence
• Broadening of eyes	showing surprise
• Smiling	used to make a tense situation comfortable
• Nodding	used to support what is said
• Moving head side-ways	indicates contradiction

And many more such body signals—plenty of them

Practice Exercise 1

Find out the frequently used body language symbols for the following purposes:

- To indicate uncertainty of your mind on some subject
- To indicate that all is fine
- To indicate that the efforts made have failed
- To indicate that you approve of something
- To indicate that you don't agree to something
- To indicate that everything is fine
- To indicate that everything is not well with the speaker
- To indicate sign of victory
- To ask a motorist for free lift or hitchhike

Practice Exercise 2

Make use of the above suggested body language in your conversation on different subjects with your friends and learning partner.

Practice Exercise 3

List out the positive body language signals to establish a good rapport between you and your listener.

Practice Exercise 4

List out the negative body language signals to avoid any frustration or a feeling of defeatism.

Practice Exercise 5

Coin your own body language signals to communicate between you and your friend when you are not permitted to speak to each other for any reason.

PART IV
SELF-EVALUATION

Knowing one's strengths and weaknesses gives us self-confidence necessary to be a winner in all situations of life.

1

SELF-EVALUATION

[Practice Exercise]

The given list of words/phrases, with their meanings, have been used in different parts of the book. You are expected to transcribe these words phonetically. Write the phonetic transcription against each word/phrase, in your practice notebook. You are allowed to refer to any good English Pronouncing Dictionary using the phonetic symbols given in the beginning of this book 'Key to Phonetic Symbols'.

Words	Pronunciation	Meaning
2 tier/3 tier second AC/first AC		kinds of berths (2 or 3) to sleep on a train
Above average		bright child—very good at studies
Academic qualification		degrees like BA, MA, PhD, etc.
Academic		relating to education
Accompanied baggage		a baggage that a passenger is allowed to carry on the same flight on which he/she travels
Account payee cheque		a cheque which can be credited only to the payee's account. Unlike a bearer cheque it cannot be encashed across the counter
Accrue		to increase over a period of time on money given on interest
Acquire		get, gain
Activity-based teaching		teaching involving classroom activities for students
Actor		a man or a woman who performs in films/movies/plays, especially as a profession

Words	Pronunciation	Meaning
Actress		a woman acting in a film/movie/play
Advance booking		when seats are booked in advance
Adverse		not favourable
Aerodrome		a small airport, used mainly by private planes
Aeroplane		a flying vehicle with wings and one or more engines
Aesthetics		connected with beauty and art
Affective domain		area dealing with emotions of a person
Affordable		you can bear easily
Agreement		an arrangement, a promise or a contract made with somebody
Airhostess		a woman whose job is to serve and take care of passengers on an aircraft
Air crew		the pilot and other people managing the flight
Airbus		plane which can carry a large number of passengers
Aircraft		any vehicle that can fly and carry goods or passengers
Airport		a place where planes land and take off and that has building for passengers to wait in
All round development		total development of a child's personality
Allowances		an amount of money paid to an individual regularly for a particular purpose
Amenities		facilities
Anaesthesia		medicine/injection given to a patient to make him or her unconscious
Anaesthetist		a doctor who gives anaesthesia
Animation		the process of making films/movies in which models of people and animals seem to move like living ones
Appetite		desire for food
Appreciation		showing pleasure at the good quality of something
Approximately		not exact (about)
Arrogance		hot temper
Assets		a thing that is valuable or useful to somebody

Words	Pronunciation	Meaning
ATM		Any Time Money/Automated Teller Machine (Money can be obtained after dialling the customer's personal confidential number)
Audience (with)		a formal meeting with a VIP
Audit		when accounts are checked by qualified accountants/auditors
Authority for payment		the right to make payment
Autopsy		postmortem of a dead body to know the cause of death
Bachelor		a man who has never been married
Baggage reclaim		where you collect luggage
Baggage		luggage
Ball-room		a room where people dance
Bank advice		bank instruction
Bank locker		a locker in which a customer can keep his personal belongings for which he pays to the bank
Bank reconciliation		tallying of accounts of an organization with those maintained in the bank
Bearer cheque		a cheque which can be easily encashed at the counter
Bearer		attendant
Bed and breakfast		room rent inclusive of breakfast charges
Belong to		birth place
Biopsy		examination of tissue removed surgically from a living body
Board and lodging		meals and a place to stay
Boarding card		a card with your seat number on it
Boeing		a type of plane
Bolt from the blue		an event or a piece of news which is sudden and unexpected
Bon voyage		good wishes for a safe journey
Book accession number		the number given to a book when bought and kept in the library. It is always a running number
Book rack		a rack in which books are kept
Book the accommodation		to reserve a room
Book-shelf		a shelf (almirah) to keep books
Borrow books		to take and use books that belong to somebody else and return them at a later time

Words	Pronunciation	Meaning
Botanical garden		a garden where plants are grown to study them
Bouncing of cheque		rejecting a cheque for payment
Box-office		the place at a cinema/movie/theatre where the tickets are sold (number of people watching a film/movie to decide its popularity or otherwise)
Breakthrough		which marks the beginning of something great
Breathe his last		die
Briefing		a meeting in which people are given instructions
Bright career		promising a success in life
Brilliant academic record		very good academic record with high percentage of marks
Broken		completely dejected—not knowing what to do
Bunk the class		same as truancy
Cab		taxi
Cabin		small room
Cable internet		internet facility provided through cable
Cable programme		a television programme shown with the help of cable instead of individual antennae
Café		a small restaurant serving light refreshment
Cafeteria		a restaurant designed for self-service
Call		to phone
Capital gain account		another kind of bank account which you have to open after selling your property with a view to saving tax on the capital gain. The money kept in this account can be spent on buying another property anywhere in the country but not for consumption purposes
Capitation fee		money charged by a school other than the prescribed fee for admission of a child
Card punching system		a system in which employees have to get their cards punched to indicate what time they reported for duty

Words	Pronunciation	Meaning
Cardiologist		a doctor who studies and treats heart diseases
Career		profession
Cargo		luggage
Caricature		a description of a person or thing that makes them seem ridiculous by exaggerating some of their characteristics
Carry on		to continue
Cash memo		receipt against cash payment
Cashier		a person whose job is to receive and pay out money in a bank/shop
Cast		actors and actresses of a film/movie/play
Casual leave		a kind of leave which you can take in case of emergency
Catalogue		a complete list of books
Cathedral		a church in a city
Cemetery		a ground to bury the dead bodies (burial ground)
Centenary		100 years, celebration of 100th anniversary
Centennial		happening every hundredth year
Chair car		a train carriage used for sitting only
Chalk board		blackboard
Challenging		which requires special ability
Chapel		a small church
Character role		a part played by an actor or actress to help the hero or heroine of a film
Chartered accountant		qualified accountant
Check-in desk		place at the airport where passengers have to report their arrival
Check-in time		reporting time for a passenger at the airport/hotel
Check-out time		the time when you leave a hotel at the end of your stay
Cheque-book		a book of printed cheques
Choreography		the art of designing and arranging the steps and movements of dance in a film/play
Christian name		first part of one's name
Cinematography		the art or process of making films/movies (technical)

Words	Pronunciation	Meaning
City station		main station of a city (to be used for both trains and buses)
Claim		demand something as right
Clinic		a place where medical treatment is given to patients
Clinical test		a test carried out in a laboratory
Closed-circuit TV		in closed-circuit TV the programme can be monitored by one person sitting at one place
Cloth-bound edition		same as hard-bound
Co-curricular activities		activities conducted by a school for the development of the child's personality
Cognitive domain		area dealing with the intellect/mind of a person
Collect call		this is when the person you ring agrees to pay for the phone call
Column		a part of a newspaper or magazine which appears regularly and deals with a particular subject
Combination		subjects offered
Come from		birth place
Comedy		a play/film/movie that is intended to be funny, usually with a happy ending
Communication		act of giving and receiving information
Commuted leave		a kind of leave, when two half-pay leave are allowed to be converted into one full-day leave on medical grounds (in government jobs)
Compartment		a smaller enclosed space within something larger
Compensate the loss		to reduce the ill effects caused by some big loss
Compere		to act as host/anchor
Complaint-book		a book kept by an organization for its customers to write their complaints whatsoever against it
Compliments		praise, appreciation
Compulsory subject		subjects which everyone has to study
Computerised branch		where the all transactions are done with the help of computers and not manually

Words	Pronunciation	Meaning
Conclusive		which concludes something
Conduct (n) and (v)		behaviour (n), behave (v)
Contribute articles		write articles for magazines and newspapers
Public convenience		a public toilet (used formally)
Conversation		talk
Conveyance allowance		an amount of money paid to one on a regular basis towards the conveyance charges
Conveyor belt		the belt which keeps moving with the passengers' luggages arrived by the same flight by which the passengers travelled
Corner		a part of the library which is reserved for a particular section of readers
Corrective measures		actions taken to correct a problem
Cosmetics		substance that people put on their face and body to make themselves look more beautiful
Cottage		a small house
Counterfoil		the part of a cheque etc. that remains after giving the other part to somebody else
Coupe		a compartment meant for two
Course of life		direction of life
CPF (Contributory Provident Fund)		an amount which is deducted from the monthly salary of an employee so that the lumpsum amount can be paid to them at the time of retirement or leaving the job
Cradle		the part of a telephone on which the receiver rests
Creativity		activities for the development of the child's originality and innovative spirit
Credit card		a card issued by a bank to its member/accountholder to enable him/her to buy things on credit upto a given limit
Credit limit		a limit to which a person can buy a thing on credit
Credit		to deposit money to one's bank account
Cross cheque		a cheque with two lines put across on the left-hand corner of the cheque.

Words	Pronunciation	Meaning
		It is credited to the drawee's account only. It cannot be encashed on the spot
Crowd puller		which attracts a lot of viewers
Crucial		important
Currency notes		paper money
Current account		a kind of bank account which is normally opened by business people who have to operate their account a number of times for deposit or withdrawal of money during a day
Curricular		dealing with the teaching subjects
Curriculum vitae		a written record of your education and employment that you send when you apply for a job
Curriculum		total activities organized by a school for the education of the child
Custody		in possession
Customer/client		a person who uses the services of an organization
Dailies		a daily or everyday newspaper
Dealing assistant		the clerk concerned
Debit card		a card issued by a bank to its account-holder to enable them to buy things against the amount they have in their account
Debit		to take away the money from one's bank account
Deceased/demise		dead/death
Deficiency		weakness
Demonstration		showing and explaining the working of something
Denomination		whether a currency note/coin is ₹ 1, ₹ 5, ₹ 10 or ₹ 100, etc.
Dentist		a doctor who studies and treats the diseases of the teeth
Dependence		the state of needing the help and support of somebody/something in order to survive
Deposit slip		a slip showing the deposit of an amount with a bank
Deposits		deposit of money
Dermatologist		a doctor who studies and treats diseases of skin

Words	Pronunciation	Meaning
Dessert		sweet dish
Detective		a person, especially a police officer, whose job is to examine crimes and catch the criminals
Detention		failing
Diabetes		a disease in which a person passes urine very frequently with sugar
Diabetic		one who suffers from diabetes
Diagnosis		identification of a disease
Diagnostic test		a test conducted to find the strengths and weaknesses of the child in the area selected
Dietitian		a person skilled in prescribing the right kind of food for patients
Dining car		a railway carriage in which meals are served
Director		a person in charge of a film/movie and who tells the actors and staff what to do
Disappear		not to be seen
Disciplinary action		an action taken by an employer against his employee to punish him for an offence committed by him/her
Discount		selling goods at a reduced price
Discriminative		which distinguishes between the two
Discursive		based on opinion
Disfiguring the book		spoiling a book by tearing off its pages or writing inside
Dishonour		to reject a cheque for payment
Dismissal		when a person is removed from a job and is not allowed to seek re-employment in the organization
Distressing		painful
Dividend		profit/gain
Divorcee		a person whose marriage has been legally ended
Documentary film		a film giving facts about something
Domestic help		a person who assists in doing domestic work
Double-locking system		the system in which a lock can be locked by one key but opened with two keys
Draft		it is like a cheque which is as good as hard cash. It is issued in favour of

Words	Pronunciation	Meaning
		an individual and the individual concerned can encash it without paying anything to the bank
Drawee		the person in whose favour a draft/ cheque is drawn
Drawn on		the name of the bank that has to pay
Dream come true		when something that you aspired happens in reality
Duplicates		one who acts for another actor
Earned leave		a kind of leave which a person earns every year of service
Educational trip		a trip that educates a person
Electronic engineer		an engineer dealing with electronic equipments
Elocution		speech (public speaking)
Emigration		permission to leave a country
Emoluments		money paid to somebody for the work they have done
Employment exchange		an office which helps persons in getting them jobs
ENT		a doctor who studies and treats the diseases of ear, nose and throat
Entitlements		right to have or do something
Entry visa		permission to enter the country
Episode		an event, a situation, or a period of time in somebody's life that is important or interesting in some ways
Erect		to build something in an upright position
Examine		to check carefully
Excess baggage		baggage for which you have to pay extra
Exchange facility		facility of conversion of currency of one country into currency of another country
Exclusive		uncommon
Excursion		a short journey made for pleasure, especially one that has been organized for a group of people
Executive		a man who acts as a manager in a company or an organisation
Exit visa		permission to go out of the country
Exit		a door to go out

Words	Pronunciation	Meaning
Experience		to feel a particular emotion
Express train		a train which stops at limited stations only
Extempore		a speech for which topic is given to the speakers on the spot
Extra co-curricular activities		activities like acting, singing, dancing, mountaineering organised by a school as a part of the school programme for personality development of the students
Faculty		members of staff
Fans		admirers
Fantastic/gorgeous/ smashing		very beautiful
Farmhouse		a building having living accommodation and attached to a farm
Fast reader		one who reads at a good speed
Feature film		a main film/movie with a story rather than a documentary
Feel completely shattered		completely dejected; broken
Film critic		a person who expresses his or her opinion about the good and bad qualities of films/movies—usually professionals
Film review		a critical examination of a film
Findings		information that somebody has discovered
Firearm		a gun that can be carried
Fixed deposit		a bank deposit made for a fixed purpose
Flight loading		when the passengers board the plane
Flight schedule		flight timings
Flight		a journey made by air, especially in a plane
Flock leader		a lady in charge of small girls (5+ to 10 yrs) called 'bulbuls' in scouting/ guiding programme
Fluency		speaking or writing well
For good		forever
Foreign exchange		used to talk about buying and selling foreign money
Foster parents		people who take another person's child into their home for a period of

Words	Pronunciation	Meaning
		time without becoming his or her legal parents
Free-studentship		when a student is allowed to study without paying the school fee
Fruitful		which gives expected results
Gas station		petrol pump
Gerontologist		a doctor who specialises in the medical problems of elderly people
Get-together		an informal meeting, a party
Give regards		same as pay compliments
Godfather		the person with whose help a person tries to go up in life
Good at		to be able to do something well
Government pleader		advocate
Grace marks		extra marks given to a student in order to pass him/her
Graduate		a person who has a university degree
Gratuity		money that is given to employees when they leave their job
Green board		chalk-board of green colour
Green channel		a channel which can be used by the passengers who have nothing to declare for customs
Grim tragedy		big tragedy
Guarantee		a firm promise that you will do something
Guarantor		a person who agrees to be responsible for somebody or for making sure that something happens or is done as per the work agreement
Guest artist		an actor or actress associated with some parts of a film/movie—usually without charging anything for the role played
Guesthouse		an accommodation for guests to stay
Guided tour		tour arranged for sight-seeing with the services of a guide
Gynaecologist		a doctor who treats diseases of women
Hail from		birth place
Half-pay leave		a kind of leave allowed to be taken on half-pay
Half-yearly		which comes out once in every six months

Words	Pronunciation	Meaning
Hand-bag		a bag allowed to be carried inside the plane
Hangars		the place where aeroplanes are parked
Hard currency		currency which is accepted in every country of the world like American dollar, British pound, German mark, etc.
Hard-bound		a cloth-bound edition of a book normally used in libraries
Hawkers		someone who carries goods from place to place to sell them
Heavenly abode		place after the death of a man
Heavily booked		when a lot of people book their seats a large number of people booking in advance to watch a movie/film play
Hero		main male character around whom the story of a film/movie/play revolves
Heroine		main female character of a film/movie
High-budget film		a film which is produced with a lot of money (running in many crores)
Hijack		to take away some aeroplane or bus by force
Hobbies		spare time activities undertaken by an individual because of personal interest
Home delivery		when articles can be received at home without going to the shop—the order may be placed on telephone or through email
Home-teacher		classteacher (used in America)
Honorarium		a payment made for somebody's professional services
Honour		something that makes you feel very proud
Hopping flight		the flight which stops at different places before reaching its destination (opposite to direct flight)
Hosiery		a word for socks, stockings and tights
Hot and cold		a room which provides both hot and cold water through taps

Words	Pronunciation	Meaning
Hotel		a building where people stay, usually for a short time, paying for their rooms and meals
Housecoat		a long loose piece of clothing worn in the house by women
Hypertension		abnormally high blood pressure
Ideal		perfect person or a thing
Image		reputation
Immigration		permission to arrive in a country
Impertinent		one who is not well-behaved
Imported goods		things bought from foreign countries
In demand		popular
In pair		two persons
In queue		in line
In search of		looking for
In twos/threes		a line of two or three people
Incentives		measures taken to motivate people to work
Industrious		hardworking
Informal		relaxed and friendly; not following strict rules of how to behave or do something
Information desk		enquiry desk
Information		facts or details about somebody/ something
Infrastructure		physical facilities
Inhibition		anything that stops from speaking
Inn		a pub, usually in the country, where people can spend the night
Innovation		to do something in a new and unique way
Insomnia		sleeplessness
Institutional planning		yearly planning for the development of different areas of the school
Inter-house		activities involving two or more houses of the school
Intra-house		activities within a particular house
Introduction		1. introducing a new person/speaker to a group of people 2. introducing a person wishing to open an account with a bank etc. is required to be introduced by someone who is already holding the account

Words	Pronunciation	Meaning
Investiture ceremony		a ceremony conducted to induct (to take in) recruits formally. It is used in case of scouts and guides
Irreparable loss		a loss which cannot be recovered
Issue clerk		a person employed to issue books to the members of a library
Issue		one of a regular series of magazines or newspapers
Jacket		coat
Jet		a plane driven by jet engines
Jocularity		amusement
Joining time		time allowed to a person to prepare themselves for joining a job on transfer or promotion
Joint account		a bank account which is operated by two persons jointly
Journal		a newspaper or magazine that deals with a particular subject or profession
Last name		family name; surname
Latch		a small metal bar used to close a door
Latest edition		the one after which no other edition has been published
Lead role		main role
Ledger entry		entry made in the ledger account
Ledger folio		same as a ledger number
Ledger number		the page of a ledger allotted to an accountholder
Leisure time		spare/free time
Leisure		spare time
Liabilities		the state of being legally obliged to pay interest on a borrowed amount
Library assistant/ Attendant		one who helps the librarian in maintaining the library, including arranging and re-arranging the books received back from the members
Library attendant		a person whose job is to take care of the books and replace them at the right place on their return
Library discount		concession allowed on the amount of the books purchased for library purpose

Words	Pronunciation	Meaning
Library management		the act of running and controlling a library
Limelight		when people come to know about somebody
Linen		clothes
Literary		related to literature
Lobby		a big room used as a living room
Lodge		a small house in which lodgings can be rented
Lodger		a person who pays rent to live in somebody's house
Long distance or overseas call		overseas calls—from one country to another
Long interval		after a gap of a long time
Long silence		no talk or contact for a long time
Lounge		same as lobby
Low-priced edition		same as paperback
Low-budget film		a film which is produced with a small budget (just a few lakhs)
LTC facility		leave travel concession
Luggage		bags etc. that you carry while travelling
Magazine		a magazine concerned with an academic subject and published every week/month.
Maiden speech		first speech
Mail train		the train with a high speed stopping only a few big stations
Maintenance allowance		an amount of money paid to an employee to maintain themselves, especially in foreign countries
Manager		a person who is in-charge of running a hotel
Mass P.T.		physical training exercises done on a mass scale, involving the whole school
Menu		a list of the food items served by a hotel
Menu-card		the card showing the names and prices of the food items to be served by the hotel
Merit		ability
Mischief		bad behaviour that is annoying but doesn't cause any serious damage or harm

Words	Pronunciation	Meaning
Miserable		very unhappy or uncomfortable
Mishap		a small accident or piece of bad luck that does not have serious results
Miss		to remember somebody
Monitoring		supervising
Monthly account		the account for a month
Monthly		a magazine or a periodical published every month
Mortgage		a legal agreement by which a bank lends you money to buy a house etc. and in return you give the bank the right to sell it if the money taken is not paid back within the agreed time-limit
Mortuary		a building where dead bodies are kept before burial
Motel		a roadside hotel with accommodation for motorists and vehicles
Movie		a series of moving pictures recorded with sound that tells a story, shown at the cinema/movie theatre
Moving bowels		discharging the waste material from the human body
Museum		a building in which objects of artistic, cultural, historical and scientific interest are kept
Mystery		something that is difficult to understand or explain
Nature of job		a type or kind of job or post
Neurologist		a doctor who studies and treats the diseases of the nerves
New arrivals		the books which are recently introduced
Not to be issued		books which are not to be issued (kept in the library only)
Notes of lessons		notes prepared by a teacher for teaching a particular lesson in the class
Nursing home		a place where people who are ill are looked after and treated
Obesity		fat unhealthily
Objective		which is based on the merit of an answer to a question

Words	Pronunciation	Meaning
Obstetrician		a doctor who is trained to handle delivery cases
Old age home		a place where old people stay and are looked after by the government or a trust
On approval		when a deal is to be made only after the items (books) have been approved
On credit		when a deal is made on the assurance that the payment would be made on some future date
On demand		when demanded or asked for
Online banking		operating the bank account on telephone and internet
Open-shelf system		a system in which books are kept in open shelves to enable the users see the books concerned before getting them issued
Ophthalmologist		a doctor who studies and treats diseases of the eye
Optional		subjects that are offered as per one's choice
Ornamental		decorative
Orthodontist		a dentist who specialises in correcting irregularities of teeth
Orthopaedist		a doctor who studies and treats the diseases of bones
Outdated		an old book which is no more relevant in terms of subject matter or data
Outhouse		a shed near main building
P.T.A.		Parent teacher association
P.T.F.		Parent teacher forum
Paediatrician		a doctor who studies and treats the diseases of children
Paperback		is a low priced edition of a book. There is, however, no difference in the contents of the book
Parish		a district under one clergyman
Pass marks		marks which entitles a student to pass an examination
Passbook		a booklet issued by the bank/ financial institution to an individual

Words	Pronunciation	Meaning
		showing his/her receipts and payments during the financial year
Passenger		a person who is travelling in a car, bus, train, plane or ship and who is not driving it or working on it
Passport control		where an official checks your passport
Past memories		thoughts of something that you remember from the past
Pastime		something that you enjoy doing when you are not working
Pathological test		a test carried out in a laboratory to find out a disease
Pathologist		a doctor who studies the scientific cause of a disease
Pay compliments		to pay regards
Pay order		similar to a draft but issued for a payment to be made locally
Payee		the person to whom the payment is made
Paying guest		a person who pays to live in somebody's house with them, usually for a short time
Pay-in-phone		a public phone which can be used by a person after paying
Pay-in-slip		a piece of paper that shows how much money a person has deposited
Payment schedule		the dates on which payments are to be made
Pension		an amount of money that a person gets after his retirement till he dies
Performance test		a test showing the performance of each student
Performance		how well you do something
Periodical		a magazine that is published every week, month, etc. especially one that is concerned with an academic subject
Periodicals		magazines and journals published periodically, e.g., a weekly/a monthly magazine
Perks		something a person receives besides regular salary/wages

Words	Pronunciation	Meaning
Perseverance		the habit of doing a thing till it is completed
Personal discussion		interview
Personality traits		characteristics of one's personality
Petrol pump		the place from where the petrol or diesel is taken for use in vehicles
Physician		a doctor who is a specialist in general medicines and not surgery
Physiotherapist		a person who gives exercises and massage to patients to cure them of their disease
Pilot		a person who operates an aeroplane
Platform ticket		a ticket that entiles a person to enter the railway platform
Popular		a book which is liked by large number of readers/persons
Popularity		when a large number of people know a person
Post-dated cheque		a cheque issued for a payment giving a future date on the cheque
Postgraduate		a person having master's degree in a subject
Postmortem		medical examination of a dead body
Prescription		medicines prescribed (advised)
Prestigious		which gives you prestige and status
Privilege leave		a kind of leave which an employee is entitled to along with other kinds of leave
Probation period		a period of trial wherein the work and conduct of an employee is watched by the employer in order to decide whether the employee concerned can be made regular
Producer		a person who is in charge of the practical and financial aspects of making a film/movie (the owner of the film)
Profession		same as career
Professional experience		the experience in a particular profession
Professional		relating to a job that needs special education or training, e.g. degrees like B.Ed., M.Ed., MBBS

Words	Pronunciation	Meaning
Project		an activity undertaken for the attainment of some educational gains
Psychiatrist		a doctor who studies and treats mental illness
Publicity stunt		done something for the purpose of publicity
Punctuality		doing something at the arranged or correct time
Pyjamas		a loose jacket and trousers worn in bed (sleeping suit)
Qualification		Engineering etc. needed for a particular profession
Quality education		education that stresses on quality and excellence
Quarterly		which comes out once in every three months
Radiologist		a doctor who is trained in using radiation to treat people
Radiology		science of use of rays in medicine
Rapport		close relation
Rate of interest		rate at which a customer is paid interest by the bank
Receipt		a paper (pay-in-slip) showing receipt of a payment from a customer
Reception		the area inside the entrance of a hotel, or an office building where visitors go first when they arrive
Receptionist		a person whose job is to deal with people arriving at a hotel/organization
Recline		to sit or lie in a relaxed way
Recreation room		a room used for the entertainment of the people staying in the hotel
Red channel		a channel meant for those who have items for customs duty
Reduced rates		at the rates lower than the normal ones
References		persons who may be referred to regarding the applicant for the job, if required
Re-fuelling		to fill something, especially a plane, with fuel in order to continue a journey

Words	Pronunciation	Meaning
Refundable security deposit		the amount which is paid by a member as a security against anything received but is refundable at the time of leaving the membership
Regular job		a job which is for unlimited time
Rehearse		to practise
Reimbursement		to pay back money to somebody which they have spent
Reinstate		to give back a job or position that had been taken away from somebody earlier
Re-issue		issue a book again
Religious		connected with religion or with a particular religion
Re-live the past		to remember the events of the past in an order in which they took place
Re-live the student life		to experience the student life once again (to remember the events of student life)
Remedial teaching		teaching provided for the removal of student's deficiency in particular subject
Re-print		printing of a book again without any changes
Requisition slip		a paper slip used to demand a book or thing in writing
Requisition		written demand or request for anything
Reserved		the books which are not meant to be issued but can be referred to in the library
Responsibilities handled		types of work handled as a part of one's job
Responsibility		a duty to deal with or take care of certain thing(s) etc.
Rest-house		a place where travellers can stay for a day or two for rest
Restaurant		a place where you can buy and eat a meal
Resume		like CV
Retail price		price charged for a thing by a shopkeeper
Reverse charge call		same as collect call
Ring up		to telephone somebody

Words	Pronunciation	Meaning
Roaming facility		when you can ring (or receive) a telephone call from wherever you are while roaming beyond the jurisdiction of network
Role-model		a person whom somebody copies in life
Romantic		concerned with love or a sexual relationship
Room rent		an amount of money that you pay for hiring a room in a hotel
Room service		which serves eatables inside the room
Runway		a long narrow strip of ground with a hard surface that an aircraft takes off from and lands on
Salesman		a man whose job is to sell goods
Sanction		bank's permission
Savings bank account		a kind of bank account on which the rate of interest a bank pays is much lower than what it pays on fixed deposits
Seasoned artist		experienced and well-tried artist
Seat-belt		a belt that is attached to the seat in a car or a plane and that you fasten around yourself so that you are not thrown out of the seat if there is an accident
Second helping		second round of food items served
Section		a separate part of a book
Sell ideas		to promote ideas (to make those ideas accepted)
Serve		to give passengers food and drink and to help them
Service charges		charges on account of the services given
Session-ending examination		annual examination
Settled in		make one's home
Settlement of bill		payment of the bill
Sheer coincidence		only by chance
Sheer disgust		out of hatred
Shoelace		a string to tie the shoe
Shoeshine		a person cleaning people's shoes for money
Shopping centre		an area of town where most of the shops are situated

Words	Pronunciation	Meaning
Shorts		short pants that end above the knee (knickers)
Side role		role which is less important than the main role
Sight-seeing		to see places of interest or the places of historical importance or natural beauty
Social		relating to meeting people, forming relationships with them
Soft paperback edition		same as paperback
Spare-time activities		activities undertaken in one's free time
Specimen signatures		signatures of the accountholder given at the time of opening the account
Sports stadium		open air arena for athletics
Statement of account		details of the account showing receipts and payments
Stationery		material used for writing, drawing and other study purposes
Stethoscope		an instrument for listening to action of heart, lungs, etc.
Stockings		that fits closely over a woman's legs and feet (tights)
Stop payment		after issuing a cheque in favour of somebody you can always stop its payment to the person concerned by issuing stop payment instructions to the bank
Stranger		unknown/unfamiliar person
Stray cattle home		a place wherein the wandering animals are kept
Streaming		grouping students on the basis of their merit/performance
Strenuous		which causes strain and tension
Strong room		a room wherein lockers are kept
Struggle		to fight for making one's place in life
Subject combination		subjects studied
Subjective		based on personal likes or dislikes
Substitution period		an extra period given to a teacher to teach some class
Superb		excellent, of very good quality
Superstar		a very famous performer, for example an actor, an actress or a singer

Words	Pronunciation	Meaning
Supervised activity		the activity undertaken under the guidance and supervision of a teacher
Surety		someone who acts as a guarantor for the working of a person as per the work agreement
Surgeon		a doctor who is trained to perform operation in a hospital
Surgery (UK meaning)		a doctor's clinic where he examines his patients
Surgery		medical treatment by operation; doctor's consulting room
Surname		family name; name by which a family is known
Surrender of locker		when locker is given back to the bank is called surrendering of the locker
Suspension		act of removing a person from a job for a period of time, usually as a punishment
Take-off		rising in the air from the ground
Tallying of signatures		comparing the signatures appearing on the cheque with the specimen signatures
Tariff		a list of fixed prices that are charged by a hotel for rooms, meals or for a particular service, etc.
Tariff		telephone rent
Taxis		when the plane moves slowly on the runway before the take-off position (to taxi—verb)
TDS		tax deduction at source
Telephone kiosk		a telephone booth
Teller system		a system in which a bank makes payment to the presenter of a cheque immediately
Temporary duty		a duty for a short duration
Temporary job		a job which is for a particular period (limited time)
Termination		when a person is removed from a job permanently
Terms and conditions		details of an agreement
Terms cash		payments by cash only
Three-dimensional film		a film having or appearing to have length, width and depth

Words	Pronunciation	Meaning
Thriller		a film/movie with an exciting story, especially one about crime or spying
Tiffin		meals
Time-barred cheque		a cheque whose date has expired for the purpose of payment
Tip		amount of money paid by a customer to a bearer of a hotel in recognition of his services rendered
Title of the account		the name under which a bank account is opened. It may be a savings a/c or current a/c. But in all cases the name (title) of the account is to be given
Titles		the names of books (a particular book or magazine)
Toiletries		things such as soap and toothpaste that are used for washing/cleaning
Tourist bungalow		one-storeyed house for tourists (those who travel for pleasure)
Tourist		a person who is travelling or visiting a place for pleasure
Tragedy		a very sad event or situation especially one that involves death
Tragic end		sad end
Transaction		receipt or payment
Transfer entry		an entry of transaction from one account to another or from one account book to another account book
Transit accommodation		where a person lives temporarily till permanent accommodation is allotted
Transit visa		permission to pass through a country with a stopover for a short-while
Trousers		pants
Truancy		leaving class/school without permission
Truant		one who follows truancy
Trunk		underwear
Tuck shop		a shop selling small things of the students' use
Turn on/turn off		switch on/switch off
Type		role

Words	Pronunciation	Meaning
Unaccompanied baggage		a baggage which is sent to its destination by a cargo plane
Undergarments		clothes worn under outside clothes, e.g., vest and underwear
Urologist		a doctor who studies and treats the diseases related to urinary system
Vacuum has been created		the gap which cannot be fulfilled up
Validate		to make valid or binding
Value-based teaching		teaching for inculcation of various values for the development of the child's personality
Vamp		a sexually attractive woman who uses this power to control men (opposite of villain)
Vest		a piece of garment without sleeves that a person wears on top half of the body
Viewers' feedback		information about how good or useful a film is according to the viewers of a movie/film
Villa		a large and luxurious country house
Villain		the main bad character in a story/play
Visa card		same as credit card
Visa		an official mark put on your passport that gives a person to temporarily enter or leave a foreign country
Voracious		wanting a lot of information or knowledge
Waist coat		a jacket worn under a coat—usually part of a 3-piece suit
Warranty		a written agreement in which a company, selling something, promises to repair or replace it if there is a problem within a particular period of time
Water-cabin		a small room with drinking water facility
Weeklies		papers which are published every week
White board		a chalk board in white colour
Wholesale		the business of buying or selling goods in large quantities
Wholesome education		total/complete education

Words	Pronunciation	Meaning
Work experience		experience at work
Working hours		time of work
Write off		an act of cancelling a debt and accepting that it will never be paid
Yearly account		account for a year
Yearly		which comes out once a year
Zoo		a place where wild animals are kept and exhibited for public

Your journey on excellence in spoken English and speech effectiveness begins here.